Gardens for the Future

Dedication

Moyra Rae Buchanan Burnett

(1927–1983)

Amaryllis Virginia Garnett

(1943–1973)

Previous page Filigreed Line, *1979, a plasma-cut aluminium sculpture which was site-generated from the landscape at Wellesley College, Massachusetts, USA by Robert Irwin.*

Right *This painted, welded steel sculpture is one of three 'garden follies' made by Thomas Balsley for a public park called Gate City in Osaki, Tokyo, Japan. This piece, made in 1998, was inspired by sedge leaves. It is entitled* Carex.

Gardens for the Future

Gestures Against the Wild

Guy Cooper and Gordon Taylor

contents

Far left, top *Fouquieria splendens, sculptural ocotillo stems in the Arizona desert.*

Far left, bottom *Part of a fabulous water feature in the grounds of the headquarters of the Banque Générale du Luxembourg, Plateau de Kirchberg on the edge of the city.*

Above *Palm oasis for 'The Citadel', Commerce, California.*

Left *These angular walls in a private garden in Phoenix, Arizona, were inspired by Alvar Aalto.*

Introduction

In 1996, we published *Paradise Transformed*, our first book on the subject of garden and landscape design at the end of the millennium. Although it is now considered to be one of the first major popular books on contemporary landscape, its publication did not mark an end to our obsessive pursuit of the subject. *Gardens for the Future: Gestures Against the Wild* represents a second phase in our compulsive journey towards some definition of private gardens and public landscapes at the end of the twentieth century. It also embraces developments in the use of materials and the principles of design that have occurred since the first book was written.

We are not cultural commentators or pundits. This is a personal selection and as such it cannot be totally comprehensive. We have tried to avoid the private language of academic landscape design. However, we have adopted the three definitions of landscape coined by Robert Irwin, the visionary American artist. Irwin refers to landscape or garden designs as being either site dominant, site adjusted or site generated. As we make extensive use of these terms ourselves, it is important that their meaning should be clear.

Site-dominant gardens have no real place in a book about contemporary design. Irwin used the term to refer to the highly influential gardens of sixteenth-century Italy, seventeenth-century France and eighteenth-century England. These are gardens that have become historical models. They are relevant to our theme only as sources of inspiration for contemporary designers.

Site-adjusted gardens draw their inspiration from a multitude of sources. In this respect the site-dominant landscapes and gardens are very important. In our Age of Information, however, the field of reference can range from ancient labyrinths to the Electro Diode Light sculpture installations of the avant-garde.

The second part of this book consists of 20 case studies of private and public landscapes which illustrate the incredible diversity of achievement at the end of the twentieth century. Of these studies, 13 are of site-adjusted designs. They include Jacques Wirtz's garden in the Tuileries in Paris which draws inspiration from European garden history, as do the designs of Daniel Urban Kiley in America and Fernando Caruncho in Spain and Florida. Ton ter Linden in Holland was influenced by the large-scale use of herbaceous perennials in early twentieth-century Germany. Other case studies reflect the influences of China and Japan.

We were amused by the notion that the British gardens of the eighteenth century could be simultaneously defined as both site-dominant and site-adjusted. They were inspired by an enormous wave of Italian influence on art, architecture and the landscape at that time, which makes them site adjusted. However, over the past 300 years, the classical gardens of eighteenth-century Britain have become so closely identified with the British landscape that they are now historical models within the context of our own cultural history and can now be read as site dominant.

It has emerged from our research that some of the most important gardens and landscapes of the past 20 years have been site generated. In simple terms, these are designs inspired by the intrinsic nature of the site. The design forms are drawn both from the physical features of the site and its surroundings and from information not visible to the naked eye, such as geology and history. These gardens and landscapes are the very antithesis of site-adjusted designs, as they evolve from the landscape rather than being imposed upon it.

Site-generated designs are a truly unique and innovative contribution to garden and landscape design in the late twentieth century. Although Alexander Pope's splendid admonition to 'Consult the Genius of the Place in all' is often misquoted, particularly in departments of landscape architecture in the United States, the best and most exciting site-generated designs to have emerged can be seen as a true, late twentieth-century adaptation of Pope's wonderful command.

Above *The International Style headquarters of the Banque Générale du Luxembourg is set in a formal landscape designed by Jacques Wirtz. Here he has combined a serpentine lawn with water to offset the austerity of the building.*

The post-industrial and post-modern realities of our time find their expression in site-generated landscape designs, which draw their inspiration from contemporary culture and the environment. They are intrinsic to our society, just as the site-dominant gardens of Villa d'Este, Vaux-le-Vicomte or Stourhead were to theirs, and as such they are a true reflection of late twentieth-century culture.

Site-generated designs seem to embody characteristics which could be defined as sense and sensibility. The 'sense' is in the shapes which emerge from a deep analysis of the site. 'Sensibility' is found in the aesthetic qualities

resulting from this process. Every aspect of the site, both visible and invisible, is taken into account and transformed into inspirational material.

Many site-generated landscapes are created on derelict industrial land. The site itself must be thoroughly analysed before the design process begins. An investigation of the history of the site is the first stage of this procedure. All visual information – including old engravings and views, sketches and photomontages – are studied alongside any written material. This historical analysis will produce a rich pool of material that can be built into the design. It will also reveal a pattern of growth and change. The effects of the climatic conditions and the seasons are also recorded, as is the annual rainfall. The site is observed during both the day and night, and the soil is analysed. This analysis includes the study of earth forms, soil textures and levels, existing drainage and drainage needs. The exploratory work is usually carried out by a multi-disciplinary, collaborative team, all pursuing the same objective.

Below Nine Spaces, Nine Trees, *Seattle, 1983. Robert Irwin's site-generated philosophy is a powerful force in landscape design and architecture.*

Site-generated Case Studies in this book show the work of Robert Irwin, George Hargreaves, Mark Rios, Desvigne & Dalnoky, D.A.ST., Thomas Balsley, and Kathryn Gustafson.

Despite the diversity of their output, the designers represented here have a common aim. They are all in pursuit of innovation. We hope that you will find their gardens and landscapes as exciting and inspiring as we have done.

Design traditions

Social context

The right style of landscape architecture for the 20th century is no style at all, but a new conception of planning the human environment.

Christopher Tunnard

Right Plant *is in Cor-Ten steel. This amusing, serial design should please all minimalist landscape architects. The Metaphysical Garden was created by a Dutch landscape architect for the Budesgartenschau (State Garden Show), Frankfurt, 1989.*

Previous page Blue Steps *at the Naumkeag Estate, Stockbridge, Massachusetts, was designed in 1926. It reflects the influence of the* Exposition Internationale des Arts Décoratifs et Industrielle Moderne *in Paris the previous year.*

The designs of gardens and landscapes create a link between culture and nature at its most primary level. In this respect, the work of the designer is of great importance and could even be seen as a significant contribution to contemporary society.

Why are people attracted to the landscape design profession? Two points of view were presented in a recent article in The Boston Herald:

> Ask George Hargreaves [a leading landscape architect and now Chairman of Landscape Architecture, Harvard Graduate School of Design] why he went into the business and he'll tell you of an epiphany on the mountaintop when he was 20.
>
> Ask Lynn Wolff to describe her purpose and she'll talk about community, people, the cultural expression of city dwellers. Others in their profession speak with passion about the poetry embodied within the contours of a hill's slope or a long stretch of undeveloped woodland.

This book is both a recognition and an appreciation of the achievements of professional landscape architects and garden designers.

Lynn Wolff explains her perception of the profession in the following way:

> Landscape architecture is not about using the cookie-cutter approach. We're supposed to design specific to the place, whether it be urban or the wilds and to the people who use it.

This positive and thoughtful view is echoed by Hargreaves, who says 'We're part of the expansion of the human settlement.'

Over the past 20 years, the landscape architecture and design profession has had to struggle to find acceptance for designs which relate to the realities of contemporary life. Even in the United States, traditionally perceived as a go-ahead and innovative society, attitudes towards contemporary designs in the garden and landscape have been slow to change. Nevertheless, a process of change is underway and even in Great Britain, where the cosy cottage or manor-house style has been the vogue for years, there is an interest in new approaches to garden and landscape design. Over the past 15 years or so design in Europe and in the United

States has begun to reflect the time in which we all live and work. The private gardens and public landscapes that are emerging on the cusp of two millennia take new, relevant and incredibly provocative forms.

The designs shown here are the contemporary NOW, rather than some historical THEN. Even those which draw on geometric or classical shapes are contemporary extensions of the basic rectilinear style of twentieth-century modern architecture.

Even the most design-conscious people seem to lose their sense of the contemporary in the garden. Take a typical, upwardly mobile, young professional couple settling into their first flat or house in London, New York, San Francisco or any number of cities in countries of the 'industrial north' of the First World. More often than not the interior spaces will be decorated and furnished in a 'classic' contemporary style: sofa by Le Corbusier, chairs by Breuer, side-lit by 'Suzy' lamps, and in pride of place in the kitchen the horned cheese grater by Starck, with prints and etchings by Warhol and Matisse. When this couple gets to the garden door, however, they often retreat to a much more conventional historical solution. A design based perhaps on the White Garden at Sissinghurst, or a variation on the formal plan of Sir Edwin Lutyens and the informal planting pattern of Gertrude Jekyll, or box hedges with terracotta pots and a tree or two for vertical contrast.

In Europe, it seems that many clients with a small to medium-sized urban garden nurse an image of some childhood garden on a far larger scale than their own.

Right *Tensile material has been put to dramatic use in an installation in France. It encloses the garden space and focuses our attention on a few, specimen plants.*

They attempt to accommodate their memory of the huge old rectory with its roses and walled vegetable garden within the narrow confines of their 7.5 x 18m (25 x 60ft) urban patch. The results are invariably incompatible with the style of the interior. Finally, the mother-in-law on either side of the marital equation often has a say in the couple's decisions about the garden, and she urges them not to be too controversial.

According to Topher Delaney, a brilliant American designer of leading-edge private gardens in California, 75 per cent of her clients would still opt for a traditional layout, as 'daring to want a truly contemporary design would be to most clients like cross-dressing in the front yard'.

Despite the entrenched conservatism that we have described here, times are changing. The gardens and landscapes shown in this book do reflect the time in which we all live. Slowly, slowly there are hints, glints, glimmers, motes and rays of change, even within some of the most conservative and traditional agencies and organizations. These changes are coupled with the early signs of a new wave of visionary commissions given to impassioned contemporary designers.

Above A Summer Caprice. *This installation was the work of a group of young Swiss designers at the Lausanne Gardens '97 exhibition. Plant cages made of rectilinear steel supports seem to reflect the nation's reputation for order.*

The change of attitude towards landscape design is reflected in journals and newspapers. Even those papers with a conservative editorial stance are beginning to show articles about contemporary gardens. In Britain a garden magazine called *New Eden* was launched in April 1999. In the first issue the editor set out his aim to:

> . . . challenge the idea that gardens can only be nostalgic, with billowing borders and acres of lawn. We want to show you that modern gardens suit modern lifestyles.

Our book represents a robust exploration of gardens and landscapes which reflect contemporary life, the life of the late twentieth century, and also act as a preview of the twenty-first century.

Cultural influences

Landscapes are culture before they are nature; constructs of the imagination projected onto wood, water and rock.

Simon Schama

Above *A contemporary New Mexico garden with drought-resistant plants softening the concrete walls. The design may reflect the influence of sculptor Richard Serra.*

Right *Glass gravel has been put to exquisite use in a private garden in Los Angeles, creating a beautiful ground cover by melding layers of crushed glass.*

Ever since the late1930s there has been a constant cross-fertilization in garden and landscape design between Europe, North and South America and Japan. In these countries landscape design often reflects the influence of twentieth-century art – from Cubism to Minimalism – and architecture – from Bauhaus to the New York Six. Within this cultural context, three great twentieth-century artists and designers have had a very specific influence on the evolution of contemporary landscape. They are the Brazilian painter Roberto Burle Marx, the Japanese-American sculptor Isamu Noguchi and the Mexican architect Luis Barragan. No university degrees in landscape architecture are needed after these names. However, formally trained landscape architects have also made their impact. Thomas Church, Daniel Urban Kiley, Garrett Eckbo, James Rose and Ian McHarg are some of the most important names to emerge since 1950. The combined effect of these diverse influences has been to inspire landscape designers and architects to think in terms of the twentieth century.

Historical styles are no longer embraced by modern designers as total models. The gardens that are created for our technological society draw their inspiration from contemporary architecture, art and film and, wherever possible, from the site itself. Late twentieth-

INFLUENCES

Abstract Art
Age of Information
Alvar Aalto
Artificial Fog
Luis Barragan
Bauhaus
Biomorphic
Roberto Burle Marx
Chain Link Fencing
Circle
Conceptual Art
Cubism
Dada
Drought Resistance
Ecological Awareness
Energy Conservation
Environmental Art
Fibonacci Sequence
Fibreglass
Fibre Optics
Glass
Global Warming
Green Architecture
High Tech
Kitsch
Land Art
Le Corbusier
Low Maintenance
Minimalism
Motor Car
Neon
Isamu Noguchi
Plastics and Polymers
Postmodernism
Scandinavian Modern
Seriality
The Serpentine
Site Dominant
Site Adjusted
Site Generated
Spiral
Steels and Metals
Frank Lloyd Wright
Xeriscape
Zigzag

century landscape design is very diverse. However, some salient characteristics can be identified. The first of these relates to the treatment of space. Contemporary designers have been inspired by modern art and architecture to think of space in three dimensions and to take a sculptural approach to its use. Gardens are no longer laid out in the traditional manner along a single axis. The notion of multi-axial, diagonal and asymmetric spaces has been inherited by our designers from the Cubists. Abstract art has had an equally important influence in design, which is reflected in curvilinear and biomorphic shapes found in the garden. Finally, and by way of contrast, geometric and rectilinear forms have been drawn from the International Style of architecture and used in contemporary garden design.

Not all of the traditional spatial models have been rejected. For example, the Ur-Islamic layout – the most traditional mode of garden design known to western civilization – marries well with the rectilinear style of twentieth-century architecture, creating a closer integration of the house and garden.

The work of contemporary designers has resulted in a greater emphasis on gardens as places for people. Designers have to confront social issues and the changes in social structures and working patterns.

Above *The Plaza of the Japanese-American Cultural Centre, Los Angeles, by Isamu Noguchi.*

Right *One of many horse pools by Luis Barragan, Mexico's great modern architect; his coloured stucco planar designs have influenced contemporary landscape architects all over the world.*

Some garden designers have even been asked to make night-time gardens that can be used by shift workers. Others have learnt how to create gardens in tiny niches which are part of the urban landscape, such as balconies, stairwells and yards.

A greater awareness of ecology is also reflected in contemporary gardens. Modern designers are concerned with the ecological health of the site, and this concern is often reflected in the planting of native grasses and drought-resistant plants.

The sophisticated technology of the end of the century has produced many new materials. Plastics, metals, fibreglass rock formations, fibre-optic lighting and artificial fog began to be used in public landscapes at the beginning of the 1980s. Now they are starting to be seen in private gardens as well.

Diversity is the hallmark of contemporary design. This is an alphabetical list that spans the many different influences upon landscape and garden design at the end of the twentieth century.

Abstract Art was one of the great, contributive influences on all of the arts in the twentieth century. Since the 1950s, some of the earliest roots for landscape architecture have been variations on either the geometric or the hard-edge form of abstraction coined by Constructivists such as Malevitch and Rodchenko, Concrete Art, practised by Theo van Doesberg and Josef Albers, or the more relaxed, organic form of the abstract used by Hans Arp and Joan Miró and referred to as the Biomorphic.

Age of Information Landscape architecture and design has begun to benefit from new technology since the invention of CAD, Computer Aided Design. This is especially helpful with larger projects. Easy access to information about historic gardens and the gardens of other cultures has opened up a rich new seam of reference for the designers of site-adjusted gardens.

Alvar Aalto The great Finnish architect, designer and artist was one of the greatest architects of the International Modern movement and contributed greatly to garden and landscape design. His combined treatment of house and garden and his Biomorphic shapes were an inspiration to Thomas Church.

Artificial Fog is another technological advance used by garden and landscape designers over the past 20 years. It is made by water being 'atomized' under high pressure. The wonderful, mysterious effect blurs landscape elements and boundaries instantly, lending a surreal, other-wordliness to the design. Man-made fog has also been used in extremely hot climates for its cooling properties.

Luis Barragan The Mexican architect is one of the greatest Modernist influences on contemporary landscape design. His square and rectangular planar wall shapes were inspired by Muslim tradition in Spain and Morocco and the architecture of Le Corbusier, the International Style and the vernacular buildings of the Mediterranean and Mexico. Counterpointing his Minimalist walls with simple pools, channels and artificial waterfalls, his elegant and simple style continues to influence landscape architects and designers throughout the world.

Bauhaus This highly important early twentieth-century school of art and architecture in Dessau, Germany, was the fount of Modernism. After it was closed by the Nazis in the 1930s, many of the artists, architects and teachers, including Walter Gropius, fled to the United States. Gropius became head of architecture at Harvard. His teaching contributed greatly to the development of landscape architecture in America after the Second World War.

Biomorphic See Abstract Art

Roberto Burle Marx was another primary influence upon landscape architecture and design in this century. He trained as a painter and applied his artistic eye to his native Brazil. His trademark was the use of large-scale, free-flowing Biomorphic drifts of indigenous native plants as exquisite ground cover. He loathed the word 'style' and viewed each of his designs as a union between art and nature.

Chain Link Fencing has abandoned its traditional role as a security barrier and begun to be used sculpturally in gardens and landscapes. Some years ago, when we first began to find out about the

Right *Cross-cultural inspiration on the Costa Cayeres in Mexico. Man's most ancient design, the labyrinth, has been used as a terrace around an invisible-edge swimming pool. In this case the design was inspired by the nave floor of Chartres Cathedral.*

contemporary garden, we saw this material being used in the landscape and we were not impressed. Years later, we understand that chain link fencing has great value as a late twentieth-century material.

Circle Along with the spiral, serpentine and zigzag, the circle is one of the most primitive marks made by humankind and has been used in endless variations over many millennia. Today these shapes are being used once more in their pure form by contemporary landscape designers.

Conceptual Art was a phrase used by the artist Sol Le Witt in the late 1960s to refer to works of art in which the idea rather than the object is most important. Its roots go back to the art of *Readymades* by Marcel Duchamp, one of the most influential artists of the twentieth century. Other important figures are Yves Klein and Piero Manzoni. Video and Performance Art were spin-offs. In the landscape, the most inspirational form of Conceptual Art is Earth or Land Art.

Cubism The name of this important modern art movement arose when a French art critic heard Matisse refer to a painting by Braque as just some 'little cubes'. Picasso and Braque were the first Cubists and they changed the use of perspective which had been primary to painting since the Renaissance. In landscape design this translates into abstraction and the creation of simultaneous points of view, which was used first by a few French designers in some gardens and landscapes in the 1920s – Robert Mallet-Stevens, André and Paul Vera, and Gabriel Guevrekian. From the 1950s American landscape architects such as Garrett Eckbo, James Rose and Thomas Church were all influenced by it.

Dada Topher Delaney and Martha Schwartz are two American landscape designers who often speak of the influence of Dada on their work. Provocation, humour and absurdity were Dada characteristics. Marcel Duchamp would probably have approved of Delaney's

Garden of Divorce and Schwartz's *Bagel Garden*.

Drought Resistance During the past 30 years there has been among landscape architects and designers a heightened awareness of the need to consider ecology and the environment. During the last 15 years the prospect of increased global warming has emerged. This is allied to important issues of resource sustainability: supplies of water which had been taken for granted for centuries must now to be husbanded more sensibly and efficiently. Plants from more arid habitats are becoming popular and are being used in garden and landscape designs in many countries of the world – even in northern temperate areas where rainfall can be optimum.

Ecological Awareness In the early decades of this century Jens Jensen was already voicing his concern about the environment in relation to landscape design. Subsequently, many prominent thinkers and landscape designers have made a contribution to the ecological debate. At the beginning of the 1960s Ian McHarg led the field. Since the 1970s it has been Richard Oehme and James van Sweden in the United States, and Ton ter Linden, Piet Oudolf and Hank Geritsen in Holland, who have made great contributions to the ecological discussion. Naturalistic plantings of varying heights characterize this style. Leaf shapes and textures create structural contrasts and there is an emphasis on the use of grasses, the beauty of spent plants in autumn and winter and planting that requires low maintenance.

Energy Conservation Allied to ecological awareness is an attempt by the profession to factor energy conservation and sustainable resources into designs for both gardens and landscapes. Reconstituted stone is used for paving, outdoor composition board takes the place of natural wood for carpentry features, retention pond systems gather run-off water for use in the landscape and 'grey' recycled water is used for water incidents, solar-powered pumps provide the energy to drive small water features and low-voltage/high-intensity outdoor lighting systems are used.

Environmental Art See Land Art here, and Section on Earth (pages 84–89)

Fibonacci Sequence This was developed by Leonardo of Pisa in 1202, and it is one of the earliest mathematical models. Out of the sequence, each term from 3 onwards is the sum of the previous two. For example, 55 = 34 + 21. The same elegant sequence of numbers is found in the petal, sepal, stamen and seed head conformations of many plants. Some designers in the United States and Japan have used the sequence in the scale and proportion of the elements in designs.

Fibreglass This inexpensive, flexible, tough, weather-resistant material is being used more and more in gardens and landscapes to make hard architectural landscape features, completely natural-looking stones and boulders in myriad shapes, sculptures, paving slabs and sections for walls.

Fibre Optics have been transforming garden and landscape lighting since the 1980s. The technology came out of research for telecommunications and medical practice. The low-voltage, high-intensity lighting is extremely flexible, and can be housed in a huge variety of cabling, both clear and opaque. Any element of the garden or landscape can be lit by the use of fibre optics. The only limitations lie within the imagination of the designer.

Below *Sand-blasted, glass-panel walls are up-lit by white neon to make a mysterious and elegant enclosure for a terrace in San Francisco. The evergreen grass stripes are* Dichondra miscantha.

Glass Advances in glass technology over the past two decades have made many forms of glass available to landscape architects and designers. Glass comes in many specifications: toughened, double skinned and even ground up and used as gravel. It is also beginning to be used as an alternative to the endless machine-made terracotta of recent years.

Global Warming Awareness of this has emerged over the past 20 years, and the more ecologically minded landscape architects and designers have tried to factor this atmospheric negative into their work. Northern climes can now take more drought-resistant-plants for the weather is much warmer.

Green Architecture Grass roof technology, turf-covered underground houses in Denmark, Germany and Mexico, solar-powered pumps for small ponds, houses made of hay, all these and many more are examples of green architecture. Designs incorporating trees within architecture are being created by American and French landscape architects; James Wines of SITE and Edouard François have been at the forefront of this work.

High Tech Every aspect of our lives has been changed by the fax and email and digital everything is on its way. In landscape and garden design, fibre optic lighting, artificial fog, videos as part of garden design: the Video Garden at MIT.

Kitsch An extremely conservative traditional landscape designer from the Deep South of the United States reckons some avant garde American landscape and garden designers in the late twentieth century have this trait. He sums up their work as ephemeral 'one-liners' with the following: 'Once you've seen a dog wearing lipstick, what else is there?'

Left *Overlapping sections of perforated steel provide security for the parking court in a Phoenix, Arizona, garden. On a sunny day the wall is semi-transparent, creating a moiré effect. On a dull day it is opaque.*

Below *The roof terrace of a multi-national bank has brightly coloured polymer material benches, silk wind socks and giant balls of ivy: a view to cheer up the computer operators inside the building. At night the terrace is lit so that it can be appreciated by the night-shift workers.*

Above *A late twentieth-century design for a courtyard in Santa Fe, New Mexico. The sound made by the falling water in this Islamic-style garden is increased by the metal linings of the raised pools.*

Land Art or Earth Art have had a significant influence on landscape architects and designers. The primary work in the mid-1960s was by many artists disenchanted with zero abstraction in both painting and sculpture. They also rejected the gallery/ curator/critic hype machine and were aware of the environmental movement. This position drew them to the endless sky and earth of the desert and non-arable wide open spaces of the western United States. Here the Earth Artists sculpted vast quantities of earth, often in shapes reminiscent of our primitive forbears' burial mounds and stone structures.

Le Corbusier Along with Mies van der Rohe, Le Corbusier was the leading proponent of the most influential twentieth-century architecture, the white rectilinear International Style. His visionary approach was not without its downside: under his influence vertical slums were built all over the world after the Second World War, and many are now being demolished. Some great single elitist compositions – the Chapel at Ronchamps in eastern France and his Villa Savoye west of Paris (the last exemplified his view of the landscape - his white architecture set in a rural picturesque landscape) alone would have secured his place in the history of twentieth-century architecture.

Low Maintenance Landscape architects and designers have been asked, even told, to include this most important basic given in their designs. Evergreens are used in place of deciduous plants, for this minimizes the need for dead leaf collecting. Ground

Above *A flower and vegetable patch designed for a plant-obsessed client in Paradise Valley, Arizona. The plants were all waiting in readiness for the garden to be completed.*

cover plants are also widely used, suppressing weed growth. Technological development since the 1980s has meant that computers and sensors can be used to control irrigation and lighting.

Minimalism is thought to have been the first modernist art movement to have emerged in the United States: Donald Judd, Sol Le Witt, Agnes Martin, Robert Morris, Richard Serra and David Smith were some of its leading lights. Their ground-zero minimalist forms, lines and groups of the same abstract geometric shapes set in seriality, cross-fertilized with the work of late twentieth-century garden and landscape architects and designers, particularly in the work of Peter Walker.

Motor Car Clients often ask us to mask or re-route the motor car and its function in relation to the house and garden. The machine must be concealed and yet accessible. Has Filippo Marinetti's notion on modern life in the *Futurist Manifesto* finally become a reality with the motor car in 1999, 'a life of steel, fever, pride and headlong speed'?

Neon This wonderful, flexible and relatively inexpensive twentieth-century design element has gone from billboards to signposting, and then to museum art installations. In the past 20 years it has found its way out into the garden and landscape. Ian Hamilton Finlay, the great British poet and designer, was one of the first to use neon art installations. Adventurous landscape designers, particularly in the United States and Japan, have been including it in their designs.

Isamu Noguchi The great Japanese-American sculptor, has had a significant influence on gardens and landscapes since the 1980s. His symbolic, sculptural garden and landscape designs included memorials, play parks and bridges. Noguchi's use of stone, water and a minimum of plants are seen in his masterpieces: Chase Manhattan Bank, New York City; Beinecke Rare Book and Manuscript Library, Yale University, and *California Scenario*, Costa Mesa, California.

Plastics and Polymers are twentieth-century materials which are now finding their way into contemporary gardens and landscapes in many different forms and configurations, such as perimeter fencing,

Above Spiral to Heaven *made from lawn and boxwood in a garden near Caen in Normandy, France.*

Right Mirror Trail, *Ithaca, New York, was made in 1969 by Robert Smithson. The effect of the snow is heightened and transformed by the use of mirrors and glass.*

retaining walls, paving, garden furniture and sculpture.

Postmodernism This term is thought to have appeared first in *Architecture and the Spirit of Man* by Joseph Hudnut, 1949, but it was popularized by Charles Jencks in the late 1960s and given form in the architecture of Philip Johnson, Michael Graves, Robert Venturi and others. It is a highly complex cluster of cultural ideas and phenomena. Just as there was a relationship between Modernism and the industrialization of society, so there is between Postmodernism and our contemporary, high-tech society. Postmodernism is a reaction against the spare, minimalist style of Modernism. It is a hybrid, full of cultural references and its forms are ambiguous. Garden and landscape designers like George Hargreaves, Adriaan Geuze, Kathryn Gustafson, Desvigne & Dalnoky all have elements of the Postmodern in their work.

Scandinavian Modern is a major twentieth century international design force. The Ant Chair by Jacobsen, Bang and Olufsen TV and music systems, and wind turbines are classic models from Denmark; Marimmeko fabrics, Arabia pottery and the designs of Alvar Aalto from Finland; Ikea of Sweden sells its products worldwide. Landscape design in Scandinavia incorporates the principles of social democracy and modern art. Sven-Ingvar Andersson, the greatest living Danish landscape architect, says that 'the very essence of our profession lies in the combination of design and architecture with ecology. '

Seriality see Minimalism.

The Serpentine is an ancient form which is used as a contrast to the square or rectilinear. The designs of Sven-Ingvar Andersson, Denmark and Ted Smyth, New Zealand, in this book provide wonderful examples.

Site Dominant is a term which was used by Robert Irwin in America. In this case it refers to the actual 'historical models' from garden history, rather than to the gardens that they inspired.

Site Adjusted is another term applied to landscape design by Irwin and used to define gardens and landscapes with a design that is influenced by the gardens of other cultures or periods.

Site Generated is a term used by Irwin to define gardens with a design that has evolved from the intrinsic characteristics of the site.

Spiral This eternal form is seen in the spiral star galaxies, and from the DNA spiral to the double spiral of florets in the sunflower or the household screw. It is used internationally in the designs of landscape architects and designers: George Hargreaves' projects

at Château de Chaumont, near Tours, and the University of Cincinnati, the public park in Luxembourg with giant water retention ponds designed by the German designer Peter Latz, and the projected public park Andoibarra by Balmori Associates in Bilbao adjacent to the Guggenheim museum are but a few.

Steels and Metals Many types of steel have found their way into the late twentieth-century landscape. Stainless steel and Cor-Ten are both commonly used to make retaining walls in gardens and landscapes. On a recent trip through Spain we saw not only handsome, cast iron, circular planters on ball feet, but long, angular sheets of steel used as pavements in pedestrian precincts.

Frank Lloyd Wright is considered the American master architect of the twentieth century, and displays enormous sensitivity towards the landscape in relation to his buildings: Falling Water in Pennsylvania and Taliesin West, Arizona, and Hollyhock House, Los Angeles.

Xeriscape Xeri means dry and this is the current American 'buzz-word' definition for drought-resistant gardening techniques.

Zigzag Along with the circle, spiral and serpentine, this is one of humankind's most ancient marks or patterns, and it is used endlessly in garden and landscape design. The origin of the word itself is unknown. It is partly symbolic, for the two different vowels do suggest two different directions, from the pattern on the columns in the Treasury at Mycenae, to the spirit bridges in Japanese gardens, to the floor plan and fenestration pattern of the Jewish Museum in Berlin by Daniel Libeskind.

We see these influences reflected in a myriad of combinations in the gardens of the late twentieth century. George Hargreaves has his own view on where this new vocabulary of landscape architecture will lead:

> With this society's shift from belief in the new to its recognition of limits and interest in what exists, the stylistic explorations in Postmodern landscape architecture have just begun. Time, nature and culture will serve as physical media and subject. Light, shadow, sky, rain, plants, dirt, debris, people of all types, and man-made elements that intensify and abstract what is already here will become the focus of simpler, more receptive compositions and non-compositions. Where this will lead and what landscapes may come to look like is, of course, open-ended.

Below Fiber Wave *is made from 150 carbon fibre rods. It was created by the Japanese architect Makoto Wei Watanabe. He refers to it as 'designless design' as the 4m (12.8ft) rods are moved randomly by the wind.*

New functions

Public spaces

At the La Villette competition, we discovered the programmatic potential of landscape, and so I explained to him [the late Yves Brunier] that, personally, I didn't find architecture particularly interesting, but that on the contrary, landscape represented an incredible potential.

Rem Koolhaas

Above *The main terrace of the Mondrian Hotel in Los Angeles designed by Phillipe Starck. Nineteenth-century Victorian flower pots have been scaled up to become giant, late twentieth-century containers for multi-stemmed bay trees.*

Previous page *Video image of the Beaubourg Centre, Paris, with a myriad of images in the* Hanging Gardens of Golders Green, *London.*

Adriaan Geuze had this to say regarding public spaces:

Green has become a kind of habit. And it has also become a cliché of its own. . . There is absolutely no need for parks anymore, because they have solved all the nineteenth-century problems and a new type of city has been created.

Adriaan Geuze is head of West 8, a brilliant architecture and landscape design team located in Rotterdam, Holland, which creates some of the newest and most exciting site-generated public spaces in Europe.

During the early part of the nineteenth century, John Claudius Loudon and his wife Jane became the first crusaders for public parks in Great Britain. Loudon was one of the first Victorian garden visionaries to think about public parks in relation to the onslaught of the industrial revolution. He believed that such parks had the power to 'raise the intellectual character of the lowest classes of society'.

In the latter half of the century, landscape design was largely dominated by the classical, Beaux-Arts style. This prevailed until the late 1920s and 30s,

which saw a radical change in the way that public spaces were designed. This change was a response to the influence of Modernism and Le Corbusier. His simple, white 'machines for living' were surrounded by quasi-natural landscapes which usually consisted of a ground plane of grass which was then punctuated by the vertical forms of trees.

Just before the Second World War, social need came to be seen as an important factor in the design of new buildings, gardens and landscapes. Denmark was one of the leaders in this field. Here gardens and landscapes were designed around new public housing projects. This early Scandinavian 'green' architecture became a source of inspiration for architects in post-war Europe and America.

Sven-Ingvar Andersson is described as the grand old man of Danish, if not Scandinavian, landscape architecture, and its greatest living designer. In his view, landscape design in twentieth century Denmark has been based on social democratic principals allied to modern art. Klee, Kandinsky, Picasso and Braque have all had an influence on Danish landscape design.

Andersson followed on from G.N. Brandt and C.Th. Sorensen, who were pioneers of landscape at the beginning of this century. It is a pity that few books in English exist on any of these visionary designers.

Below *The Citadel, the former Uniroyal Tyre and Rubber Company building, Commerce, California. Its façade is reminiscent of an Assyrian temple, and was the inspiration for the oasis of palms planted there in 1991. The 'ghosts of tyres past' are made in concrete and used for sitting and for protecting the palms from cars.*

Below *One of 26 follies on grid points of the Parc de la Villette, the largest public park in Paris. Bernard Tschumi, the designer, described the design process in the following way: 'First we decided that we were not going to be contextual . . . We were determined to literally start from a pure concept.'*

Andersson credits Brandt and Sorenson with managing to combine Denmark's rural landscape with advancing urbanization and modern art. They were influenced by the use of the abstract which was displayed in modern architecture and painting. The public plazas and parks that they built represent another layer of the Scandinavian Modern style.

During the 1960s and 70s, landscape architects became increasingly concerned about the plight of the landscape after a century of rampant industrialization. From this time onwards, an awareness of ecology became integral to landscape design.

In the northern industrial countries, the last 20 or 30 years have seen a huge growth in the garden and landscape spaces created for public use. The public

park now has the highest profile in contemporary 'place-making' – to quote Capability Brown, that great designer of eighteenth-century landscapes. Many of Brown's picturesque landscapes have been transformed into public parks since the end of the Second World War. Blenheim, Bowood, Chatsworth, Longleat, Petworth and Weston Park: all these are now open.

It should be remembered, however, that public access is not an entirely modern concept. Many stately homes, gardens and landscapes could be viewed by merely contacting the head gardener or housekeeper and paying them token fees for the 'tours'.

This is not the place for a complete history of the public park. However, it should be noted that the provision of open space for sporting amenities dates back to the 1870s in England.

There are many differences between the parks of the nineteenth century and those that belong to the twentieth. The four projects which are described here are intended to reflect the diversity of contemporary public spaces. One of the most striking contrasts between these parks and those of the nineteenth century is their location. Traditionally the park was found in the centre of a town or city. Today it can be

situated anywhere. It might be on the very edge of an urban area or some distance away from it.

Parc de la Villette

Parc de la Villette was built in a Parisian suburb in the 1980s. The project represents another seismic shift in the design of the public park. This park has become a watershed in recent thinking about the creation and function of public spaces.

The 70-hectare (175-acre) ex-abattoir and cattle market site is the largest park in Paris. When the competition for the design was announced, its aim was 'to realize on the same site the largest Museum of Science, Technology and Industry and a Music Centre'. Grand words for an unbuilt public park project at pre-competition stage, but in the event, Parc de la Villette did prove to be a uniquely creative and inventive place.

The La Villette project attracted 471 entries from 41 countries. The competition was judged by an international jury of 21, with the late Roberto Burle Marx as its chairman. It was won by Bernard Tschumi, architect and chairman of the school of architecture at Columbia University. Tschumi describes his design in the following words:

> La Villette was called a park, but it was not a park; it was a new type of city. I have always said it is the largest discontinuous city building in Paris. Like many of our urban projects today, we were starting with an old industrial area, the site of slaughterhouses.

Below *The Guadalupe River Park flood control project was a site-generated design created in the 1990s in San Jose, California.*

The enormous site has been organized on a point grid. At 26 points of intersection there are 26 pure red, metal follies. Some of them are abstract metal sculptures and others function as kiosks where drinks and ice cream are sold. Tschumi designed two other layers of lines in the form of raised walkways.

Alexandre Chemetoff designed the Bamboo Garden – which lies below the soil grade – and Vexiard, also a French landscape architect, designed the formal Vineyard. Some young designers have been disappointed by their work. However, Lodewijk Baljon, a Dutch landscape architect of about the same age, was more impressed:

> The result is a Mannerist plan. It is characterized by unrest, movement, passion and a tendency towards elegance. It aims to evoke a fantastically ordered chaos with an ingenious mental game; it is admirably suited to a cultural amusement park.

Below *The Interopolis Garden, Tilburg, The Netherlands. The triangular, 2-hectare (5-acre) site is near Breda, southeast of Rotterdam. A large, tectonic-shaped lily pool is finished with wooden slabs that can be used as seating.*

Duisburg North Landscape Park

The 200-hectare (500-acre) site of a derelict steelworks at Duisburg in the Ruhrgebeit area of central Germany has been transformed. Four years after the works were closed it was suggested that the site should be made into a park. An international competition for the design was won by Professor Peter Latz and his colleague, Anna-Liese Latz. In 1994 the park was opened, but work will continue here for many years.

Duisburg North is budgeted at £28 million and it is part of a 300sq km (117 sq m) regeneration project in an area which boasted some of the most advanced steelworks in the world. In fact the works buildings and the enormous machinery have been left intact and incorporated into the design.

Initially, an analysis was made of the existing vegetation, all the major structures and the railway network which formerly served the works. Latz saw the

railway, with its complexity and superb engineering, as a form of land art and he incorporated it into the design. Where the railway structure had broken down, he designed high-level walkways to improve access and to give views over the site.

Many of the existing materials on site have been recycled. Aggregate for cement has been made from salvaged bricks and large metal plates made of pig iron have been blasted clean with compressed air to become giant pavers laid in sand to make a plaza: the Piazza Metallica. The run-off water from pavements, roofs and roads has been channelled into a polluted waste water canal which has been diverted into former cooling tanks and old settling basins. As a result, the water on the whole site has been purified.

The design concept for the landscape is not entirely unified because the site is so large; it is a design realized in several layers. Latz initially submitted plans for five separate parks which would have been superimposed on one another during installation. On further consideration, he designed seven satellite areas nearer to the workers' housing and away from the main park. Here he located sports grounds, children's playgrounds and other areas defined by leisure activities.

Latz has a clear view of the role of the Duisberg Park: 'This is to become a historical park, but the history starts now and goes forward as well as backwards.' The park is well used by the local population. Rock bands play in the open air, groups of mountain climbing enthusiasts scale the taller blast furnaces and ex-worker families promenade on the overhead walkways.

Guadalupe River Park

The Guadalupe River which runs through the city of San Jose, California, can become a destructive and

Below *The Minneapolis Federal Courthouse Plaza contains sculptural earth mounds, based on glacial drumlins and logs. These are symbols of inherited memory. They represent the hills and trees seen by the first settlers in Minnesota.*

Above *The former Thyssen steelworks in Ruhr, Duisburg-North, has been transformed into a public park. This is the spring garden in the former pig iron smelting area.*

raging torrent when it is at flood tide. The city did not want the standard government-agency solution of ugly concrete culverts enclosing the entire 4.8km (3m) stretch of water in order to protect the town and its citizens when the river was on the rampage. It was for this reason that Hargreaves Associates were asked to solve the problem of creating a preventative measure that was also aesthetically pleasing.

George Hargreaves headed a multi-disciplinary team which consisted of civil, hydraulic, structural and geo-technical engineers, and environmental consultants, as well as 14 additional review agencies. Their collective aim in this project was to realize the city's vision for their river and its use.

The design concept consisted of two layers. One, the 'underlay' as George Hargreaves calls it, was to increase the depth and the width of the river channel so that it could accommodate the flood tide. Two, the 'overlay', involved shoring up the banks with runs of gabions (tough wire cubes containing either rocks or soil for planting) to retain the river bank organically and to underpin the path and planting system.

In section, the plan was to read from river to the gabion to a generous path for walking or bicycling to, in parts, graceful stone retaining steps doubling as seats. Trees and shrubs have been planted along the entire section of the river. These plants look very attractive and they also help to stabilize the earth structure of the bank.

In places the river bank was totally flat. Here raised and shaped earth forms were designed, both for their visual impact and so that they could act as a reinforcement during flood time. The total cost of the project was $50 million.

Scan Park

Scan Park was designed by Sven-Ingvar Andersson in 1997. The completed park is an example of his

Above *Scan Park, a small public park in Copenhagen, Denmark, has beautiful walls retaining undulating grassed land forms.*

Centre *The serpentine pond walk creates a contrast with the sculptural, rolling wave land forms in Scan Park.*

most skilled work as a mature designer. It is a small public park which is situated in a bleak industrial suburb of Copenhagen. The project was initiated when a developer wanted to build a business centre that would be used by many companies. As an initial move, the developer wanted to create an attractive park at the entrance to his land. The competition for the park was won by Andersson.

Andersson has played sinuously with the main elements of the design. The largest part of the ground planes is a lawn consiting of six rolling earth forms. Seen in section from the street side of the park, Andersson has retained the rolling shapes with a run of close-set pale yellow concrete stone palings. The curved tops of the palings are a striking variation on the rolling forms of the lawn: a sturdy, simple and beautiful design element.

The lawn-covered forms slope down to meet seamlessly at a large pond with an undulating serpentine edge, which has been created by a generous asphalt path retained by neat rusty steel sections; the serpentine shape is further reinforced by a ribbon beach of pebbles which runs along the pond. It is a serpentine with a difference, recalling the image of Alvar Aalto's rippling modern classic vase design, the Lake.

Gentle troughs next to the path contain groups of tall aquatic plants creating a contrast in height, colour and texture. The tallest vertical contrasts are two 8m-high (25ft-high) pipes at the shallow end of the pond, one rusty and one stainless steel, and water flows out from the tops of them. Andersson was inspired by the stems of tall bamboo.

On the opposite side of the pond is a 2m-high (6ft-high) wooden fence. It echoes the vertical foliage of the aquatic plants and fountains and masks the near-derelict site beyond. Andersson is pleased to see that the park has become a playground for the children from a nearby housing estate.

Private spaces

Residential design is the most intricate, specialized, demanding and frustrating field for the landscape designer.

Garrett Eckbo

The private garden has not been a focus of attention for landscape architects and designers since about 1980. Their energies have been devoted to the design of public spaces. This trend reflects an economic reality. Only by accepting large-scale commissions can they be assured of a sufficient client base to support their offices. In other words, they have had to 'follow the money' . . . .

Two very distinct strands of design for private spaces have emerged in the latter part of the twentieth century. The first is naturalistic and is characterized by mainly herbaceous plantings.

Left *The spines of agave leaves in the foreground were the inspiration for the large, sculptural shapes of the structures in this Arizona garden.*

Below *The Barragan-inspired walls in a suburban garden in south San Francisco. The owner of the garden is an Indian expatriate. The walls washed in the vivid colours of the sub-continent personalize his private space.*

The other, opposing strand might be called a 'smartening-up'. It is characterized by a sculptural approach, inspired by the intrinsic nature of the site.

The naturalistic approach to design has its roots in the planting style of German parks, and is now also popular in Holland and the United States. At the end of the 1980s this trend in civic design triggered a formulaic, ecological and naturalistic style of planting in contemporary private gardens. At their best, the results are simplistic. At their worst they represent a 'dumbing down' of landscape and garden design.

Below *In this private Arizona garden an iridescent, serpentine wall clothed with green glass mosaic encloses a terrace used for entertaining.*

The opposing, more sculptural style of design is practised by some designers in the United States and Europe who are not concerned solely with plants *per se*. By using various contemporary materials they make gardens which reflect certain aspects of contemporary culture and have something to say something about this particular moment in history.

These two approaches to garden design are very distinct. However, they both reflect the fact that the private garden has had to adapt to social and economic pressure. Generally, private gardens are very much smaller than their counterparts in the nineteenth and early twentieth centuries. This is due largely to the enormous social changes wrought since the Second World War, such as the high cost of maintenance and labour. Ground cover plants have become more popular because they reduce maintenance costs to a minimum. The suburban lawn has begun to be modified as more and more young couples create simple, tough gardens that suit the needs of their growing children and the family pets. Environmental change has also left its mark as dry, or even drought conditions predicate a corresponding plant palette. Finally, a renewed interest in naturalistic, ecological plantings has reduced the popularity of exotics. This has led many garden centres to narrow the choice of plants that they offer.

The naturalistic, ecological style was thoroughly investigated during a series of lectures given in London

Right *A bold and simple design for a private garden in Holland. The paths and fences are attractively made and there are stepping stones in the pond.*

in March 1999. The event was an opportunity to hear the views of landscape architects and designers such as Piet Oudolf of Holland, Dan Pearson of Great Britain and James van Sweden of the United States, all of them practitioners of a mainly naturalistic style.

By the end of the day, we both yearned for some structure which went beyond the hard landscaping of just a few roads, paths and the occasional summer-house (admittedly of a highly contemporary design). Our senses were clamouring for any structure beyond that provided by perennial herbaceous plantings.

Oudolf, Pearson and van Sweden all spoke at length about the sculptural beauty of dried stems and seed heads in the autumn and winter. We felt great sympathy for Mary Keen, the British garden writer and designer, whose view of naturalistic planting is rather similar to our own. As she put it, a garden which is 'basically brown' (said in her unique, orotund and ironic tone) for four or five months of the year is not terribly attractive. Mary Keen also criticized the intrinsically limited palette of naturalistic, herbaceous planting. Like us, she felt that the endless drifts of sedums, rudbeckias, salvias and polygonums were not really diverse nor interesting enough to fully engage the eye and brain.

This book offers several examples of gardens which stand in opposition to the naturalistic approach. Many of them could be categorized by Robert Irwin's definition of the site-generated design. One such example is a private garden in London which was designed to take account of the intrinsic nature of the site, the history of the house and, most important of all, the personal interests of the client.

Above *Sky reflected in the dark grey interior of a swimming pool in a private garden in Madrid. The clipped mounds of escallonia are reminiscent of the organic shapes of azaleas in Japanese gardens.*

The design evolved in the following way. The designers were invited to meet the clients and to see what they described as 'a very small garden patch at the back of the house and a few broken-down plant containers at the front.' The initial discussion was stereotypical, covering all of the usual questions relevant to a small, London garden. The breakthrough occurred when the designers were invited up to the drawing room. Here they saw that their client was a collector of works by young British artists. The bookcase was filled with books about Land Art and modern artists such as David Hockney, Gordon Matta-Clark, Frank Stella and Andy Warhol. At this point, the idea of a nice, conventional solution to the design of the back garden was abandoned in favour of something that would reflect the client's own interests. Given this opportunity, the client declared that he would really like to see stone, metal and moss used in a low-maintenance garden.

Over the next three months the design gradually evolved. It encompassed a pink, Indian stone terrace adjacent to the house. Moss was planted along the fractured edge of one side of the terrace. A smooth, concrete, 1m-high (3ft-high) diagonal was built from the house, across the terrace and then into the lawn at its grade level. This structure, which provides seating on the terrace, is edged along its entire length with a narrow stripe of blue mosaic in Hockney, Los Angeles swimming-pool blue. Steps on one side of the terrace lead to the upper level of the garden. Here, the ground plane is surfaced with bitumen-set gravel.

Three rusting, cast iron, eighteenth-century European-style urns from China were arranged on the concrete seating structure. These were a reference to the house, which is also eighteenth century, and they could be used as planters for seasonal flowers. A circular pavilion measuring 3.5m (11ft) in diameter was also installed. It is built of the steel mesh used for reinforcing concrete and has a blue circular cover made of tensile material which can be roped on in summer.

The wittiest element of all is an arc of lawn which runs along to one side of the circular pavilion. This amused the client as it was a reference to the arc work of Robert Matta-Clark. The client also understood that it doubled as a reference to the English lawn. Even though it was only 3m (10ft) long and 10cm (4in) wide, he wondered if he would be able to maintain it to a sufficient standard!

Sites like this small, London garden and the naturalistic style (which was described earlier in the chapter) represent two main strands of landscape architecture and design. Viewed in this way, they give some idea of the diversity of work being done in the latter part of the twentieth century.

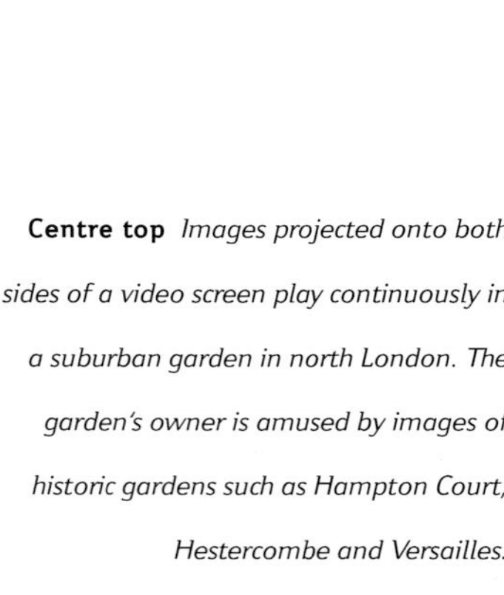

Centre top *Images projected onto both sides of a video screen play continuously in a suburban garden in north London. The garden's owner is amused by images of historic gardens such as Hampton Court, Hestercombe and Versailles.*

Centre bottom *An international businessman uses this Johannesburg garden for meditation. The carp pond bounded by rocks is evocative of the serene courtyard gardens of Japan.*

Far right *A Tokyo courtyard garden created by a leading Japanese artist, potter and film maker. The brilliant effect of his 'river of moss' proves that gardens can be made by non-landscape artists.*

Right *These fish stepping stones are on the Sea Terrace of the Jonathan Parker Abramson Safe Harbor Roof Garden at the Beth Israel North Hospital in New York. Recuperating children use the rubber stepping stones as an aid to retrieving a sense of balance after long illnesses.*

Healing gardens

Left *Convalescing children regaining motor control at water and sand tables. The rubber tubes in the background are part of a 9m-long (30ft-long) rubber sound sculpture connected to the Octopus Table. The sculpture is activated by children talking into the tubing.*

A landscape for people with life-threatening illnesses is going to be a different kind of place from your typical open park. It should have enclosed, connected rooms that provide a safe haven. A family huddled together sobbing, you don't want to share. And there should be lots of botanical complexity, but it should be ordered not sloppy. Disease represents disorder, and that's the last thing a patient needs.

Topher Delaney

Left *This 6.5m (20ft) metal fence encloses the terrace of the Safe Harbor Roof Garden. It was made by Sarah Keizer, who encloses children's fantasies within cartoon silhouettes of the 20 Manhattan bridges.*

Delaney is a leading American landscape architect and artist who designed her first healing garden near San Francisco while recovering from cancer. Latterly, she has designed healing gardens for the San Diego Children's Hospital, New York Beth Israel Hospital, a garden for Alzheimer's syndrome patients south of San Francisco and a meditation garden at the Norris Cancer Center in Los Angeles funded by a family whose daughter had died at the Center. Healing gardens create a sense of community and in no other area of garden and

landscape design is this more relevant. The gardens designed by Delaney have often been built with volunteer labour and funded by donations.

The idea of the garden as a place of healing has its roots in ancient history. In Egypt, gardens were designed specially for patients with mental illnesses. Gardens of healing, solitude and sanctuary were also part of the life in the great monasteries and abbeys of medieval Europe. Montecassino in Italy, Cluny in France, Monserrat in Spain and Fountains Abbey in England were some of the most historically important.

Healing gardens reflect an understanding of the human need to be in contact with nature and the natural processes of growth and renewal. The instinct to create gardens of this kind has emerged once again in the late twentieth century. This is the century which has brought us keyhole surgery, chemotherapy and laser technology, but despite huge medical advances, the high-rise hospitals of our time cannot provide all of the curative answers. Environmental and behavioural psychologists have been working to prove the benefits of bringing gardens and landscapes to patients.

Research at Harvard University has shown that the response of patients is improved by contact with a natural environment.

In the United States there are over 150 hospitals and day centres which have gardens or greenhouses devoted to horticultural therapy programmes. By creating therapeutic gardens, they are also taking a lead in humanizing the 'hard settings' of most hospitals and hospices. A therapeutic garden often has to meet the needs of two different categories of patient. There are those needing short-term rehabilitation and those with long-term degenerative diseases.

Dr Roger Ulrich, an environmental psychologist at Texas A & M College of Architecture, has undertaken a ten-year research project focusing on the relationship between patient well-being and environment. He has found that patients whose rooms overlook brick walls need more painkillers and longer recuperation time than patients who have views of a natural landscape from their beds. Similar studies show that maximum sunlight and contact with the natural world reduce patient anxiety levels.

Several gardens have been designed on the 21-hectare (52-acre) campus of the new 80-bed acute-care department of the St Michael Health Care Center, Texarkana, Arkansas. The gardens are the result of an environmental psychologist and a landscape architect working together to provide a more humane setting for the hospital's patients.

James Burnett, the landscape designer on the project, had seen his mother die in a small room overlooking a gravel roof. Talking about the experience, he said: 'I would like to have gotten her out of there. She lived on a lake and she just wanted to go home.' He was left with the conviction that his practice should change direction and devote itself to the design of gardens and landscapes for hospitals.

The architect D. Kirk Hamilton worked together with Burnett. Their aim was to create buildings and gardens that would provide compassionate settings for healing as well as dignified places in which to die. In describing his motivation, Burnett says: 'It's tragic that people today have to leave the planet in these unbearable situations. They're like prisons: tiny little rooms with people coming in and jabbing you and TVs blaring all down the hall.'

On the St Michael site, Burnett preserved as many existing trees as possible and planted more in the gently rolling woodland divided by two streams. His master plan included nine fountains, a lake fed by wells which became the reservoir for irrigation, and a series of jogging paths through the woods. The circulation paths are logical and well marked. In the large courtyards of the hospital, a simple bicolour paving pattern was used and one of the fountains offers access for wheelchair users. Seasonal plantings include azalea, grape myrtle, pear trees and spiraea.

In the early 1990s David Kamp, a landscape designer who used to plan estates in Connecticut, decided that he would devote his professional time and skills to designing gardens for AIDS patients. His first project, The Schnaper Memorial Garden, was a terrace adjacent to the AIDS section at the Cardinal Cook Hospital in New York City. The powerful medications the patients take make their eyes very sensitive to bright sunlight. To counter the over-bright, sunny aspect of the terrace, Kamp designed shaded seating. He also provided low planters which would allow wheelchair-bound patients to garden actively. They grew herbs, vegetables and flowers which were picked and used to brighten up the patients' rooms.

Kamp worked with the Tamarind Foundation, a non-profit-making organization in New York. He and Bruce Detrick, another founding member, worked to achieve the group's goal of helping to ensure an

Left *An* Art in Hospitals *project in Worthing, England. This piece is called* Shell, *and it was made by Peter Randall-Page in 1997. The sculptural bench is by Steve Geliot. It creates a contrast with the restrained plantings of* Sedum spectabile *'Autumn Joy' and the grass* Stipa arundinacea, *which lends gentle sound and movement to this healing garden.*

improved life for AIDS sufferers. As with so many other healing gardens in existence, this project was funded by private donations.

Sedgemoor Commons, Falmouth, Maine has a garden designed for Alzheimers patients by Robert Hoover, a local landscape architect. His design for the 2-heactare (5-acre) site is based on what he calls 'remembrance therapy'. He views the disease as 'life in fast-forward reverse'. He has identified three stages of the disease which he sees as a reversal of the normal ageing process. At the onset of the disease, Alzheimer patients are adults. The 'reversal' to which Hoover refers means that they end their lives as infants.

Right *The courtyard healing garden was created from a sterile space in the Marin Cancer Center, north of San Francisco.*

Sedgemoor Commons is built in the shape of a clover leaf. Each wing is named after a major American poet: the Hawthorne wing is for residential care, Longfellow is for nursing care and the Millay is for advanced nursing care. This continuum of care is unique in the treatment of Alzheimer's. Hoover has made a garden for each wing of the hospital. The gardens are designed to help patients at each stage of the disease. All of them have extremely secure fencing and generous, easily identifiable paths.

Above *The Norris Cancer Center, Los Angeles, is a large meditation garden. The walls reflect the influence of Luis Barragan.*

The Hawthorne garden is used by patients with the early stages of Alzheimer's. Honeysuckles, roses and lilacs are planted here, to help patients focus on earlier times in their lives. A clothes-line, basketball hoop and gazebo are intended to give the patients some sense of autonomy, exploration and control. Another of Hoover's main objectives with these gardens is to 'bring back choice into the lives' of people institutionalized and suffering an irreversible disease.

The Longfellow garden is centred on the second stage of Alzheimer's, which is the emotional equivalent of adolescence. The pergola provides a sense of enclosure and safety. Eight hawthorn trees are spaced in pairs on grassed plots around the garden's main quadrangle. The plantings emphasize tones of green rather than flowers. The planting includes arborvitae, viburnum, spiraea, periwinkle and magnolia.

The much smaller and more intimate Millay garden is for the third stage of the disease and beyond. Hoover emphasized security and serenity in this Japanese-inspired space. Here there is a dry stream bed with glacial river stone and specimen weathered field stone within plantings of Siberian iris, snow-in-summer and kousa dogwood. Lilac, roses and honeysuckles on either side of a path reinforce the sense of safety and security. The adjacent beds are planted with Himalayan birch, hay-scented fern, witch-hazel and bayberry.

Patients with long-term mental impairment or psychological problems also benefit from contact with plants and gardening. Dr Oliver Sacks, a neurologist and the author of *Awakenings* and *The Man Who Mistook his Wife for a Hat*, refers to the stress-reducing qualities of plants on his patients: 'I had people who were so anxious in the hospital that I would do my consultations in the greenhouse. They would often feel less pressured there and have less ticks and involuntary movements.' He has watched patients in deep dementia – 'who could not tell a knife from a fork' – begin to plant: 'They do not put a plant upside down, and no matter how estranged the mental state, they have a deep sense of how plants grow.'

In England, the West Dorset Hospital in Dorchester and the Royal Brompton Heart and Lung Hospital in London both have courtyard gardens for their patients. At St Thomas Hospital in London, the Thames-side garden next to the hospital doubles as a public park and a garden for the patients.

A new design aesthetic

Place

Previous page *The Trump Towers, Fifth Avenue, New York City. More property developers should consider planting trees on the façades of their unimaginative steel and glass skyscrapers.*

In the landscape, the context is everything, from the cosmos to the park, so the real question is, 'What idea arises out of that?'

George Hargreaves

Above *This former steelworks in Germany has been transformed into a public park. Trees have had a humanizing influence on the site. The blast furnaces are lit at weekends.*

Post-industrial sites, the plazas of new towns, office buildings, shopping centres, corporate headquarters, river and harbour sites, healing gardens, memorial and sculpture parks: it is in these contexts that contemporary landscape and garden designers work. They focus on improving the site, making it more useful, more expressive and capable of giving greater pleasure to the public.

In the past, landscape architects and designers were employed almost entirely by clients wanting grand, private or quasi-private gardens. Today, the situation has changed entirely. While the designers of the past invested heavily in creating a sense of place in a limited number of private gardens, today's designers are concerned chiefly with the transformation of a huge and diverse range of places.

Robert Irwin, an abstract painter turned landscape designer, was commissioned to design the Lower Central Garden for the Getty Center, Los Angeles (see pages 104–111). Irwin's designs are always site generated. This means that the design is inspired by the natural features of the landscape in which it is to be created. It develops from the existing site, rather than being imposed upon it.

Since the 1980s Irwin has become internationally famous for his site-generated works in public spaces. In these works he often makes use of topographical features and natural plantings. He made the following statement in relation to his design for the Getty Garden in Los Angeles:

I began with a set of circumstances. As such, every decision had to make sense within the context of a set of cues. In this case, of course, the surrounding architecture was key. This was not going to be a garden off in a field some place. I accepted its architectural setting – which was all but overpowering – but that, in turn, raised other questions. For how do you go from such a surround – from buildings like that – down to a flower? So you can see this petal,

Left *A series of pools in a garden on the edge of Lake Lucerne, Switzerland, with the 'borrowed landscape' of the mountains.*

that stalk? I began to think in terms of starting from geometry, compounding the geometry to pattern and the pattern to texture. And in doing so in both directions – from the flower out to the buildings, and from the buildings back to the flower.

Irwin is not alone in creating site-generated landscapes. At the beginning of this chapter we quoted George Hargreaves as saying that 'the context is everything'. This is another way of defining the basis for site-generated design. An article written by Melinda Wortz in *Artforum* in 1981 provides a detailed analysis of Irwin's philosophy of design:

> The content of Irwin's art derives from the presence of the site where the artist works. Presence for Irwin is so much more than just visual phenomena – it is the impression the site presents to all of the senses of the body and the mind. The physical structure expressed in a response to this presence acts as metaphor for the location it occupies. The art's content is both autonomous in its presence [and] wholly integrated with its context. In the end, the work assumes a symbolic power, in the true meaning of the word 'symbol'. Unlike the traditional symbols, Irwin's work does not refer to the presence of some other thing, but to what is immediately here.

One of Irwin's earliest site-generated works was created at Wellesley College, outside Boston, Massachusetts, in 1979. During an initial visit to the college, Irwin was 'struck by the grace of the nature on the campus. How beautiful it all was, and without any intrusion by me.' He created Filigreed Line, a line or low wall of brushed stainless steel 36.5m (120 ft) long that sliced through the landscape of venerable trees and gently rolling lawns. It spans a low hollow between some beautiful trees, fronting a pond in the middle distance. Abstracted leaf and branch patterns were cut out randomly along its length using a highly sophisticated plasma metal-cutting technique. At its two ends, the metal wall is only a few centimetres above the ground. In the middle it rises to 1m (3ft) where it is supported by concrete footings. When the

Below *The asymmetrical design of this contemporary, rooftop garden makes a striking contrast with the spectacular view of the ultra-conservative City of London below.*

shadows from the leaves and branches from the nearby trees play on their metal cut-out images, it is a subtle and beautiful fusion of art and nature – an effect aimed at by many landscape designers. Some time after the installation, Irwin wrote:

> The Wellesley site was so lovely and pastoral, it really didn't require anything additional from me. All I was trying to do with my gesture, in the most subliminal fashion I could manage, and thanks to the reflectivity of the steel and the shimmer of the pond beyond it (the screen often just seemed to disappear) – was to, in a sense, underline the beauty and perceptual vitality of the site as it already existed.

The subtlety of much of Irwin's work in the landscape may not capture the immediate imaginations of many onlookers, but his influence on gardens and landscapes and on the sense of place in the late twentieth century is of great importance and has far-reaching consequences. It is all about seeing the context.

Left *A site-generated sculpture in a eucalyptus grove at the University of California, San Diego. The blue, chain link fencing takes its colour from the bluish cast of the leaves.*

Below *A garden makeover design, including a swimming pool, on a Phoenix, Arizona, hillside, overlooking Paradise Valley suburb. Indigenous planting around the pool reinforces the sense of place.*

Space, scale & form

**Designs shall be three dimensional.
People live in volumes, not planes.**

Garrett Eckbo

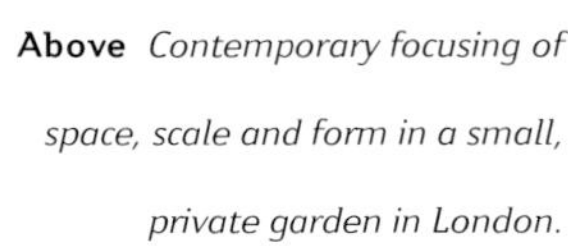

Above *Contemporary focusing of space, scale and form in a small, private garden in London.*

Space and scale create and reinforce each other. In the contemporary garden and landscape we find a great diversity of designs. There are those that use perspective and the orthogonal, and others based on the diagonal, the sculptural, or the ecological. In the midst of this diversity, the force of the formal and geometric can still be felt.

The great formal gardens of sixteenth-century Italy and seventeenth-century France were four-square, perpendicular ground extensions of the 'footprint' of the villas and palaces that they embellished. When perspective was rediscovered in Renaissance Italy by Brunelleschi and Alberti, great architects patronized by the Medici, it became a prime tool for establishing the centre line or axial spine of a garden. This was often a wide central path, as at the Boboli Gardens in Florence or at Versailles, from which all the other elements were scaled. Transverse paths, square or rectilinear flower beds, *allées* of trees, urns, basins and water jets were all common features.

Above *There is an interplay between the different forms of the undulating lawns and immaculate walls in this large garden surrounding a multi-national, corporate headquarters near Paris.*

Garden designers such as Michelozzo in Italy and Le Nôtre in France adopted many painterly tricks. A flat plane could be made to seem three dimensional through the use of one, two or three lines leading back to a vanishing point. Converging parallels created an illusion of space on a two-dimensional ground plane, a trick that exaggerated the depth of the site. Finally, geometric shapes were used to foreshorten both the garden space and the objects in it. Orthogonal space and scale were most widely used during the nineteenth century in Europe and the United States, where the style was defined as the Beaux-Arts.

In this century, the use of orthogonal, formal principles of space and form has been reinterpreted by designers such as Daniel Urban Kiley in the United States and Fernando Caruncho in Spain. Examples of their work are shown in the Case Study section (pages 196–201 and page 176–179).

The diagonal use of the garden space is unique to the twentieth century. This new approach, which is rooted in the 1930s, is in direct opposition to the orthogonal layout. The Beaux-Arts style of the nineteenth century eventually gave way to a new form of twentieth-century landscape architecture. This new style drew on the influences of Cubism, Art Deco, the International Style of modern architecture spearheaded by Le Corbusier, and the work of the Bauhaus personified by Walter Gropius.

Gropius became the head of architecture at Harvard University in 1938. There were three students in the landscape architecture department who were especially inspired by his lectures: Daniel Urban Kiley, James Rose and Garrett Eckbo. Rose and Eckbo were to have a major influence on the profession in the years after the Second World War. Two other influential figures from the pre- and post-Second World War period were Thomas Church in California and Christopher Tunnard in Great Britain.

Eckbo is an iconoclastic and truly revolutionary landscape designer. Seen as a representative of the modern in landscape architecture both in the United States and abroad, he is credited with two primary innovations: freeing the landscape from the axial designs of traditional, Beaux-Arts formality and the rediscovery of the diagonal, the zigzag and the sculptural.

These new modes of dealing with space and scale were inspired by Picasso, Theo van Doesberg, Mies van der Rohe, Vassily Kandinsky and Naum Gabo. The influence of their work led Eckbo to make use of the abstract in his designs. He was also profoundly influenced by Gabriel Guevrekian and Pierre-Emile Legrain, Cubist or Art Deco designers from Paris in the 1920s. It was a design by Legrain which gave Eckbo his life-long obsession with zigzag paths for establishing space and scale, especially in small, urban gardens.

Below *Swirling drifts of ground plane planting contrast with the verticals of pampas grass in this garden in Brazil.*

Right *Sculpted yew hedges enclose the spaces of this naturalistic garden made by a Dutch plantsman.*

Eckbo wrote an article defining his concept of space and scale in landscape architecture and its relationship to sculpture:

> Architecture (like sculpture). . . works with three-dimensional volumes, but their arrangement is governed by the human activities they must shelter. . . . Yet sculpture is also analogous to landscape design, for the handling of ground masses can be carried out with a truly sculptural set of forms in relation. In fact, landscape architecture may be considered more analogous to sculpture, since its forms are moulded and carved and grouped, whereas those in architecture are constructed.

Although Eckbo designed gardens for private clients in Bel Air, his true obsession was with integrating aesthetic and social values. Many of his most visionary projects involved public housing for migrant workers at the end of the American Depression. He described his work as 'the arrangement of environments for people'. He may have been inspired by Bauhaus theories regarding the social responsibility of all the arts.

As a student, Eckbo published a paper entitled 'Small Gardens in the City' containing 18 different layouts for a standard, rectangular, fenced, urban garden. The layouts show an oblique skewing of the ground plans, terraces, walkways, plantings, abstract

Above: *A geometric planting of thistles in a meadow at the garden festival at the Chateau de Chaumont in France demonstrates a witty use of space.*

arcs and, in each case, some use of the diagonal. Eckbo drew his inspiration from the art of the early part of this century. This may account for the continued relevance of his designs, as this period in the history of art continues to hold sway today.

In 1993, Eckbo gave a reworked commentary on his 1937 small gardens model:

- Gardens are places in which people live out of doors.
- Gardens must be the homes of delight, of gaiety, of fantasy, of illusion, of imagination, of adventure.
- Designs shall be areal, not axial.
- Design shall be dynamic, not static.

We were fortunate to meet Eckbo briefly in December, 1997. We took the opportunity to ask him what he thought was Gropius' single, most important influence all those years ago at Harvard. Eckbo replied most succinctly: 'Art was the ground-breaker.'

Ecological awareness, which began to emerge in the late 1960s and early 70s, became a primary influence upon the design of gardens and landscapes in the late twentieth century. In an ecological project, the scale is determined by the indigenous plants and trees on the proposed site. The ability to respond to the ecology of a site has become a part of every landscape architect's and designer's battery of basic, professional skills.

Above *Allée of fastigiate oaks screening the offices of the Banque de Luxembourg from the property line of an adjacent garden.*

Ian McHarg leads the field on the subject of ecology in landscape design. He has been teaching landscape architecture at the University of Pennsylvania since 1954. His course, entitled 'Human Ecological Planning', has provided a basis for the ecological planning movement worldwide. McHarg published *Design with Nature* in 1972 and it has become an ecological manifesto for the planning and design profession and for urban ecologists. The book was an attack on the uncontrolled building and desecration of natural habitats that occurred after the Second World War.

Inevitably, it was felt that some university landscape departments and professional landscape architecture practices over-emphasized McHarg's vision. It was said that the aesthetic – a vital aspect of

Below *A contemporary minimalist, serial form of spatial design is used to organize a traditional potager in the courtyard of a* ferme omée *in northern France.*

landscape architecture and design – had become subservient to planning and ecology. McHarg responded to this criticism with the following words:

> I can't believe that design can proceed without knowledge of the natural environment and the social environment. . . . [Design and planning] are complementary. . . I don't think [they are] adversarial at all.

Our personal view is that if you over-emphasize the importance of ecological considerations in determining the space and scale of a landscape, you end up ultimately denying history and culture, with all the riches that they can bring.

The concepts of space and scale in contemporary gardens and landscapes have been fundamentally influenced by three men: Luis Barragan, Roberto

Burle Marx and Isamu Noguchi, who have the status of icons within the landscape profession.

Above *This Mexican-influenced design in El Paso, Texas, demonstrates a sculptural use of form and scale.*

Barragan originally trained as an engineer. The Minimalist, rectilinear aesthetic of his work has inspired three generations of architects and landscape designers. Islamic influences from Spain and Morocco can be seen in the space and scale of his projects. This merged neatly with his interest in the buildings of Le Corbusier and the International Style. Planar walls, often washed in the bright colours of his native Mexico, planes of water in square or rectilinear pools, and more water falling from the channels at the ends of linear walls are all features of his designs.

Burle Marx studied painting in Berlin during the 1920s. A visit to the botanic garden in Berlin led him to discover the beauty of plants from his native country, Brazil. The paintings of Joan Miró and the Biomorphic sculptures of Jean Arp inspired him to design drifts of rounded, free-flowing planting on a huge scale. The scale of his garden and landscape designs attracted modern architects. His designs were perceived both as an adjunct and contrast to the buildings that they enclosed. Oscar Niemeyer commissioned him to design the landscape for Brasilia. Burle Marx's other masterpiece is in Rio de Janeiro. It is the 5km-long (3-mile-long) Copacabana promenade with its bold, serpentine, bicolour pattern; a hard landscaping variation on the drifts and swirls of planting in his gardens and landscapes.

Noguchi was a Japanese-American sculptor. As a student in Paris he worked with Constantin Brancusi. The space and scale of Noguchi's work in the landscape was an amalgam of both the western ideas and the eastern aesthetic. Modern materials such

Right *In a park adjacent to a main railway station in Barcelona, seating takes the form of a large, multi-level spiral edged in ceramic tiles and defined by trees which provide shade. The 1992 Olympic Games were the impetus for a series of public parks created across the city by architects, civil engineers and artists.*

as steel and marble fountains were juxtaposed and contrasted with large natural stones.

Noguchi's last great work is called *California Scenario*. It is located in the plaza of some office buildings at Costa Mesa, California, south of Los Angeles. The design was inspired by the image of the early settlers trudging across the Sierra Nevada and Cascade Mountains to the Golden State. Noguchi has abstracted from that experience and yet conveyed its reality: a serpentine water course dives down the angle of a sluice shape used for processing gold, an angled grass and flower meadow is bounded by redwood trees, and a sandy, gravel hillock is planted with cacti. Two stainless-steel fountains here are an allusion to twentieth-century mechanization. The use of space and scale in this layout continues to inspire landscape architects and designers today.

GREEN

Colour & texture

A good garden must be a piece of art. The basic principles of contrast, texture, dimension and proportion. [are] very important to understand. But there must be an idea!

Roberto Burle Marx

Colour and texture of amazing diversity have emerged in garden and landscape design since 1980, the moment at which garden designers and landscape architects began to use a more varied and brighter palette in their designs. This new range of colour can be seen in both the natural and the artificial materials shown in this book. Many of them are the 'signatures' of the work by designers in the Case Studies section.

The tendency to use a brighter and more exciting range of colours is the result of a diverse collection of influences over the past century. At the end of the nineteenth century and the beginning of the twentieth, there were the wonderfully mad mosaics by Antonio Gaudí in Barcelona and a few of the major Art Nouveau icons such as Charles Rennie Mackintosh and Joseph Hoffmann, who are still an influence in architecture and the contemporary landscape today. Art Nouveau brought a wide and divergent range of colours and textures to all of the arts. That movement also paved the way for the many forms of abstraction which were to emerge during the twentieth century and continue to be a source of inspiration today.

New, colourful twentieth-century landscapes also reflect the influence of the works of painters such as Joan Miró, New Realist sculptors such as Niki De Saint Phalle, Jean Tinguely, Yves Klein and Christo, and works of Pop Art, and its Dada precedent in the 1950s and 60s, represented by Andy Warhol, Jasper Johns, Roy

Above *These words were cut out of a field of corn using a template projected at night from a negative transparency. It was part of a crop art project undertaken by Pierre Vivant at Warwick University, England, in 1993.*

Left *'If a plant is dead, then paint it!' This was the concept of a landscape artist and former stage designer who remade a Virginia garden of dead shrubs by grabbing cans of enamel spray paint and letting rip.*

Right *Coloured plastic bottles stacked on rods are the basis of a recycled watering system designed in 1998 by a French fashion and cinema designer with technical help from an architect.*

Lichtenstein, Claes Oldenburg and Robert Indiana in the United States, and Richard Hamilton and Eduardo Paolozzi in Great Britain.

One of the leading landscape architects whose work has been much affected by Pop Art is the American Martha Schwartz. Witty, artful and iconoclastic, but above all colourful, Schwartz has, over the past 20 years, outraged, enlightened or amused her public. She has also caused fury among conventional landscape architects. Having attended the International Federation of Landscape Architects congress in Florence a couple of years ago, where most of the speakers should have been either statisticians or accountants, we are not surprised by this reaction.

Schwartz's use of colourful materials ranges from the purple aquarium gravel on the ground plane of her notorious Bagel Garden, built in Boston in 1979, to the astroturfed biological shapes in the Splice Garden created in Cambridge, Massachusetts, in 1986. In 1988, she designed the Rio Shopping Centre in Atlanta, where the central incident was serried ranks of plaster frogs painted gold and pointing regimentally towards the main water feature. The 1997 Nexus Kashi 3 Development car park is defined by ranks of giant orange discs (we think of rising suns brought back to their native land. . .).

Above *Gene splicing meets Ryoan-ji meets Boboli! A tiny courtyard becomes an amusing sculptured box of colour and texture viewed from the lunchroom of a microbiology research centre. The principal elements are fake boxwood, green gravel, paint and astroturf.*

In 1996, Schwartz designed the garden of the Davis House in El Paso, Texas. The space is divided into a series of compartments with walls washed in pinks, blues, purples and dark yellows, the colours of the American southwest.

The use of the sumptuous, bougainvillaea colours of Mexico washed onto pure, planar, rectangular or square walls is characteristic of the architecture of Luis Barragan, the great Mexican architect. His use of colour has been a primary influence on gardens and landscape in the latter part of the twentieth century. Among the many designers influenced by Barragan are two with practices in northern California: Topher Delaney in San Francisco (see pages 44–46 and 184–189) and Peter Walker in Berkeley.

Kathryn Gustafson is a designer who shows great sensitivity to texture in the landscape. This may in part

be due to her background in fashion design, where both colour and texture are of paramount importance. She maintains that the move from fashion to landscape was nothing more than a change of medium. Instead of making sketches of her design, she now encapsulates her initial concept in clay as a bas-relief. Some of her earlier influences were twentieth-century artists such as the painter Richard Tuttle, and Dennis Oppenheim, the sculptor.

Hard elements, such as stone, brick, plaster and metal, all bring texture to the twentieth-century landscape. There is an enormous variety of texture to

Above *Images of the terraced rice paddies of the Far East realized in 1997 by students from the Ecole Mediterranée des Jardins et du Paysage de Grasse, France. Woven chestnut wattles sculpt the land and retain the rice plantings.*

be seen in the Case Study section of this book. Stone is used in numerous different ways. There are Daniel Urban Kiley's stone retaining walls in Connecticut, layered stone grid patterns by Arata Isosaki in Japan, and the solid stone block seats of Thomas Balsley in Long Island City. There are also satellite-dish sculptures used by Mark Rios in Long Beach, the bougainvillea-coloured plaster walls of Topher Delaney in California, rusting steel retaining walls designed by Robert Irwin

Right *Glass gravel has been used to create the impression of cones of harvested rice and salt, evoking memories of the designer's home in Vietnam. The gravel's appearance changes constantly in sunshine and moonlight. The garden has been built on a Los Angeles hillside and planted with agaves, lemon grass and orchids.*

in Los Angeles, aluminium sculpture and screening by Ted Smyth in New Zealand and cones of sand made by the D.A.ST. artists in Egypt.

Soft landscaping elements can also bring colour and texture to the design. The Case Studies include Fernando Caruncho's wheat parterres in Spain, Jacques Wirtz's undulating yew hedges in Paris, the grasses and herbaceous plantings of Ton ter Linden in Holland, the tropical plants of Raymond Jungles in Florida, Jack Lenor Larsen's dune garden in Long Island, a grid of fruit trees designed by Desvigne & Dalnoky in France, Walter Beck's and Lester Collins' mosses at Innisfree in New York State, and the grassed land forms of Kathryn Gustafson, George Hargreaves and Charles Jencks.

Above *Plantings of delicate waving grasses and dense stolid succulents: an excellent example of naturalistic planting in large drifts.*

Jacques Wirtz excels at designing gardens with interesting colour and texture all year round. One of his largest Belgian gardens is Le Petite Garenne near Antwerp. Here he uses beech hedges and raised, triangular beds solid with pennisetum and molinia grasses, randomly planted with widely spaced cornus and roses. This use of plant material creates a great interplay and variety of texture. The spring grasses contrast lightly with the vertical of the cornus. The summer green of the grass contrasts with red roses. Finally, in autumn and winter, the pale beige tones of the grasses are a stunning counterpoint to the red-gold of the beech hedges which form the basic structure of the garden.

Rhythm & movement

Flux and reflux – the rhythm of change – alternate and persist in everything under the sky.

Thomas Hardy

'Rhythm is the most important single attribute in landscape design. It is the quality that gives life and joy, motion and repose. It is poetry and song.' So said Will Curtis, an American landscape designer and creator of the Garden in the Woods, near Boston. Whether or not one agrees totally with this, he has captured aspects of that elusive quality in his design in a most attractive way.

Rhythm and movement in the contemporary garden derive from the relationships between earth forms, planting and water incidents, all of which give unity and direction to a design and create an expressive variety of experience. Paths and the movement that they allow, the framing or screening of views, the position of focal and viewing points, changes of level, and the movement of elements such as water and

Far right *Strong, meandering benches make a rhythmic counterpoint to other hard landscaping elements in a public park in Auckland, New Zealand.*

Inset right *Here the ground plane rhythm is established by serpentine bands of contrasting indigenous grasses and wild flowers, enhancing this contemporary landscape in the Napa Valley.*

MINOLTA

Above *An alternating rhythm and movement to right and left and from bottom to top of a hillside at Castelledefels near Barcelona, Spain, is established by steel section retaining walls.*

Right *The pure square has been used as the design module for the terrace of this San Francisco house, creating a strong sense of rhythm and movement.*

plants are all important. The combination of these features creates contrast, the single most important element in any design.

The first element in a garden or landscape upon which the architect or designer must focus is the ground plane, for all of the other elements in a design are governed by it. For at least two millennia – and longer if one includes the Egyptian dynasties in the chronological count – the ground plane of traditional gardens has been defined by a grid. This means that the site is squared off and divided into regular square or rectangular elements. The earliest example of gardens designed in this way were the square or recti-linear mud-walled enclosures of the Egyptians, the pleasure grounds of the ancient Persians and the peristyle gardens of the Greeks and Romans. The pattern was perpetuated in the cloister gardens of medieval monasteries, and the Renaissance palace and manor house gardens throughout civilized Europe. Finally, the traditional grid was still being used in the nineteenth and early twentieth century, when gardens were created in that pot-pourri of earlier European historical styles.

The organization of the ground plane is the basis of any garden or landscape design, whether formally or asymmetrically designed.

A splendid example of the grid and its contemporary use can be seen in Kathryn Gustafson's design for Rights of Man Square at Evry, one of five new towns built near Paris during the 1970s. By the late 1980s the population of Evry had reached 80,000. The decision to build a new city square was an attempt by local and regional authorities to create a sense of unity in the rapidly growing city.

Gustafson, in collaboration with the architect Gerard Pas, won the competition for the design of the 1-hectare (2.5-acre) site in 1989. The competition organizers set the Rights of Man as the underlying motif for the design. Gustafson responded to Article II of the Rights of Man: freedom of expression. She created the square as a place for both public and private activity. There were to be municipal events and performances of music, dance and drama. The square was also the town's platform where any of the inhabitants could give soap-box speeches. Finally, it was a pleasant place to meet friends or have a meal within the sight and sound of water, and among plantings which brought the countryside into the newly built town.

By lowering the ground plane of the square, Gustafson created a definite boundary and removed the sunken space from the constant hurly burly of the traffic which runs past. This was a brilliant design stroke. The square is bounded by various important public and municipal buildings which have been designed by noted French architects. The

Autoroute du Sud from Paris to the south runs down one side. The magnificent new cathedral and cloister of Saint Corbinien by Mario Botta, the Swiss-Italian architect, creates a central focus.

The main paving is pale grey Celtic granite which is overlaid with a grid of white granite. The grid is continuous, even when there are steps and ramps. These changes of level reflect each of the buildings surrounding the square. For example, the large granite staircase which leads down into the underground car park corresponds to the huge scale of the arc of Botta's cathedral.

Being a leading contemporary designer, Gustafson has revised the traditional arrangement of vertical and horizontal elements. She has organized them in ways that reflect her aesthetic and that of the late twentieth century. Their positions govern the contrasts of rhythm and movement intrinsic to the design.

The Dragon Basin is a superb raised pool of massive proportions made of green Brazilian granite. It is 130m (416ft) long and varies from 5m to 8m (16 to 25ft) wide. It is angled at one side so that it overlaps the grid ground plane and creates a visual connection between the town hall and chamber of commerce on one side of the square and the cathedral on the other.

Another design stroke relating to the rhythm of the layout is the division of the Dragon Basin into two sections linked by steps providing access to two levels of the square. This means that a pedestrian has no need to walk the entire 130m (416ft) of the basin in order to get from one point to another. This is an aesthetically pleasing and extremely efficient aspect of the rhythm and movement of the design.

Gustafson has designed two rectangles within the grid ground plan. The first is a rectangle of water which is called the Simmering Pool. A pattern of water jets churn up the surface of the water. Adjacent to it is a rectangular pavement area of a similar size. The area is patterned with holes from which 153 programmed jets can play vertically. The lighting of the Dragon Basin, the Simmering Pool and the pavement adds another dimension to the rhythm and movement of Gustafson's design.

Above *In this design, which is entitled* The Wave Field, *a sense of movement is evoked by natural light and shadow and by people walking on the grassed earth waves or sheltering among them. The waves, which rise from ground level to a maximum of 1.8m (6ft), give rhythm to the piece. Maya Lin designed the site in 1995. It occupies an area of 8sq m (676sq ft) at the University of Michigan, Ann Arbor.*

Right *Low undulating rolling land forms contrast to angled parallel stone-edged canals for the Esso/Exxon headquarters garden near Paris.*

Another superb example of rhythm and movement can be found in the design for a raised terrace garden in San Francisco by Topher Delaney. Here the ground plane is paved in lines of white, concrete pavers. The lines between them are made from dark green grass *Dichondra miscantha*. The verticals are provided by climbing plants against the white plaster perimeter walls. The other boundary walls are made of glass – but glass with a difference. They are double-skin glass panels 3m (10ft) high with a 20cm (8in) space between the two sections.

At the bottom of the space Delaney has placed strips of white neon to up-light the glass panels. Some of the panels fronting onto the terrace have been shot blasted and some of the rear panels are mirrored. The effect of this treatment is both beautiful and wonderfully elegant. It demonstrates the way in which the artist's or designer's imagination can elevate a contemporary material. Continuing the design module of the square, Delaney has created a square pool in which there are nine slightly raised, square planters, all of which are planted with white zantedeschia lilies.

Site-generated references abound in Torres' and Lapeña's design for Constitution Square, on the edge of Gerona in northern Spain. The project was conceived by the municipal government of Gerona, which had decided in 1983 to dedicate a square to the new Constitution of Spain, ratified in 1978. A vaguely triangular site was chosen in a newly developed area

of the city. It is bounded along one side by a major road, Gran Via de Jaume I, and a new building for the Bank of Spain, and on the other by an access ramp which leads to an underground parking facility and a school playground.

Torres and Lapeña decided initially that the square should become an urban garden, bringing a shard of nature into the heart of the city, just as a flower pot brings a small token of nature into a house. Beautifully finished concrete was used to raise the level on one side of the square. The resulting ramps slope down to key into the pavements at their far end. Concrete was also used to define the edges of the site. Triangular, asymmetrical shapes and sections of the concrete were raised in parts in order to serve as seating and to establish and emphasize the rhythm and movement of the triangular site.

The raised concrete on one side of the square serves as a wall for the ducting vents to service the underground car park. Torres and Lapeña have designed the entrance to the car park as a sharp, long triangle within a part of another raised wall, making the entrance discreet, recessive and at one with the rhythm and movement of the design.

Time & change

The elementary living entity would from its very beginning have had no more wish to change, if conditions remained the same; it would do no more than constantly repeat the same course of life. In the last resort, what has left its mark on the development of organisms must be the history of the earth we live in and its relation to the sun.

Sigmund Freud, *Beyond the Pleasure Principle*, 1921.

The Age of Information has brought new meaning to the concepts of time and change. In our high-tech environment we are capable of keeping in touch with the reality of daily life all over the world. We also know more about history than ever before and we have a much better idea of the relationship between time and change and the history of gardens.

Great gardens from the past have much to teach us. Their existence today is due to a deliberate policy of conservation. We will never know to what extent their past survival was dependent on chance. Some gardens have been cared for over many centuries by the same family. This is often the case in Italy, where it has been a

good recipe for survival. Private citizens who take on the stewardship of a historic garden have often proved themselves to be saviours. The seventeenth-century gardens of Courances in France were rescued from dereliction in the twentieth century by the de Ganay family. Similarly, the long abandoned estate of Désert de Retz was restored by Olivier Choppin de Janvry.

More recently, governments or charities have taken on the task of preserving our garden heritage. In Denmark there has been a concerted effort by the government to restore and conserve the formal gardens of the seventeenth-century Rosenberg Palace and the eighteenth-century gardens of Frederiksborg Castle and Fredensborg Palace. Similarly, in Japan the Great Stroll Garden of Katsura Imperial Villa Gardens has been preserved as far as possible in its original state, as have the Lake Garden of the Golden Pavilion and the Gravel Garden of the Silver Pavilion. Ryoan-ji Zen Garden and the other small but immensely important Zen Buddhist gardens of the sub-temples in the Daitoku-ji precinct have also been preserved. In both Japan and Denmark the garden landscape forms part of the traditions of art, architecture and design that are intrinsic to society.

There are also international organizations in existence which are dedicated to the discovery of historic gardens and monitoring them as well as identifying those of particular importance. The Benneton Foundation awards certain grants for the preservation of historic landscapes. Worlitz Park in Germany and Désert de Retz in France have both benefited in this way.

Other organizations are dedicated to the conservation of plants. Botanic Gardens Conservation International is based at Kew Gardens in London. It actively promotes plant conservation among its 500 member gardens across 110 countries. Many of the botanic gardens that it sponsors are of great historic significance. Among its members are Padua and Pisa in Italy, Rio de Janeiro, Oxford, Cambridge and the Chelsea Physic Garden in England.

On the Making of Gardens, published in 1909, is Sir George Sitwell's hymn to the great sixteenth-century gardens of Italy. It is a wonderful homage to time and change in the garden:

Left & below *One of the stunning earthworks by James Pierce in his 'garden of history' in Maine.* Earthwoman, *1976, seen in three of her time and change transformations: clipped, overgrown with grass and wild strawberries, and at the summer solstice.*

> Yet in truth such a garden as that of Lante is a world possession, and the builder of it a great poet who has influenced the life of thousands, putting them in touch with the greatness of the past, lifting their thoughts and aspirations to a higher level, revealing to them the light of their own soul, opening their eyes to the beauty of the world.
>
> Architecture, the most unselfish of the arts, belongs to the passer-by, and every old house and garden in which the ideal has been sought is a gift to the nation, to be enjoyed by future generations who will learn from it more of history and art and philosophy than may be found in books.

Time combines with the weather to affect change in garden landscapes, whether they be contemporary or historic. The designers of contemporary site-generated or contextual landscapes make references to the effects of time in their designs. Geuze and West 8 in Holland, Desvigne & Dalnoky, Gustafson in France. Ariola and Piol and Torres and Lapeña in Spain and Stig L. Andersson in Denmark all use time and change to some degree in their designs. An outstanding example of this practice is found in the work of George Hargreaves. The central idea of Hargreaves Associates, based in Cambridge, Massachusetts, and San Francisco, is the connection between culture and environment and between the land and the people. In their designs, time and change become part of an ecological approach and the notion of sustainable landscape.

Hargreaves' design for Byxbee Park on the edge of San Francisco is a good example of the references to time and change in his designs. The land forms in the park are planted with indigenous grasses which change throughout the season. At Villa Zapu in the Napa valley he planted grasses and wildflowers in serpentine patterns.

The ephemeral gardens of the Chelsea Flower Show focus our minds on time and change. The Chanel Garden in 1998 was a temporary example of a classical seventeenth-century French formal garden. It was installed over three weeks, seen by the public over five days and dismantled in three days. This act of defiance in the face of time contrasts with *Earthwoman* by James Pierce. *Earthwoman* is an example of land art based on ancient earthworks and built between 1970 and 1982. She is now biodegrading slowly.

Every aspect of the Chanel Garden flew in the face of time. Tom Stuart-Smith, the British landscape architect responsible for the design, first met Karl Lagerfeld, design maestro for Chanel, in January 1997. At this early stage it soon became evident that white camellias, in quantity, would be required, for they were Mlle Chanel's favourite flower. It mattered not that camellias were only introduced to Europe in the nineteenth century, or that they bloom in late winter.

Stuart-Smith did his best to dissuade the Chanel people from their choice, but to no avail. The fashion house already had its camellia range of products in process. Lagerfeld chose the name *Le Bosquet de Chanel* for the garden.

Time and change were certainly a problem for the camellias. The first batch was frost damaged. A replacement batch was housed first in a frost-free tunnel, then in a dark cold store and finally under clear glass. By late May they were in full bloom.

On the Kennebec River near Hinckley, Maine, James Pierce makes earthworks on 6.8 hectares (17 acres) of meadow and woodland. His work has many primitive, elemental associations. 'My medium is the landscape itself, its earth, rocks and trees. I work in these materials because I feel their elemental power.'

Pierce's *Stone Ship* makes references both to Viking burial and to Norse explorations of the Atlantic coast of North America. Stone boulders outline the ship on its raised earth platform. This is an explicit reference to the ancient burial rituals of the Vikings during the Bronze Age.

The Kiva is a 3m-wide (9.6ft-wide) subterranean chamber similar to those built by American Indians for ceremonies. The spoil from the chamber was used to make the Triangular Redoubt and the Burial Mound. These are references to English and French settlements in the eighteenth century. Finally, the Turf Maze is linked to European gardens of the seventeenth century.

Pierce calls his earthworks 'a garden of history'. They represent his own perception of history and the meaning of time and change. In his own words, they are 'a relatively harmless means of satisfying desires for control, security and immortality, while re-living the history of the race and discovering one's humanity in physical union with nature.'

Sadly, Pierce is surrounded by changes that may eventually threaten his site. A paper mill has been built nearby and it can be seen over the tops of the trees.

Above & left Le Bosquet de Chanel *garden, Chelsea Flower Show, London, 1998. Designed by Karl Lagerfeld and interpreted by Tom Stuart-Smith, it shows time and change at their most complex. The makings of the garden – its beech hedges, box bushes, Chanel 'Cs' and all – were bought by an Irish lady for her own garden.*

New elements

Earth

I think earth is the material with most potential because it is the original source material . . . I found that, in using it, I could have a fairly complete vocabulary.
It brought up all kinds of things about the prehistoric or preliterate past, and referred to a lot of traditions about art that were more interesting than looking at works of art in the Louvre or the Metropolitan Museum.

Michael Heizer

Earth and Land Art have emerged as design forms truly unique to the gardens and landscapes of the latter part of the twentieth century. They are truly Postmodern, but they have the most ancient antecedents – how's that for an anomaly?

Landscape architects and designers have been profoundly influenced by Earth Artists, who work directly with the land as their medium. Allied to this practice is a new awareness of the natural processes and uses of the earth. The imaginations of landscape designers worldwide have been fired by this approach, which they find useful on post-industrial sites.

In the late 1960s there were many Earth Artists. They were often painters or sculptors who recognized the ecological movement as an artistic antidote to the impact on the landscape of rampant late nineteenth and twentieth-century industrialization. These artists were also reacting against the increased hold of the international gallery owner/museum curator/art critic cabal on the art marketplace – not that its overwhelming grip has loosened any in the late 1990s. It should not be forgotten, however, that Virginia Dwan, a New York gallery owner, underwrote the first work by Heizer and Smithson, two of the most important Land Artists. Land Art emerged from these two cultural and economic circumstances.

Preceding pages La Brume et Les Saules *– mist and willows with a difference, at Château de Chaumont-sur-Loire, the site of a unique International Festival of Garden and Landscape. Willows were planted and woven into living sculptures, made mysterious by the autumn mist.*

Left La Terre en Marche *(*The Earth in Motion*), at the Chaumont Garden Festival, is entered through a random grove of fibre glass rods. A gravel path ascends a spiral mount which offers views of the Loire river and the nearby Château de Chaumont. Serpentine, grassy beds and white perennials create a contrast to the spiral.*

Land Artists chose wild, untrammelled and desolate places for their work (Utah and New Mexico), and in doing so, they seemed to be rediscovering what was known by our ancient ancestors: the interrelationships in the universe between space, infinite time and art.

Robert Smithson and Michael Heizer moved many tons of earth and rock in the deserts of Utah and Nevada to create massive earth sculptures which echo the earthworks and mounds of primitive and ancient peoples. Between 1969 and 1970, Heizer created *Double Negative* in the Nevada desert. It consisted of two cuts in a high, rocky tableland or mesa, which displaced 240,000 tons of earth. The cuts were 450m (1,500ft) long and each one was 9m (30ft) wide and 15m (50ft) deep. John Beardsley, whose books on Land Art and Earthworks are the authoritative Ur-texts on the subject, described the *Double Negative* as '. . . a consecrated space in which one experiences sensations of great distance, aloneness, and silence that inescapably recall the sublime.'

Michael Heizer wrote about his discovery of 'real space' in the desert in the following words: 'The position of art as malleable barter-exchange item falters as the cumulative economic structure gluts. The museum and collections are stuffed, the floors are sagging, but real space exists.'

When Heizer talked to Beardsley he said: 'I don't care about landscape. I am a sculptor. Real estate is dirt, and dirt is material.' He referred to the western landscape of the United States as 'that kind of unraped, peaceful, religious space artists have always tried to put into their work.'

Below right *Earth design at Wadi Rayrn in Egypt. This was the result of a project given to French landscape architecture students in 1995. They were briefed to create a design without water or plants and supplied with a length of rope and two boards. The rest was left to their imaginations.*

Below *An earthwork interpretation in Maine of Janus, the Roman god of many faces. Here he has four eyes and four noses. He can be read from any perspective. The summer solstice sun rises through one of his eyes.*

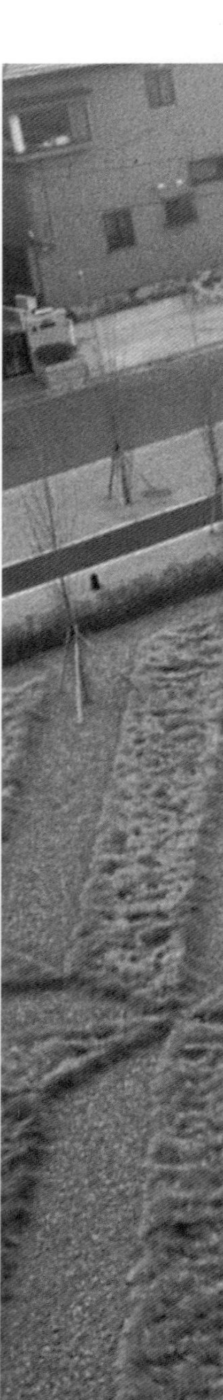

Double Negative was not portable art merchandise. Perhaps more important still, it was not sculpture in the traditional sense, as it was not a constructed form or a mass, it was a sculpture from the space created in the two giant cuts in the earth of the mesa. Despite these distinctions, photographs of Heizer's Earthworks do change hands for ready money in art galleries across the world.

In this section on earth, we will focus on the use of the spiral. This is both because it has caught our interest as designers and writers and because it has inspired a large number of contemporary landscape architects and designers whose projects span a wide range of designs.

The spiral has been 'rediscovered' in the last 20 years as a land form. It was first made, along with other primitive marks such as the circle, the serpentine and the zigzag, some say, 17,000 years ago, when it was incised into bone tools and weapons and painted on cave walls. We can still see these primary, primitive shapes much later in the stone and wood henges, or circles, of western Europe, in the giant stone outlines of the Nazca in Peru, in the huge snake and water-spider Earthworks of the Missouri and Mississippi River valleys of middle north America and in the labyrinths of earth, stone and turf that are found in all cultures of the world over many millennia.

We see the use of these primitive shapes by artists and landscape architects in the late twentieth century as part of a splendid, contemporary leap of the imagination. They represent a grand historical trajectory back over the sweep of garden history.

Below *Large, sculpted earth shapes below the Tokio Marine Oyama Training Centre, Tochigi Prefecture, Japan. The forms are enhanced by lines of grass and gravel referring to ancient farming methods and contemporary abstract painting.*

The starting point is the current English granny-gardener, with her cottage or manor house formal plan and informal planting inspired by Hidcote, Sissinghurst, Arts and Crafts, Robinson and Jekyll. We refer to this as the 'chintz loose-covers inside and herbaceous borders outside' school of design. The arc then spans the Victorian and American Beaux-Arts historical pastiche, the Italianate landscape or 'landskip' C. Brown style, Versailles style, the Italian Renaissance style based on villa gardens of Rome and Greece, the enclosed gardens and landscapes of Persia and Egypt, and finally over millennia of unknown and undocumented garden history, the cave dweller! The labyrinth, circle, zigzag, serpentine and spiral still have resonance today. Their use reconnects contemporary design to the earth.

The creation of *Spiral Jetty* by Robert Smithson was a very significant moment in the history of Land Art.

Below Spring Tide on Earth *is an earth, turf and Cor-Ten steel construction in Belgium.*

The primitive spiral made of earth, black basalt and limestone was built out from the shore into the water of the Great Salt Lake in 1970. It is 450m (1,500ft) long. Smithson was initially attracted to the site because it was covered all over in industrial junk and derelict vehicles which were left over from a failed oil extraction project. He believed that both this project and the large-scale Earth Art projects which he made from reclaimed mine sites in Ohio and Colorado made a positive statement: 'Art can become a physical resource that mediates between the ecologist and the industrialist.'

The spiral form of salt crystals when viewed under a microscope was a major source of inspiration for Spiral Jetty. Smithson was also very taken by a micro-organism in the lake which colours the water dark pink. His giant, macro, spiral form came from a minute, micro-analysis of an aspect of the lake's composition. After 28 years, the earth and rocks of the jetty, once proud of the water of the lake, are now beginning to be submerged. It has become what Smithson predicted:

'. . .matter collapsing into the lake mirrored in the shape of a spiral.'

The spiral is a shape widely used in contemporary landscapes. Its genesis is universal, ancient and arithmetical. In nature, the living mathematics of the spiral can be seen in the spirals of the ammonite and the nautilus. Some of the arithmetic and geometric precedents of the shape are the Spiral of Archimedes, the Spiral of the Golden Section, and taken from it are mouldings of classical architecture: ogee, astragal, cyma recta and ovolo are some, and the plant and flower spiral formations discovered by the thirteenth-century Italian mathematician, Leonardo of Pisa, known as Fibonacci. The Fibonacci Series of Numbers follows an arithmetic sequence which can be found in the seed and leaf formations of plants. Equally profound and exciting are the Fibonacci spirals found in the cross-section of the growing tip of a plant shoot or generative spiral: the primordia. Fibonacci's thirteenth-century theories, taken from Hindu-Arabic texts on the spiral nature of plants, were borne out by the twentieth-century epic discovery of the spiral of the DNA by Crick and Watson at Cambridge.

There are many other examples of contemporary spiral land forms. One of them is to be found in the Egyptian desert at El Ghouna near the Red Sea. Desert Breath consists of two interlocking spirals of precise positive and negative conical volumes of sand, ascending in height and descending in depth from the common centre of a circular pool 30m (96ft) in diameter. (See pages 202–205). In Scotland Charles Jencks has designed a 15m-high (50ft-high) grassed earthwork which he refers to variously as 'a snail', 'a mound' and 'a mount'. (See pages 146–151). At Villa Zapu, in the northern end of California's Napa Valley, George Hargreaves designed a pair of spiral bands of wild grasses and flowers around a mount. The spirals progressively unfurl into serpentines, which flow towards and then underpin the rest of the garden and the house.

Centre *Lower Manhattan's Jacob Javits Plaza was a featureless space improved originally by Richard Serra's* Tilted Arc *sculpture. This proved too controversial and was removed. In 1997 this new design was created. It consists of 'topiary' made from misting grassed hemispheres, 1.8m (6ft) high, which cool the air for office workers relaxing on the swirling, double-sided benches.*

Below *Double spirals of earth and grass for the Cité des Arts, Paris, 1991, recall the* parterres de broiderie *of French formal gardens. Here the parterres are realized as twentieth-century, sculptured Land Art.*

Water

'What pleases me most in these new fountains,' said Claudio Tolomei, 'is the variety of ways with which they guide water, turn it, lead it, break it, make it rise and fall'. This sixteenth-century account of Roman fountains and decorative waterworks would do very nicely to describe the amazing variety of contemporary water features and incidents in gardens and landscapes 400 years later.

The high-tech water engineering which has been made available to contemporary garden and landscape designers over the past 25 years would, in its magical effects and diverse configurations, dazzle Signore Tolomei. He would be amazed by the artificial

The thing about water is that it can do what nothing else can do. Daniel Urban Kiley

fog which can be created at the flick of a switch connected to some very expensive engineering and computer technology.

Water has been praised and extolled throughout history on account of the practical and aesthetic pleasures that it offers. In gardens and landscapes, water is the most mutable design element, and now it is also the most manageable. Perhaps it is true to say that water is the most sensuous element in the garden, and often the most visually exciting. It can either be the gentlest or the most dramatic part of the design, whether it is found in the smallest of private gardens or the largest public display. Wind, wildlife and humans are the only other capricious and changeable participants in a garden scene.

In Europe, the distinctions between the uses of water in the north and south has always been determined by geography and climate. In regions north of the olive tree cordon in upper Provence, there is a preponderance of both natural and man-made lakes, pools and ponds which act as wonderful, dark mirrors to draw down the sky and clouds. Perhaps, the cooler, greyer, rainier skies of the north need fewer fountain jets.

The countries where the olive flourishes lie below that 'invisible' geographical line which all northern Europeans love to cross in order to find the heat, the

Left *In the Crystal Garden Lobby, Sea Hawk Hotel and Resort, Fukuoka, Japan, there are 16m-high(52ft-high) waterfalls made from serpentine ribbons of glass. When the water is turned off, the glass ribbons become giant sculptures.*

Below *The ground plane of the still pool in Arata Isosaki's Nagi Museum of Contemporary Art is the setting for a stainless-steel sculpture by Aiko Miyawaki.*

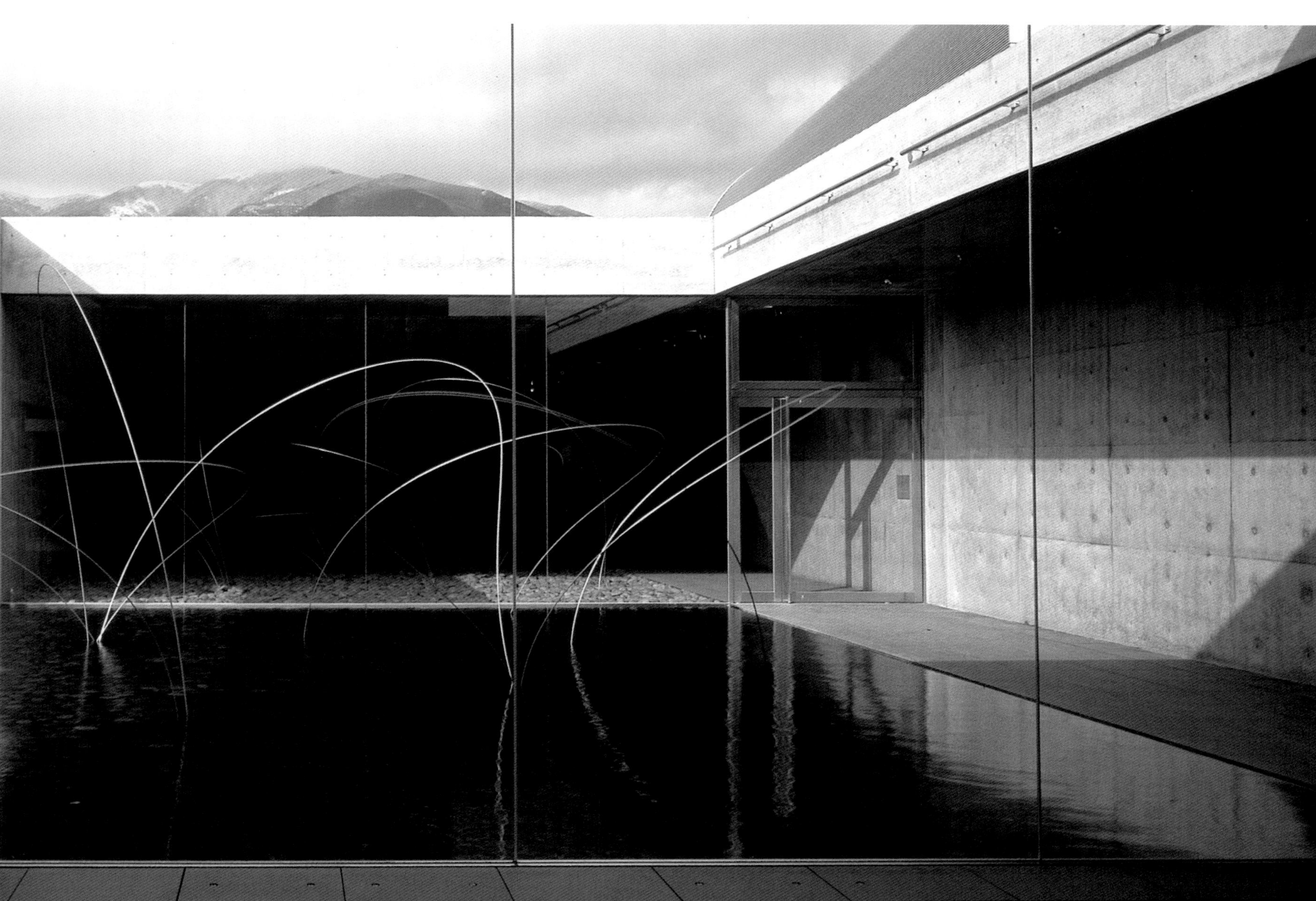

sea and the sand. Here, the long, hot days of the Mediterranean summer inspire gardens containing water in every possible form. Waterfalls, sprays and splashes, indulging the senses of both sight and sound.

In 1989 we visited 45 Italian gardens between Lake Maggiore and Naples. Here we saw every possible variation on the use of water, from the still nymphaeum pool of the Villa Barbaro near Venice to the greatest conflation and variety of Renaissance waterworks at the Villa d'Este, east of Rome. Here we recovered from the heat in the black shade of a giant and mythic cypress tree, seeing and listening to the wonderfully refreshing play of Pirro Ligorio's fountains.

Below *Sphagnum moss, wire mesh and steam are the main elements of the mysterious* Puffing Mosses *set in a pool at Stockholm's annual Rosendal garden show in 1998.*

Ippolito d'Este, the cardinal who was Ligorio's patron, ordered his workmen to alter the course of the nearby River Aniene so that a limitless head of water was provided to gravity feed Ligorio's extensive and magical designs. Where, oh where are such patrons of garden design today?

If only today's advanced water engineering had been available to André Le Nôtre in seventeenth-century France. Then the beautiful fountains that he designed for Louis XIV on the flat ground below the palace of Versailles would have played continuously. As it was, Le Nôtre depended on a complex set of hand signals between the garden boys hidden in the hedges through the garden.

Today, electronic and digitally programmed computers, micro-piping and jets, fibre optic lighting, and even artificial fog, created by water atomized under high pressure, are all available to garden and landscape designers. Another major technical improvement in the use of water has come from the development of polymer and butyl membrane liners for the waterproofing of pools and lakes, enabling reservoirs to be made on a much larger scale, and on terrain usually considered unsatisfactory. This has allowed large lakes and reservoirs to be created on desert sites in the countries of the Middle East. Used to contain both fresh and salt water, they service the needs of the population and the newly constructed palace gardens of the ruling class.

Liners have replaced the traditional puddling mode of waterproofing, when workers would stamp in a mixture of heavy clay and sand to make the

Right *The Water Garden jets at night in Fragments of Garden History, the public park at Terrasson, France.*

impermeable lining of ponds, lakes, embankments and canals. When the eighteenth-century Moon Ponds at Studley Royal were drained, some workers' footprints were found intact.

Although waterproof liners are widely used today, there are some situations in which traditional puddling is more effective. We puddled the 0.6-hectare (1.5-acre) lake that we created in 1990 on the Elton John Estate. The puddling was not done with the stamping feet of our workers, however, but with the front buckets of large earth-moving equipment which worked a layer of clay onto the bottom and sides of the lake area.

Water can be used to create a vast variety of effects. It can be incredibly subtle, as in the almost imperceptible sheen that spreads serenely down both the rough and the cut faces of a large rock which Isamu Noguchi has placed in the Japanese wing of the Metropolitan Museum of Art, New York. An exquisite murmuring sound comes from the water hitting the surface of the reservoir under the boulder. The surrounding area is masked by pebbles.

The low, vigorous waterfalls in the Fountain Plaza, Dallas, Texas, are designed by Daniel Urban Kiley. He has set 200 mature swamp cypresses in circular planters among the waterfalls and water jets, creating a refreshing environment for workers from the adjacent 60-storey, I.M. Pei office building, and for passers-by escaping the relentless heat of the midday sun. The flow of water for the falls and jets is controlled by a complex set of computers.

The Kiley garden is an excellent example of the use in large public gardens and landscapes of 'grey' or recycled, non-potable water, in place of fresh water, a natural resource which is becoming more and more precious. 'Grey water' is the sane and sensible path towards the conservation of a diminishing natural resource.

Below *Technically advanced pumps activate this* carrousel d'eau, *an installation built in a French garden in 1996. The still water of the central pool contrasts with the waves, bubbles and ripples created by the various pumps.*

Some twentieth-century landscape designers and architects have had a great influence on the way that water is used in contemporary gardens and landscapes. Alvar Aalto, the great Finnish architect, designed the first free-form, curvilinear swimming pool for the Villa Mairea outside Helsinki. Thomas Church, the innovator of the California style of garden design, was inspired by Aalto's designs and imported his distinctive stools, chairs and vases to San Francisco. We think that Church's pool at El Novillero near Sonoma was directly inspired by Aalto's pool at Villa Mairea. Church's beautiful design for the pool and garden are counted as twentieth-century masterpieces. When looking down on the garden from a nearby hilltop, the shape of the pool echoes the distant, curving salt marshes below the northern reaches of San Francisco Bay. The design of Church's pool was picked up by various magazines – hence the endless, bright blue, kidney-shaped swimming pools which proliferated in the back yards and gardens all over southern California.

Frank Lloyd Wright, with his design for Fallingwater at Bear Run, Pennsylvania, is another architect who has had a profound influence on future generations of landscape architects, designers and the other environmental professions. Fallingwater is brilliantly sited. It seems to be interwoven with the trees, the rocks, the stream and its waterfall. From a distance, the strong horizontals of the house are in perfect harmony with the landscape elements. If only the clients had followed Wright's suggestion that the horizontals of the main structure should be covered in a dull gold leaf. Then the house would have become truly at one with the golden colour of the autumn leaves.

Fallingwater was Wright's greatest achievement and most original contribution to architecture. Here he demonstrated his new concept of space by creating rooms which overlap both vertically and horizontally. He made subtle use of natural lighting and provided woodland or stream views from every room. Rooms were defined by function and there was a constant interplay between indoors and outdoors, all underpinned at Fallingwater by the constant sound of the stream from the waterfalls beneath the house.

Carlo Scarpa, the great Italian Modernist architect, had a profound influence on landscape architects and designers. He created quiet, subtle planes of water in the form of shallow pools adjacent to his private houses and in the courtyards of his public buildings. Scarpa was a follower of Frank Lloyd Wright's architectural style, rather than the prevailing International Style of van der Rohe. The American and German architects' antithetical views represented a cultural divide similar to the division between Matisse and Picasso. In each instance, the division is still debated by 'culture vultures' on both sides of the Atlantic.

Scarpa's shallow pools of water reflect and soften the buildings. Some examples are important to note. On the garden side of the Casa Veritti in Udine, the arc edge of the pool is a variation on the curved roof of the house; the arcs contrast with the triangular shape of the double-height glass walls of the drawing room. The shallow, rhomboid-shaped pool at the Casa Ottolenghi is fed from the water running off the roof. In the courtyard of Palazzo Querini-Stampalia, Venice, he created a maze of low square and rectangular pools which feed into a central double square pool in which white water lilies grow.

Scarpa's masterpiece is the Brion Family Cemetery, Treviso. Here his shallow water incidents lead the visitor inside the boundaries of the cemetery. A long, formalized rill diminishes in width as it focuses on the

two sarcophagi under their protective arch. The family chapel sits on the diagonal in a low square pool. Water lilies embrace its sides. The modest water incidents strike a correct, recessive note in the cemetery.

Luis Barragan makes water fall from narrow spouts at the ends of rectangular planar walls stuccoed in brightest Mexican-bougainvillea colours. Barragan was much inspired by the traditional wooden aqueducts which were created to carry water over the villages of his native Guadalajara. One of his Minimalist masterworks is the horse trough he designed between 1958 and 1962 at Las Arboledas, near Mexico City. Here he employed the simplest of materials: the water was in a raised trough. At one end there were two rectangular walls, one white to gather the shadows from the grove of tall eucalyptus trees, and one blue to suggest distance, thus achieving a Minimalist grandeur. Barragan has had a potent and continuous influence on landscape architects and designers in the United States, Europe, and even as far away as Australia. His style is now being carried forward by the architect, Ricardo Legorretta.

Noguchi is also a master in the use of water. His skill is evident in his smaller scale courtyards such as the Plaza of Chase Manhattan Bank, Wall Street, New York City, *California Scenario,* Costa Mesa, California, and the Beinecke Rare Book and Manuscript Library, Yale University, New Haven, Connecticut.

Above *The mirrored water of the moat of Schloss Hunnefeld, Bad Essen, Osnabruck, Germany, is the site of a floating, minimalist installation created by Tage Andersen, the noted Danish florist, for the castle's 850th anniversary.*

Left *A courtyard garden in Santa Fe, New Mexico, seen in winter. It has a contemporary, black granite pool and a waterfall inspired by the traditions of the southwest.*

Sculpture

My intention is not to improve on nature but to know it – not as a spectator but as a participant. I do not wish to mimic nature, but to draw on the energy that drives it so that it drives my work also. My art is unmistakably the work of a person – I would not want it to be otherwise – it celebrates my human nature and a need to be physically and spiritually bound to the earth. Andy Goldsworthy

Right *Nature and culture 'dance' into the twenty-first century. An evergreen holm oak and a concrete triangle* assemblage *by Mauro Staccioli at the Museum of Contemporary Art, Tortoli, Italy.*

Below *Iron, water and bark are juxtaposed in Anne Jones'* Between Earth and Sky, *1996, giving wonderful reflections of the sky and the surrounding landscape.*

Sculpture is no longer sited as a single focal point or 'eye-catcher' in contemporary gardens and landscapes. It is either integrated into a garden or landscape, or the concept for its creation arises directly from its situation. Another characteristic which is peculiar to contemporary sculpture is the loss of its religious and political connotations. During the 1990s landscape architects and designers were drawn to works of sculpture inspired directly by nature. These pieces had a sense of belonging to a specific garden or

landscape. In other words, they were site-specific site-generated sculptures as opposed to works inspired by a different historical period and a different culture and set of beliefs.

The twentieth century has been unique in its exploration of new designs and materials for sculpture, and the use to which these sculptures are put. Picasso, Matisse, Arp, Miró, de Kooning and Calder created sculpture which was, in the main, portable. Even the large pieces for public display could be moved – with a crane in some cases.

Portability is no longer relevant to leading-edge contemporary sculptors. Their work is either on such a huge scale, or made of such fragile natural materials, that the portable aspect is null and void. The portable, saleable record of their work, which has become the 'work of sculpture' is either the concept sketch or a photo of the finished work. Some major examples from the 1970s and 80s are Christo and Jeanne-Claude wrapping the Reichstag in Berlin with tensile material, or *The Running Fence*, miles of tensile fabric-covered umbrellas 'intervening' in long lines through the landscape of northern California.

The beauty and originality of work using natural objects has aroused a deep interest in the natural landscape. Andy Goldsworthy, with his 'found' materials of twigs, ice, sand and clay and his leaf patterns on trees and in still pools, is at the forefront of this movement, as is Richard Long with his arrangements of 'found' rocks and flowers. Work of this kind has had an enormous influence on garden and landscape designers worldwide.

This is a quote from Goldsworthy's book *Touching North,* a section which refers to one of the most ephemeral of his sculptures:

> Its energy is made visible in ice and snow. When I work with winter I work with the North. The further North I go the stronger its presence. I want to follow North to its source – to try and come to terms with it – in the same way I work with a leaf under the tree from which it fell. I want to understand the nature of North as a whole. Unlike the summit of a mountain, the North Pole has no distinctive feature

to tell you are there – there is no land – only snow and ice. There is little difference between the Pole and the surrounding five hundred miles. It is more of a feeling than a place. It belongs to no one – it is the earth's common – an ever-changing landscape in which whatever I make will soon disappear.

The twentieth century has also seen a change in the public display of sculpture. We now have temporary, travelling exhibitions in public parks, sculpture parks with permanent collections and, most important of all, the development of Land, Earth and Environmental Art, based on the concept of the site-generated.

Right *Christo and Jeanne-Claude's* Wrapped Trees, *Fondation Beyeler and Berower Park, Riehen, Switzerland 1997–98: the latest project of artists who have been working on, among other things, wrapping trees for 32 years. Here 178 trees have been wrapped in 55,000sq m (588,500sq ft) of woven polyester fabric and 23km (14 miles) of rope.*

Below Secret Life IV, *1998, Peter Randall-Page at Wenlock Priory, Shropshire, England. Sir Roy Strong says that Randall-Page: '. . .stands at the end of the line which stretches back to Celtic crosses and down to William Morris.'*

Contemporary landscape architects and designers are concerned with sculpture inspired by nature that has a sense of belonging to its natural surroundings. In other words, they prefer the site-generated, and tend to avoid works that are the product of a different historical period. This is very different from the position taken by practitioners in the past, when garden artefacts were seen as a statement of wealth. In contemporary gardens, sculpture is an integrated part of the design.

Public sculpture gardens began to be made in the early twentieth century in Scandinavia. Gustav Vigeland made a highly personal sculpture garden on an island in a fjord near Oslo. It is famous for its amazing pillar sculpture of writhing bodies. In Stockholm, the Carl Milles Garden is on a series of terraces with pools and fountains, on which light and airy sculptures stand at various levels, silhouetted against the Swedish skies.

Scandinavia's largest public sculpture garden is the Louisiana Museum, 30km (19 miles) north of Copenhagen. It is one of the earliest and most successful combinations of landscape, architecture, painting and sculpture. Its holdings of international modern art rank with the major collections elsewhere in the world, such as the Tate Gallery in London. The garden is on the site of a nineteenth-century manor to which glass and wood corridor galleries have been added, adjacent to the wooded boundaries of the site. The sculptures are set within the woods, some are out in the open and others are situated within a variety of enclosures which are connected by carefully designed paths. In 1986 the patrons of the museum added *The Gate in the Gorge*, a site-generated sculpture by Richard Serra, and in 1994 Per Kirkeby's untitled brick sculpture.

The Kroller-Muller Museum in the Netherlands was built in 1961 on an 11-hectare (27.5-acre) site in a former hunting forest. Again, glass-walled galleries have been used to divide the formal approach to the museum from the more irregular woodland clearing and the lake. The sculpture is placed between the open views and the more enclosed wooded areas of the site.

The Kroller-Muller and Louisiana Museums have been the models for sculpture parks in many different countries on diverse sites, often covering large areas. In New York state, the Storm King Art Center, north of New York City, covers 80 hectares (200 acres). In Great Britain, the Welsh Sculpture Park at Magram has a stunning 352-hectare (880-acre) site which includes an Iron Age fort and wooded park land with lakes and formal gardens close to the museum. On the former Bretton Hall estate in Yorkshire, the Sculpture

Above *The Star of David Pavilion, 1991–1996, by Dan Graham in the moat of Schloss Buchberg, Austria. Sculpture, glass architecture and two-way mirrors magically transmute the landscape, brilliantly fooling the senses.*

Park covers 105 hectares (263 acres). These large landscape sites demand sculpture on a larger scale to harmonize with the longer views.

Garden or courtyard sites are more harmonious for the display of smaller scale sculpture. Noguchi's courtyard masterpiece for the Beinecke Rare Book and Manuscript Library, Yale University, New Haven, Connecticut and his sculpture gardens for Chase Manhattan Bank, Wall Street, New York City, along with his design at IBM Headquarters in New York state are but three of these. Also in New York City is the exquisite garden for the twentieth-century sculpture of the Museum of Modern Art designed by Philip Johnson and James Fanning.

In Great Britain, two important twentieth-century sculptors have created landscape or garden settings for their work. The first is Dame Barbara Hepworth in St Ives, Cornwall, and the other is Sir Henry Moore at Much Hadham in Hertfordshire.

There are three important late twentieth-century private gardens in Great Britain which must be noted for their sculpture. The first is in the Pentland hills south of Edinburgh. Here the poet Ian Hamilton Finlay has made what some critics describe as the most original garden to be created in Britain since 1945. Sculpture is used here to make Finlay's philosophical and polemical points about antiquity and the revolutionary nature of the human spirit.

In Hertfordshire, the architect Sir Frederick Gibberd created a sculpture garden of 'found' architectural objects and also sited sculptures by contemporary British sculptors whom he had encouraged during the 1960s and 70s. Similarly, Lord Carrington's interest in contemporary sculptors has made his garden in Buckinghamshire into a showcase for the new generation of sculptors in the 1980s and 1990s. The collection includes splendid, large-scale stone acorns, pine cones and fruit pieces by Peter Randall-Page.

Site-generated sculpture collections have emerged all over Europe and the United States over the past 20 years. In Europe, Grizedale in Cumbria is particularly important, as is Domaine de Kerguennec near Josselin in Brittany, France and Villa Celle near Florence in Italy.

At the Abington Arts Center, Pennsylvania, USA, there is a fascinating permanent installation called A Reclamation Garden by Winifred Lutz. She has been making her name as an artist working in both paper and wood, and here she is asking and answering contemporary questions to do with art versus nature, culture versus nature and larger questions about the permanence of the garden.

Lutz shapes her installations from the branches and twigs of the woodland near the arts centre. Names emerge from the shapes she creates: *The Deadfall Dome*, *The Red Oak Portal*, *The Impact Zone*; all of these are impermanent and give the illusion of being naturally formed. The only permanent shape is the 4.5m (15ft) stone tower which is definitely man-made and will have a longer life than the installations made from the 'found' woodland materials.

These modest woodland site-generated sculptures are not the vast bulldozer-made signs on the earth made by Michael Heizer or Robert Smithson in the 1960s and 70s. However, they pose a similar set of questions about being and non-being, existence and non-existence.

Above *Section of a spiral of standing stones from 'The Mist Garden' created in France, 1998. The spiral is punctuated by spaces, or 'windows', onto the surrounding landscape. Mist animates ammonite forms in stone slabs and also nurtures the ferns planted among them.*

Left *By the pond in the Hannah Peschar Sculpture Garden, Surrey, England, are these figures made from galvanized steel mesh by British sculptor David Begbie. The female is called* Limber. *1998 and the male* is Lean, *made in 1996.*

Robert Irwin
Douglas Reed
Daniel Libeskind
Ton ter Linden

Thomas Balsley
Ted Smyth
Desvigne & Dalnoky
Rios Associates

Charles Jencks
Jacques Wirtz
Jack Lenor Larsen
Arata Isosaki

Raymond Jungles
Kathryn Gustafson
Fernando Caruncho
Walter Beck & Lester Collins
T. Delaney & Co
George Hargreaves
Daniel Urban Kiley
D.A.ST.

Case studies

Twenty Case Study gardens and landscapes by leading international landscape architects and garden designers from France, Germany, Greece, Holland, Japan, New Zealand, Spain and the United States, follow showing the diversity of contemporary landscapes.

The influence of art, science and technology has brought about extraordinary developments in garden and landscape design since the 1980s. The gardens in this section are a reflection of contemporary culture. They display new aesthetic principles and often employ materials new to gardens and landscapes, such as metals, glass, plastics and tensile fabrics. Plants have not been relegated to a subsidiary role, but are often used in some of these Case Studies as an element of sculpture in a design, rather than as showpiece specimens. Some of the gardens are totally plant-inspired.

Most of the designers work in public spaces. We think that many of them display a primary advance in the thinking and practice of contemporary landscape architecture and design. Their work is largely contextual or site-generated.

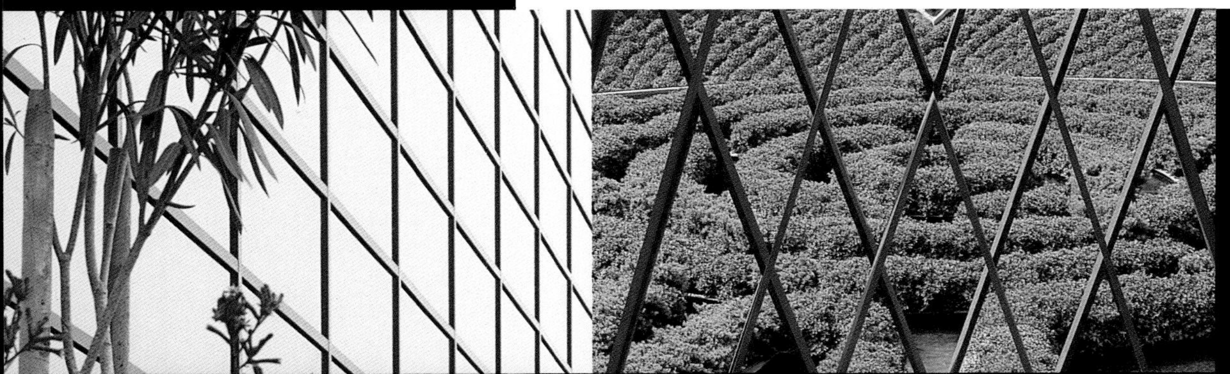

Play it as it lays.

Robert Irwin

Robert Irwin

Lower Central Garden, The Getty Center, Los Angeles, California

'A sculpture in the form of a garden aspiring to be art.' This became Robert Irwin's mantra when he was working on his design for the Lower Central Garden of the Getty Center. The Getty garden is a splendid example of site-generated design – a concept that has inspired some of the most creative landscape architects and garden designers in the United States, France, Holland and Spain. The shapes and forms of the design are drawn from within the site, rather than being imposed upon it in the traditional way. In Irwin's own words, this amounts to 'playing "it" as it lays'.

Far right *Robert Irwin's splendid 'trees' designed for the plaza of the Lower Central Garden of the Getty Center. Made from concrete reinforcing rods, the trees provide vertical interest and make excellent climbing frames for bougainvillea.*

As we drove up the San Diego Freeway on the Interstate 405 from Long Beach, we saw a striking group of buildings perched on the point of an escarpment above the Sepulveda Pass. At first we thought that they might be a 1950s Veterans' Administration hospital, but as we got nearer, we realized that it could only be the Getty Center, designed by Richard Meier. Pity the community of Brentwood residents below the complex were so intransigent about the project. They quashed Meier's brilliant idea of brushed stainless steel for all of the metal façades. They had to be painted white or off-white. The steel contrasting with the stone would have been superb; a splendid design opportunity lost.

The Getty is the richest centre of art in the world. Thirteen years in the making, it covers 44 hectares (110 acres) high above Los Angeles. On a clear day, Catalina Island in the Pacific is visible to the west and Mount Baldy to the east. Meier's hilltop campus, which was built at a cost of $1 billion, consists of the J. Paul Getty Museum (54 galleries) and five cultural institutes, including a concert hall. The

GARDEN STATISTICS

Client: The Getty Center
Budget: $8.5 million
Designer: Robert Irwin
Area: 1.4ha (3.5 acres)
Climate: Southern Californian
Soil type: Sandy topsoil
Aspect: West
Date of completion: 1997
Number of gardeners: 5

buildings are faced in off-white travertine, cut from ancient quarries near Rome. Some 37,000 tons of this stone were used.

The Getty Board, who should be eternally thanked for their vision, wanted 'an artist's sensibility', as they put it, to be applied to the design of the lower gardens. Robert Irwin was appointed to design the Lower Central Garden on the 1.4-hectare (3.5-acre) west-facing slope of a natural canyon (a deep valley with steep sides, often with a stream flowing through it) below the buildings.

This is said to have caused Meier no end of anguish. His first reaction was to demand a 9m-wide (30ft-wide) *cordon aesthetique* of lawn between his buildings and the edge of the valley where the garden was to be. When telling us about this, Irwin's tone of voice was similar to that of a patient Montessori nursery school teacher: 'It was hard for him to have someone else paint on his canvas.' We presume that Meier did not want any trees and shrubs to blur the mathematical rigour of his buildings.

Irwin's working life as a leading American artist is also a précis of modern art in the latter half of the twentieth century. It begins with his paintings as an Abstract Expressionist in the 1950s. In the late 1960s he chucked out his art supplies and began his journey from what he calls 'ground zero' as another kind of artist. He investigated Art and Technology, Installation Art, Light-and-Space Art, Los Angeles 'Look' Art and

Above *The dramatic, Mogul-inspired waterfall feeds into a circular pool on which pink and red azaleas create an ancient maze pattern*

Left *An elevated view of Richard Meier's Getty Center. The museum is on the right and the art history centre, encompassing Robert Irwin's design, is on the left..*

Above *Irwin's early coloured presentation plan of the Lower Central Garden reveals its giant stem and flower form.*

Below *Irwin's model delineates the circle, maze, serpentine and zigzag, the major design elements of the garden.*

Above *Irwin went to Montana and South Dakota to select the rocks for the serpentine stream. He arranged them down the centre of the original canyon site to orchestrate the sound of the running water and create the maximum visual impact.*

Centre *Teak benches on the stone path provide a place to enjoy the sound of water and the shade of the plane trees.*

Public Art. These different art forms are all 'site-generated', or 'site-conditioned'.

With the Getty project, Irwin moved from 'site-generated' projects inside buildings to an exterior site. When he accepted the challenge he confirmed that he was not a gardener. However, we consider the Lower Central Garden a masterpiece of site-generated landscape design. Its main elements have emerged from Irwin's deep analysis of the site (his main aim was to restore and adapt to the canyon site), but they also reflect some of the most important metaphors in garden history. The design incorporates the serpentine, the zigzag, a Japanese reverence for the placing of stones, the formal *allée*, the circle, the bosque, the labyrinth, the terrace, viewing points and a unique and expressive use of plants. And, viewed from above, the circle of terraces, with the pool with labyrinth of azaleas, becomes a splendid parterre. The configuration of the circle and water course aerially hallucinate into a giant flower and stem.

Irwin has designed a central serpentine line of water down the slope which is divided by a wonderful zigzag stone path. This is a perfect example both of Irwin 'playing it as it lays' and of the 'site-generated'. In his original plan the paths were straight down the sides of the water course. Irwin was then confronted by the Los Angeles ordinance on wheelchair access. This meant adapting the path to a zigzag ramp, yet another design stroke among the many in this garden. Where the triangular sides of the ramp meet the lawn area, they are retained with up-stands of Cor-Ten steel. Since the Getty Center is open two nights a week, Irwin designed tall standard lights to illuminate the ramp. When seen from above, the lamps outline the form of the serpentine and circular elements of the garden and, as Irwin puts it, provide 'a drawing of the garden'.

Between each crossing of the zigzag ramp, Irwin has placed rocks that he selected himself in Montana and South Dakota. These are arranged so that they 'tune' the water to different decibels at each level of the garden. At the first level the water is only heard, not seen, under the rocks. As one descends the slope, the water is visible and the sound is more pronounced. It reaches a climactic roar as it falls from the 15m (50ft) waterfall into the pool at the bottom of the plan. The rough boulders get smaller and more ordered, until at the plaza the water course has become a shallow fast-running channel lined with a diamond pattern of stone sets and narrow steps, allowing visitors to step down to the stream's edge. This is Irwin's variation on the

Right *Exquisite, small stone setts on the stream bed contrast with large boulders and rocks. The main zigzag path of stone changes to teak wood bridges over the stream.*

Persian and Mogul chuddar waterfall, which is angled and stepped to give more sound and glitter to the water as it falls. On the edge of the pool, above the waterfall, there is a bronze arc, which acts as a safety balustrade and a handrail. It also looks like a stylized setting sun, giving an Art Deco reference to Hollywood in the 1920s and 30s – just one more example of Irwin's sensitive and visionary grasp of design.

The planting is carefully calibrated from the top to the very bottom of the water course. Under the plane trees at the top, grey-leafed plants predominate. Midway down the slope the leaf colours turn to red, purple and dark green. Irwin uses these dark colours to contrast with the pale walls of Meier's stone and metal buildings. Finally, at the lowest level, the plants are pale green with yellow flowers. When questioned by members of the more conventional landscape architect community about his diverse selection of plants, the high levels of maintenance that they would require and their mutability, Irwin replied: 'Let's assume this garden is art.' He believes that the Getty should curate the garden just as they do the art objects in the museum.

The plaza is a generous, open space, a splendid contrast to the serpentine water course, the zigzag ramp and the interlaced labyrinths of azaleas that embrace the pool and appear to be floating on the water. During the flowering season, one gardener has the sole duty of plucking off the spent azalea blossoms. Irwin has designed a ladder down to the pool specifically for this purpose.

The lower tiers of shallow, amphitheatre terraces above the pool are planted with hundreds of species of perennial and annual plants and encircled with crape myrtles. Irwin chose the myrtles for their deciduous nature, as he believes that 'bareness is beautiful'. On the top tier of the amphitheatre are serried ranks of grasses. These look wonderful all year; even when they have been cut back in the winter they have attractive, sculptural shapes.

Where the ramp enters the plaza, there are two trios of monumental, bronzed 'tree' shapes. Each one is 3.6m (12ft) high and is made of concrete reinforcing rods. The structures will eventually be clothed in *Bougainvillea* 'Tahitian Dawn'. Their crucial role now as tall, arboreal shapes will be transferred to the *allée* of London planes (*Platanus acerifolia* 'Yarwood') on either side of the water course.

Above *The zigzag paths, required for access by the disabled, made the final design stronger. Cor-Ten steel upstands retain the earth of the flowerbeds and support bronze handrails.*

Left *Honeysuckle, roses and heliotrope combine with many other scented plants to create an* omnium-gatherum *of herbaceous and annual plantings. Irwin's advisor on the planting was Jim Duggan. The garden manager is Richard Naranjo. Any negative reactions from the American landscape architecture profession become irrelevant when one watches visitors of every kind enjoying the variety of scent, colour and leaf in the garden.*

Irwin believes that every garden and landscape has a 'power site'. In this case, it is here, at the mid-point, when one turns away from the LA panorama and looks back over his garden embraced by the buildings of the Getty Center.

The treatment of the view from the slope has led to another heightened discussion with Meier. In his original plan for the garden, the grand staircase and terraces would have made his buildings completely open to the view. Irwin's solution is more exciting as it includes some elements of surprise, such as the plane trees of the water course. Irwin had the following words carved into a stone at the bottom of the serpentine water course and they are an accurate reflection of the triumph of this garden:

Ever Present, Never Twice the Same
Ever Changing, Never Less Than Whole

Above *Contrast is another characteristic of Irwin's design game. Here a green lawn abuts Cor-Ten steel retaining walls. Sculptural clumps of grass rise out of the softer herbaceous and annual plantings.*

These have a potential height of 36m (120ft). When they reach 18m (60ft), Irwin predicts that they will 'read' in scale, improving the space vertically below and relating to Meier's buildings on either side of the garden above. Even now, they provide welcome cool shade after the blistering travertine stone setts of the arrival plaza.

The French wicker café armchairs scattered about the plaza create an informal atmosphere and also serve as a design reference to the relaxed street life of France and *La Vie Douce*.

The simplest and yet perhaps the most effective element of Irwin's design is centred on the top tier of the amphitheatre above the oval pool. Here the Cor-Ten steel walls retain gravel and provide a daring contrast to the arcs of the planting on either side. Angular crossovers are not only a design variation of the ramps across the serpentine stream, they also provide the visitor with a vast panorama of Los Angeles at a garden exit.

The Therapeutic Garden demonstrates that human interaction with the landscape is a dynamic and vital experience that offers the promise of awareness, recovery and transformation.

Douglas Reed

Douglas Reed

Therapeutic Garden for Children, Wellesley, Massachusetts, USA

Garden Honoured with President's Award of Excellence, 1997 American Society of Landscape Architects

Gardens have been perceived as places of sanctuary and healing for many thousands of years. This tradition is now manifest in the healing gardens of hospitals and hospices today. Contemporary healing and therapeutic gardens are being designed and made to help AIDS patients, Alzheimer and stroke sufferers, and many types of extreme psychological and traumatic disorders.

A sense of sanctuary is basic to the healing work of Douglas Reed's Therapeutic Garden for traumatized children near Boston. Reed was commissioned to design the garden by Dr Sebastiano Santostefano, director of the Institute for Child and Adolescent Development, a treatment centre for children suffering from the traumas of a variety of emotional and behavioural disorders. Santostefano and his therapists work on hidden trauma. Children who have witnessed illness, violence or death are often his patients. He explains his approach by saying: 'Early intervention is the basis of the Institute's work. It operates in an elementary school in Boston, testing even the kindergarten children.'

Far right *A young patient delights in the Therapeutic Garden for Children designed by Douglas Reed. Exploration of the garden, and the dialogue between therapist and patient that results, constitutes an important part of the treatment at the Institute.*

Santostefano has definite views on restoring the mental health of children. They are never treated on the analyst's couch, nor in the clinical and often oppressive conventional psychiatric facility. His success rate since 1993 has been excellent. It has been shown in subsequent studies that if testing and help can be given to children with traumas before the age of ten, then they will have three times less chance of developing behavioural or learning disorders in their teens.

GARDEN STATISTICS

Client: Institute for Child and Adolescent Development

Budget: $250,000

Designer: Douglas Reed Landscape Architecture Inc.

Area: 0. 4ha (1 acre)

Climate: Zones 4–5

Soil Type: Acidic loam

Aspect: South east

Date of completion: 1996

Number of gardeners: Contractor

For many years Dr Santostefano had wanted to transform the rambling. 0.4-hectare (1-acre) garden behind his large, three-storey Victorian house. By creating a purpose-built garden, he hoped

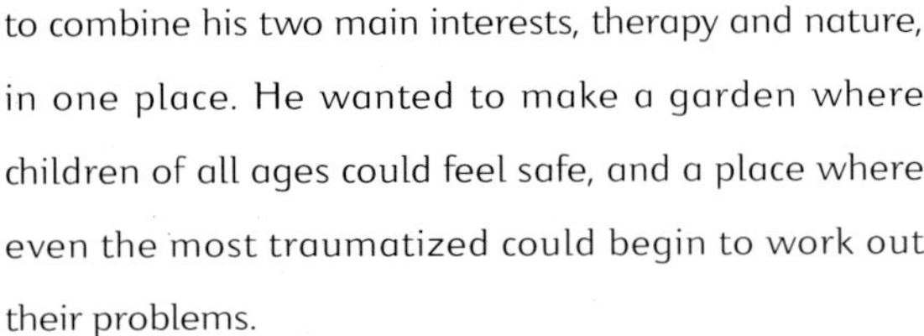

to combine his two main interests, therapy and nature, in one place. He wanted to make a garden where children of all ages could feel safe, and a place where even the most traumatized could begin to work out their problems.

Douglas Reed was eager to accept the commission. It was a challenge as it was the first garden of its type that his office had undertaken. He talked to Santostefano at length about the psychological implications of the landscape on therapy. They worked together to research the brief for the project by touring areas of natural beauty around Boston.

Reed described his role in the design process in the following words:

> The director had long dreamed of developing a garden for use in therapy, and developed clear ideas about what the landscape should provide. My role as a landscape architect was to give form to those theories and ideas.

Below *The flowing lines of one of Reed's earliest sketches for the garden reflect the inspiration that Reed drew from his discovery that there had once been water on the site of the Therapeutic Garden.*

Mature stands of existing trees and a 2.75m (9ft) change in elevation were the sources of inspiration for Reed's first drawings. In his own words, 'The design expresses the narrative of a water course that weaves its way through the site, linking a sequence of spaces that correspond to the stages of a child's recovery.' The sunken area of the site was once the path of a stream. The knowledge that there had once been water on the site led Reed to use it as the major design element. To him it symbolized life (as it has in gardens for millennia) and in this garden it also became a symbol of recovery.

The serpentine water course was inspired by the one at Rousham House in Oxfordshire. Rousham, one of the most admired and poetic of the eighteenth-century landscape gardens, was designed in 1738 by William Kent. Reed's water course, the major unifying element of his design, is a low, 20cm-wide (8in-wide) steel-sided trough, partially filled with gravel. The water begins its journey on a stone terrace to one side of the Institute. Reed thinks of the terrace and garden as a seamless extension of the building. The head of water rises first from a low, circular grey-green granite basin, spills gently over the edge and flows out through five stainless-steel pipes in a wall. It then falls into a rill which the children follow through the garden.

When the garden was judged for the American Society of Landscape Architects award, one of the judges commented: 'I can just imagine a child putting something – a leaf, a stick, a sailboat – in this trough and watching it make its way through the landscape.'

Reed envisaged his design as 'a series of archetypal land forms carved by water.' Following the rill as it falls from the terrace, they find a sequence of shapes. Some of them are extrovert shapes which rise

Right *The fluid contours revealed by a model of the garden dramatically illustrate Reed's attempt to create a landscape which seems to have been moulded by the forces of water.*

Above *The rill running through the garden was inspired by the water course at Rousham, the great eighteenth-century garden by William Kent in Oxfordshire, England.*

up from the garden. There is a knoll, a mount, a bridge, an island and an upland wood; others, such as the cave, the ravine, the shallow pond and the glade, are obviously introvert.

Reed wanted spaces to correspond to levels of recovery: a dark, narrow cave-like ravine conveys a sense of safety, an upland wooded area is for exploration, the steep and shallow slopes of the grassed-earth forms beg to be climbed and there is a large, sunny glade for playing and running.

The different areas of the garden are defined by plantings of native species. In the upland section, among the existing red and white oaks, he planted Norway maple, and there are river birch with native grey and red osier dogwoods, common witch hazel and arrowhead viburnum. The decorative shrubs include common box, Japanese, longstalk and inkberry holly, mountain laurel, mock orange, lilac and oakleaf hydrangea. The cave, for hiding and huddling in, is built from a shelter of transplanted Japanese yew. Liquidambar and pagoda dogwood, American beech and woodland hydrangea are included with birches to furnish the ravine and ridge slopes. The island itself is actually a thicket of swamp azalea, clethra

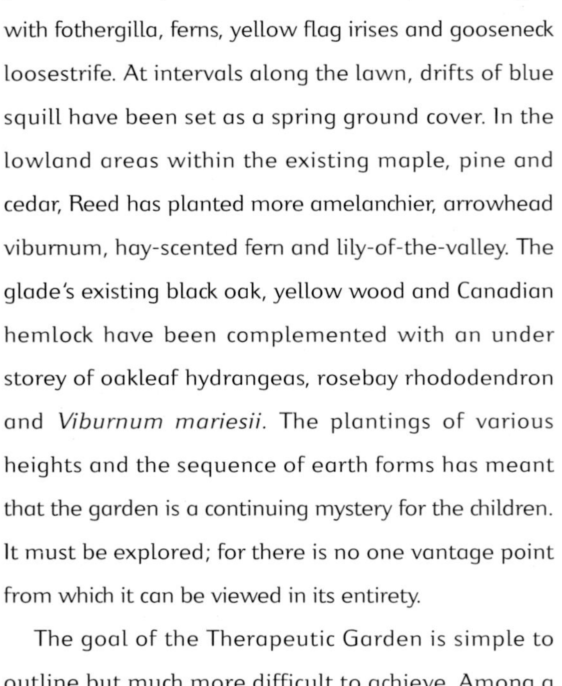

(summersweet) and amelanchier. The pond is edged with fothergilla, ferns, yellow flag irises and gooseneck loosestrife. At intervals along the lawn, drifts of blue squill have been set as a spring ground cover. In the lowland areas within the existing maple, pine and cedar, Reed has planted more amelanchier, arrowhead viburnum, hay-scented fern and lily-of-the-valley. The glade's existing black oak, yellow wood and Canadian hemlock have been complemented with an under storey of oakleaf hydrangeas, rosebay rhododendron and *Viburnum mariesii*. The plantings of various heights and the sequence of earth forms has meant that the garden is a continuing mystery for the children. It must be explored; for there is no one vantage point from which it can be viewed in its entirety.

The goal of the Therapeutic Garden is simple to outline but much more difficult to achieve. Among a variety of therapeutic techniques employed at the centre, Santostefano now includes the exploration of the garden. The therapist and child establish a bond through the elements of the landscape. The behaviour of a child at each of Reed's design incidents is documented by the therapist on a copy of the garden plan. Santostefano explains that 'some memories are unlocked by sensation'. He recalls the case of an adolescent girl's realization about her generalized anger while lying face-down on the mound in the garden. She told the therapist, somewhat hesitatingly, that she felt she was lying on the belly of a pregnant woman. Further discussion revealed that the girl's early trauma came from her mother having given birth to a stillborn child.

Dr Santostefano's dream of a therapeutic garden was realized with the help of Judy Pillsbury, a Paris art dealer. Santostefano had treated a member of her family, and she spearheaded a drive to raise the first $200,000 needed to pay for the garden. The work of the Institute goes beyond the boundaries of Douglas Reed's design, for the good doctor is using the garden as a training ground for the para-professionals who will work on the Institute's outreach programme for adolescents in the socially and economically deprived South End area of Boston.

Reed thinks that the garden is one of the most satisfying he has ever designed. It is truly rewarding to see the tangible results among the children who have been treated there. The following passage, written by Mac Griswold, a leading American garden historian and writer, gives a marvellous insight into the purpose of the garden:

> Sanctuary has lost the power of repeated common ritual and shared community memory. Instead, what establishes a sacred public landscape in contemporary times is our often individual and nearly unconscious response to its peace and safety and beauty. Actions dictated by the design of the place itself, such as sitting, staring off between the trees, moving through space on a path, listening to the sound of water, or watching the slow patterns of shadow, are what restore power, hope and psychological stability.

Below *The terrace with a low, green granite basin, the source of the rill which leads the children on a therapeutic journey of discovery through the garden.*

Left *The stone retaining wall of the terrace pierced by stainless steel pipes fed by the basin on the terrace above. A catchment pool then feeds the rill meandering through the garden.*

Daniel Libeskind

E.T.A.Hoffmann Garden, The Jewish Museum, Berlin

I imagine that many people have read E.T.A. Hoffmann at some point... I have always loved E.T.A. Hoffmann, and I was stunned when I started working on the Museum to discover that he was a lawyer in the Altbau, in the Kollegienhaus.

Daniel Libeskind

The Jewish Museum is adjacent to the Kollegienhaus, a Baroque public building designed by Philipp Gerlach in 1725. Hoffmann worked there as a judge. The E.T.A. Hoffmann Garden was designed by Daniel Libeskind as an extension to the theme of the museum building. It is named after Ernst Theodore Amadeus Wilhelm Hoffmann (1776–1822), the great nineteenth-century romantic writer.

Hoffmann is considered to have been Germany's most important story-teller. Even though he had prepared himself for a legal career, music was his true vocation. He was also a brilliant caricaturist and this caused him trouble among the conventional bourgeois society of Posen as he caricatured local officials. The satiric drawings cost Hoffmann his job as government assessor and he was exiled to the dull town of Plock. He continued to divide his time between drawing and music and his first short literary work was published in 1803, *The Letter from a Monk to his friend in the City.* He continued to write while pursuing his legal work, until his death in 1822.

Far right *The rose was the only plant allowed to be grown in Jerusalem. A skewed grid of red and white roses is a link between Daniel Libeskind's Jewish Museum and his E.T.A. Hoffman Garden, a Garden of Exile and Emigration.*

There are three routes through the museum, which Libeskind prefers to call 'roads'. The first long one calls up the history of Berlin and its long continuity and leads to upper-floor exhibition galleries. Of the two others, the longer route goes to the dead-end 'road of the Holocaust void' and the shorter to the memorial Garden of Exile and Emigration and two spaces of contemplation. The garden is Libeskind's metaphor, combining the image of so many Jews who left by sea and also a reference to the soil of Berlin. The memorial garden form is in a hypostyle (group of columns) supporting a roof grid of 7 x 7 rough unclad concrete columns. The square of columns will eventually support a green roof.

GARDEN STATISTICS

Client: Berlin Senate

Budget: DM111.8 million *(building and garden)*

Designer: Daniel Libeskind

Area: 22 x 22m (70 x 70 ft) *(garden)*

Climate: North European

Soil type: Sand

Aspect: North

Date of completion: 1999

Below *The asymmetric pattern of stone setts in a variation on the pattern in the Paul Celan Courtyard.*

In the top of each of the 49 columns there has been planted a willow-oak shrub (*Elaeagnus angustifolia*), and these are watered by an irrigation system which runs underground. These plants will grow together, forming a green canopy over the columns. The centre column of the grid has been filled with earth gathered from Jerusalem and stands for Berlin, the other 48 contain earth from Berlin and symbolize 1948 when the state of Israel was formed. The hypostyle has been placed on the ground which slopes in two directions and all the columns are tilting as a mass towards the museum. It is the only orthogonal right-angled square form to be found anywhere in the museum, the design being right-angled both in section and in plan.

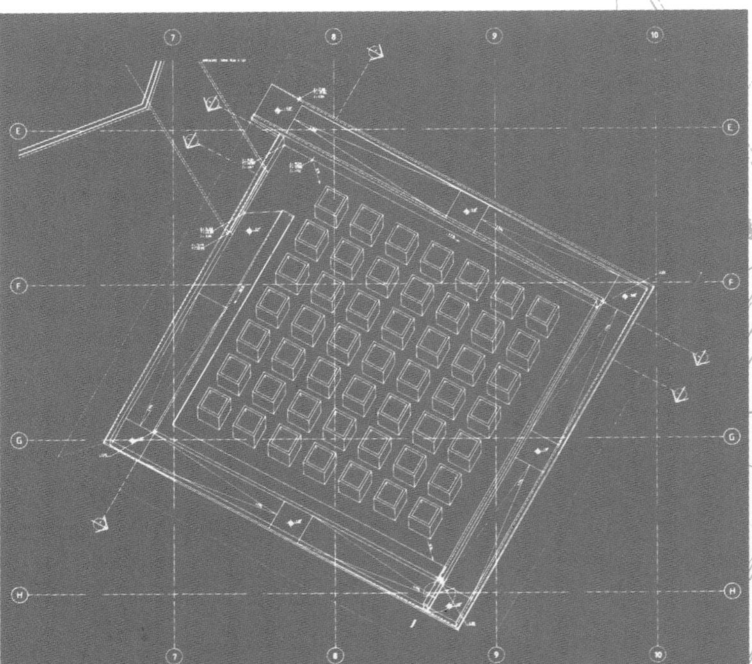

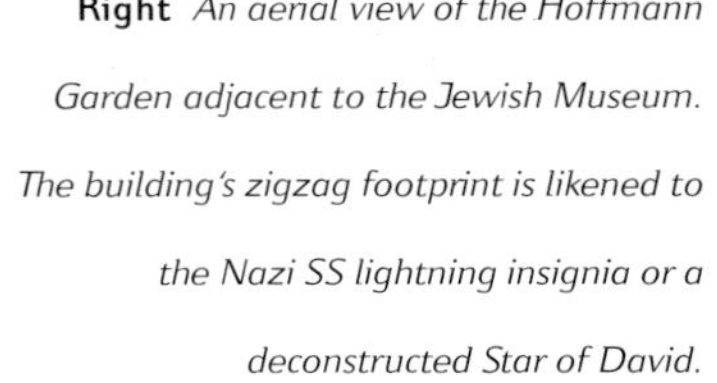

Right *An aerial view of the Hoffmann Garden adjacent to the Jewish Museum. The building's zigzag footprint is likened to the Nazi SS lightning insignia or a deconstructed Star of David.*

The garden has a disturbing effect after experiencing the asymmetricality of the interior of the museum.

Libeskind's purpose was to disorient the visitor. It was to represent the 'shipwreck of history'. He wanted the visitor to feel unstable and even somewhat seasick. The garden and architecture of the building are to be experienced with both the head and the feet. Libeskind thinks architecture should first be experienced with the feet and then, later on, one can think about it. Libeskind has also called the garden of memorial the 'upside down' garden, a further metaphor referring to the displacement of Jews prior to the Second World War. Images for that experience are drawn from Libeskind's idea that Berlin looked very different to the exiles and even to Berliners who remained. The upside down aspect of the garden emerges from the earth inside the concrete columns, the hard ground below, the roots at the top of the columns and the willow-oak shrubs forming their canopy high above – inaccessible.

Other landscaping around the memorial garden consists of old species red and white roses planted in 2m (6 ft) squares. The grid pattern is turned or skewed 15 degrees in relation to the museum, so 'the roses dance with each other', according to Jan Wehberg who consulted on the landscaping. The rose was chosen for its symbolic past associations, the thorny rose as a model for life in that it has the power to both injure and reconcile. The rose was also the only plant which was allowed in the ancient city of Jerusalem. Existing maple trees became part of the landscape design. A grove of spiny locust trees were planted as a contemporary inversion of the mythical motif of the Garden of Eden, the garden of paradise. The landscaping was designed by Cornelia Muller and Jan Wehberg, landscape architects who work in Berlin.

The garden was placed on an open side of the museum so that it engages street life of the city. It also invokes many other images. The route to the garden from underground is through a glass door which calls up the notion that freedom comes only through exile. The hypostyle grid of columns has associations with the urban grids of cities massed with skyscrapers, perhaps an image of haven for the Jews fleeing from Berlin.

Finally, there is a kind of garden in another courtyard of the museum. It is the Paul Celan Courtyard in honour of the Jewish poet, author of 'The Death Fugue'. Planted in the courtyard is Celan's favourite tree – a single paulownia.

Far left *A plan of the E.T.A. Hoffmann Garden of Exile and Emigration. The only orthogonal element in Libeskind's Jewish Museum design is the garden grid.*

Below *A transverse view of the Hoffmann Garden.* Elaeagnus angustifolia *grows from the tops of the columns, its horizontal growth forming a green roof over the hypostyle grid of 7 x 7 columns.*

Ton ter Linden

Ruinen, Drenthe, Holland

I see each border as a water-colour; light is all important. I like to use tall airy plants so you can see the light fall through them.

Ton ter Linden

Impressionism and Pointillism: two definitions drawn from the history of painting that could be used to describe this extraordinary garden in north-eastern Holland. Ton ter Linden, the creator of the garden, is himself a fine painter. Early on, he experimented in oils, but found them too thick and opaque for his flower and plant subjects. Water-colours became his preferred medium. They embodied the lightness and transparency that he expresses wonderfully both in his plant paintings and his gardens. Piet Mondrian, the great Dutch Abstract artist of black-and-white grid paintings with blocks of colour, also comes to mind when looking down at the strictly rectilinear plan of ter Linden's garden.

Far right *Ton ter Linden's gloriously informal massed planting within his strict square and rectangular ground plan.*

Ton ter Linden is a self-taught artist and garden designer. While growing up in Amsterdam, he loved the flowers his mother placed in the house. When he was older he began making pencil sketches in the local parks, teaching himself about structure and line from the trees. Later he ventured into colour and its myriad variations. It was in the Thysse Park in Amsterdam that he noticed the organic methods employed by the gardeners. Since then he has never used pesticides or chemical fertilizers again. Ton ter Linden bought his 1.6-hectare (4-acre) site in the rural province of Drenthe on a bleak, rainy day 20 years ago. It is an area of peaceful, open meadow land, with a scattering of small farms with thatched or grass-covered roofs. It was the perfect place to paint and garden.

For many years, ter Linden had dreamt of creating a garden. Here, the land was cheap and he could realize his ambition. His new home consisted of a small, run-down farm complete with disintegrating brick farmhouse, dilapidated barns and neglected meadows. The only thing of beauty was a venerable apple tree, now over 100 years old. Ton ter Linden used the tree as a look-out and as a vertical reference while he was in the process of designing the garden.

GARDEN STATISTICS

Designer: Ton ter Linden
Number of staff: 2
Area: 1.6ha (4 acres)
Climate: Northern temperate
Soil type: Peat
Aspect: South
Date of completion: Ongoing
Number of gardeners: 2

Hanne Cannegeiter, ter Linden's assistant, is very clear about the way plants are used in the garden:

> Ton's love of water-colours is apparent throughout his garden. There are no sharply defined areas of colour next to one another, rather a moving interplay, one colour drawn on by another. This style leads to a planting arrangement Ton calls 'weaving', for which he may make use of so-called 'weaver-plants' spread through a border, simulating the effect of a mist in merging colours. For this purpose, some of his favourite plants are artemisia, nepeta, *Physostegia virginiana speciosa* 'Bouquet Rose'.

Gradation of height is the conventional Gertrude Jekyll legacy for the classic Arts and Crafts border, a historical norm flouted by ter Linden. He often plants tall, upright subjects at the front of a border to give a sense of transparency and depth. He succeeds in this because of his vast knowledge of colour, flowering times, leaf and plant form. In autumn and winter, seed and flower heads add beauty to the foreground of a planting, rather than being massed in the background.

Right *Grasses in one of ter Linden's six 'water borders'. Ter Linden calculates the areas for the borders and positions his plants freehand, without the constraints of a paper plan.*

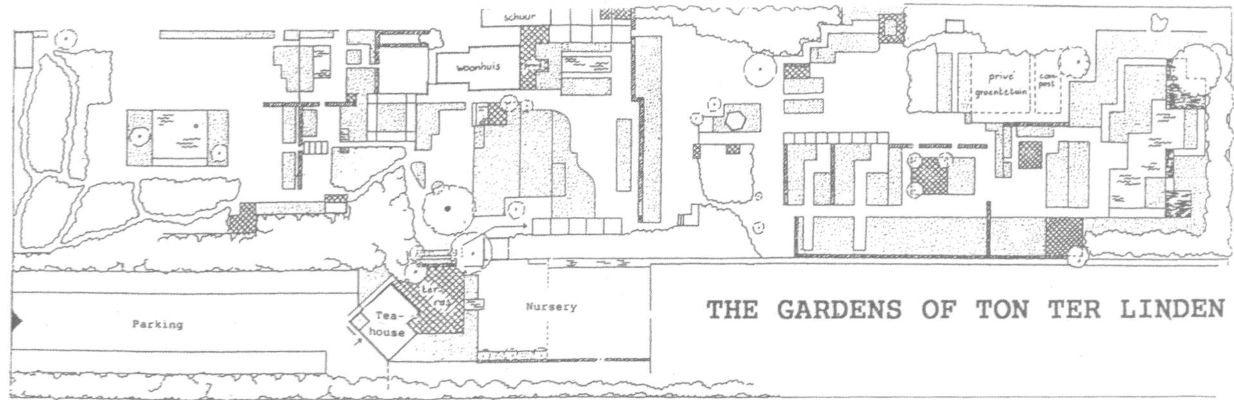

Below *The master plan of Ton ter Linden's Garden not only recalls the grid paintings of his fellow countryman, the artist Piet Mondrian, but also calls to mind the super-precise agricultural field patterns of their homeland.*

The Yellow Garden is not the usual pale, almost monochromatic one to be found in other Dutch gardens or in some of the more prissy manor gardens in England. Ton ter Linden's vigorous artist-plantsman, eye lays down a yellow core, then 'weaves' in red, terracotta and orange from plants selected to reach a climax in August. Solid blocks of colour are descried, he graduates tones of alchemilla, alstroemeria, helenium, oenothera, solidago and verbascum, creating his painterly plant composition. Roses are planted for contrast on the pergola and on 2.5m (8ft) frames.

As you might expect, the Sun Border is in full sun. Conceived on a large scale, it is 29m (95ft) long and 6.5m (21ft) at its widest point. Here is the exception to ter Linden's 'taller plants at the border front' rule. Though mainly at the rear of the border, they flow through its length in ribbons of colour. Two of his favourite 'big chaps', being both tall and luxuriant in growth, are *Veronicastrum virginicum album* and *Verbena hastata*. Both create a dramatic impact. He uses a broad colour palette and contrasts plant shapes artfully.

In autumn the dried seed and flower heads create a splendid visual effect. Leaving them uncut also has a practical purpose. It provides insulation for plants in the border's under storey, and according to the garden's guide book:

> It is forbidden to pick anything. In our way of gardening it is important that seeds are spread round the garden in a natural way.

Most of the taller plants need staking and quantities of brushwood are used. In ter Linden's own words:

> Birch is ideal because it is so pliable but I also use a lot of oak twigs. I start staking plants like delphinium and thalictrum when they are about 2ft [60cm] tall but I also stake surrounding plants. In this way I create a network of brushwood which I hope will survive the inevitable gales. After staking I cut away all the superfluous wood, so nothing remains in sight.

Ter Linden waits until spring to work on his borders – the big clean-up. First, he removes and burns all of the spent brushwood. The dead stems of the herbaceous plants are then cut with secateurs into 20cm (8in) lengths and spread over the bed. Here they become a layer of mulch fertilizer, aiding moisture retention during the summer. When this job is complete, ter Linden can embark on the weeding.

To vary the garden pictures for both adults and children, ter Linden has built a wooden platform which he calls the belvedere. It is only 1.5m (5ft) high, but it offers the same perspective of the garden as that enjoyed by a low-flying bird.

Ton ter Linden's dislike of curves is played out in the herbaceous beds as well as the six 'water borders'. The leaves of plants and the arching stems of the grasses are mirrored by the surfaces of the pools.

The garden changes, not only with the seasons but also with its owner's constant care and painterly eye.

Above *A mature climbing rose behind the serene pool on a summer's evening. Its rounded, organic shape is an effective contrast in form to the geometric lines of the pool and benches.*

What I hope drives the approach to Queen's West is sensitivity to the past.

Thomas Balsley

Thomas Balsley

Gantry Plaza State Park, Queens, Long Island City, New York

Long Island City is the site of the Isamu Noguchi Museum, where sculptures and a sculpture garden have been established for the work of Noguchi – one of the greatest influences on late twentieth-century landscape and garden design. We feel the shade of Noguchi must be smiling benignly down on this new, 0.8-hectare (2-acre) waterfront plaza park, if for no other reason than the strong and sculptural use of stone that Balsley has employed in his design for the site.

Far right *Local Long Island City residents are seemingly oblivious to the magical New York City skyline as they focus on the game in Thomas Balsley's Gantry Plaza State Park.*

The spectacular views from the park across the East River to the skyline of Manhattan are a splendid bonus. The park was named for the huge black steel gantries which were used to hoist railway cars and other cargo onto river barges for the westwards journey, and Balsley was determined that they should not be swept away. They were cleaned up and have become stunning, post-industrial frames for some of the most imposing buildings of the 'electric' metropolis across the river. One view is a 'shot' of the United Nations headquarters, designed by the great Brazilian architect Oscar Niemeyer; a second and equally stunning view is of the Empire State Building and the Chrysler Building, rising up within the amazing skyscraper-scape of that 'wonderful town'.

Queens West is part of a major redevelopment at the western end of Long Island. It is designed to be a combination of commercial and residential buildings, over some 29 hectares (73 acres). The site, which is called Hunter's Point, covers a 182km (114-mile) linear, waterfront strip on the edge of Long Island City. The total cost of the development is to be $2.3 billion. This will fund the construction of 19 high-rise buildings, open spaces and parks amounting to some 10 hectares (25 acres).

GARDEN STATISTICS

Client: Development Corporations: New York and New Jersey

Budget: $15 million

Designers: Thomas Balsley Associates

Area: 0.8ha (2 acres)

Climate: Zones 4–5

Soil type(s): Clay and loam

Aspect: South and west

Date of completion: 1998+

Below *Balsley designed robust split-faced granite blocks to retain the river bank and to act as a park amenity.*

Local community alarm bells began to ring in the existing neighbourhoods of Long Island City when the redevelopment project was initially announced. The inhabitants predicted that the proposed new buildings would be detrimental to their homes, and at the very least screen them from the waterfront and might well cut them off completely. All too predictably,

Right *The sculptural gantries were retained by Balsley as an historical reference to the railroad and river barge trade of the past.*

their suspicions were soon confirmed by the construction of a monolithic, 42-storey tower, designed by Caesar Pelli. The height of this building alone confirmed the community's need for new open spaces and public parks. In response to the local outcry, Hunter's Point Community Park was built in 1996. It is situated on a relatively narrow patch of ground at the end of the main shopping street of Long Island City. Here Balsley was able to experiment with both hard and soft landscaping materials, which he would return to later in Gantry Plaza and the other parks. The stainless-steel street furniture with geometric patterns punched into it, the metal light fixtures and the sail-shaped canopies combine to give the area both a stylish as well as an industrial quality.

Balsley has been commissioned to design three other public spaces within the Gantry Plaza project. The major works of North Gantry Park and South Gantry Plaza were completed in the spring of 1998. The Peninsula, which will span over 0.4 hectare (1 acre), has yet to be installed.

North Gantry Park to the south of the Peninsula is the arrival and mid-point of the entire Gantry Plaza State Park design. It is best to arrive at the park on foot from Long Island City. Balsley has designed a circular fog fountain sitting in a small plaza which is backed by a wall on which 'Queens West' is written in large letters. The most immediately striking features here are the giant gantries. As Balsley says, 'they create this moment that dominates your consciousness, but you have to think of them in context.'

Lee Weintraub,who collaborated with Balsley on the project, agreed with his statement that the gantries represented a historical 'take' and confirmed their use as sculptural design elements within the setting

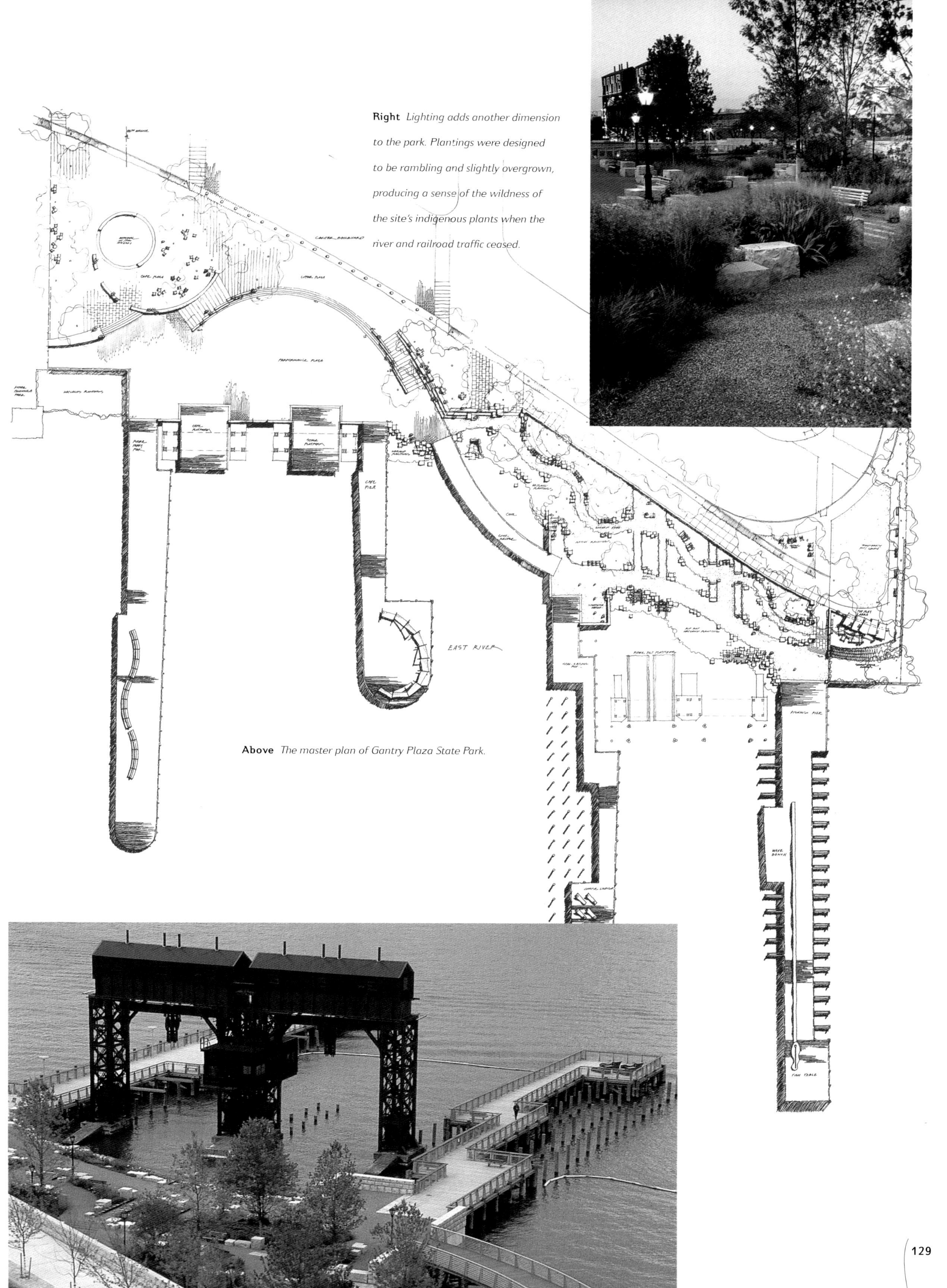

Right *Lighting adds another dimension to the park. Plantings were designed to be rambling and slightly overgrown, producing a sense of the wildness of the site's indigenous plants when the river and railroad traffic ceased.*

Above *The master plan of Gantry Plaza State Park.*

Below *Anglers' bait, catch and other equipment can all be left on this metal table. It is also equipped with stools and a water tap – a good setting for those discussions about 'the one that got away'.*

of the park. As Weintraub said, 'the gantries were always going to be a focus, or screen, through which to see the back wall of the space – the east side of Manhattan'. They provide a strong vertical aspect to the design as well as a pleasing intermediate shape between the land and river, with its amazing panorama of skyscrapers.

The name of the locality, Long Island, is painted on the gantries in bold red-and-white-trimmed letters from the late nineteenth century. The developers' preference was for the name 'Queens West', which appears in North Gantry Park. Balsley pushed for the use of the original name. 'We wanted to build on the history of Long Island City as a centre of manufacturing, a place where people actually made things.'

The ground plane leading to the gantries has strong pairs of honed stone, paved stripes, which link and lead to pairs of railway rails at the gantries. These are references to the time when the gantries' function was to heave up railway cars onto river barges. The rail motif continues, leading the visitor out to the gantries and also to the four piers jutting out into the East River. Each pier has been designed with a different function, although they are all linked by the common elements of metal-pipe balustrading capped by rounded wooden railings. One pier is equipped with benches and it

might eventually house a ferry terminal. The next has a raised metal counter like a bar and was described by Weintraub as 'a place to sit down, put your elbows on a table and eat lunch'. The third pier looks more private, with its stylish, gently wavy, slatted wooden loungers. Finally, the fishing pier has a serpentine bench along its length and at the end is a metal table designed for cleaning fish and bait in the purpose-built sink. Now it also has a tape measure fitted by one of the fishermen.

In all areas of the design. Balsley has played with a wide range of materials: stone, gravel, metal, wood and planting. The variations have come from his site-specific or site-generated approach to the design. The cut-stone arcs of steps and wall seats are inspired by the curves of the river bank. The hefty chunks of the split-faced granite steps are stacked at the water's edge, helping to retain the bank and bring visitors to its edge for Manhattan-viewing. To Balsley, the stone blocks suggest 'the ruggedness of the railroad, and reinforce the notion of the power of industry and its effect on this site.' Gravel paths are sited among the asymmetrical planting beds, punctuated with more stone blocks and elegant wooden benches.

The plantings have a purposely overgrown, unkempt and slightly wild feeling, as though they were successors to the indigenous colonies of plants that grew up when the gantry, railway and barge operations stopped.

The Interpretative Area, which includes one of the gantries, was conceived as a 'place to think about the past'. Weintraub's view, which could be a controlling part of the inspiration, is that:

> this area, including the gantry, was intended to suggest the way the place might have looked after the last rail car was loaded onto a barge, and the workers left – a kind of stabilized ruin.

Right *A view of the wave-pattern wooden bench on one of the four river piers in the Balsley park design.*

I pay no homage to the traditions of standard English-based picturesque garden-making. Where the landscape is deliberately man-made as in this situation, a designer doesn't have to relate to the natural context. I am driving this thing.

Ted Smyth

Ted Smyth

The Sanders' Garden, Auckland, New Zealand

A native New Zealander and Aucklander, Ted Smyth has never travelled out from his native country, but his outlook could hardly be called 'regional'. His garden designs are extremely Modernist and sophisticated. He says that he may have been influenced by the painting of Kandinsky and Modigliani, and by the music of Schoenberg, along with a 'sighting' of the work of Noguchi. We wonder if he has secretly read *Topos* and *Domus*, the high-brow landscape and architecture journals, or even the occasional issue of the more middle-brow *Architectural Digest*?

While growing up, Smyth was always interested in gardens. In high school he was fond of art and would cycle for miles to sketch the landscape. He has always thought of himself as an artist. At one point he worked as commercial artist. Later, to pay for time to paint, he became a manual labourer.

Ted Smyth is a self-taught garden designer who has created his own, distinct language of design. As he says:

> I have always ignored the traditions. I prefer to define space structurally, sometimes with planting, sometimes with hard materials. I enjoy setting up volumes of space. An architect sets volumes of space as a mass, sometimes I like to set it up in reverse.

Far right *The strong, sculptural shapes of the subtropical plants used by Smyth provide excellent foils for the white, International Style house and pool.*

He has been influenced very little by the major strands of contemporary garden design. Having always thought of himself as an artist, he only began to design gardens because he had to pay the bills. This compelled him to redirect his considerable, and now brilliantly realized, creative energies to the landscape. Smyth recalls his early days as a designer of gardens somewhat wryly:

GARDEN STATISTICS

Client: Darrin and Leslie Sanders

Budget: NZ $650,000

Designer: Ted Smyth

Area: 1,987sq m (21,388sq ft)

Climate: Temperate sub-tropical

Soil type: Varies – all imported

Aspect: North

Date of completion: 1996

Number of gardeners: 3

I used to have nightmares about making landscaping into art. There was the problem of fitting in the lifestyle commodities, which are the antithesis of art! It was important for me to keep believing I was an artist.

Two other artists of influence on contemporary landscape design in the twentieth century, Luis Barragan and Isamu Noguchi, also redirected their creative energies from architecture and sculpture to garden and landscape design. They would be considered self-taught too.

Smyth is now becoming, quite correctly, internationally recognized as a garden designer. We first saw his work in the *Harvard Design Magazine* in 1997. The article featured the Sanders garden in Auckland, the subject of this Case Study. The house is a white, Modernist, angular, glass and stucco design built in the 1980s. It was designed by Rolly Adams of the Auckland practice of Adams Langley.

Smyth was first asked to revamp the entry courtyard. Then he was commissioned to rework the entire garden, an empty rectangle with two trees. He was made designer and overall project manager for the year of garden installation.

In the rectangular garden space, Smyth has played with the design, echoing the curves, ellipses and rectangles in the architecture of the house. The patterns and shapes are repeated in the paving, the swimming pool and the perimeter walls – constructed of both plaster and metal. Achieving a harmony between the house and the design of the garden was a particular concern of Smyth's:

The integration of the house and the garden with the architecture is very important, important with this particular house because it is so very strong. But it's important with virtually every garden. Landscape architects/designers shouldn't decide to use structure in a garden and wilfully ignore the architecture of the building. But many do. Generally, landscape architects/designers in New Zealand haven't yet learned to integrate their work with architecture either overtly or poetically.

Smyth has used a typically restrained range of materials: stainless steel, stone, marble, water and sculptural plants. He defines his attitude to the materials of hard landscaping in the following words:

I like the anonymity and modernity of materials. They shouldn't be too animated like terracotta, brass or gold which are like busy, noisy animals. They interfere too much. In order to create serenity and spatial quality you have to reduce the personality of the materials. Even the plants, although they are sculptural and striking, have to work with the other elements.

The swimming pool area is the largest design element in the garden. It is extremely attractive for it is a generous enough size for a good swim. Smyth's detailing has made the pool visually exciting. It is minimal-Modernist-ornamental, if that's possible! Instead of the conventional rectangular or kidney-shaped pool, Smyth has used zigzag or stepped corners, a pattern repeated on the profile of a

Below *A side view of the Sanders' house and garden, for which Smyth created the landscape elements and also supervised the construction of the house.*

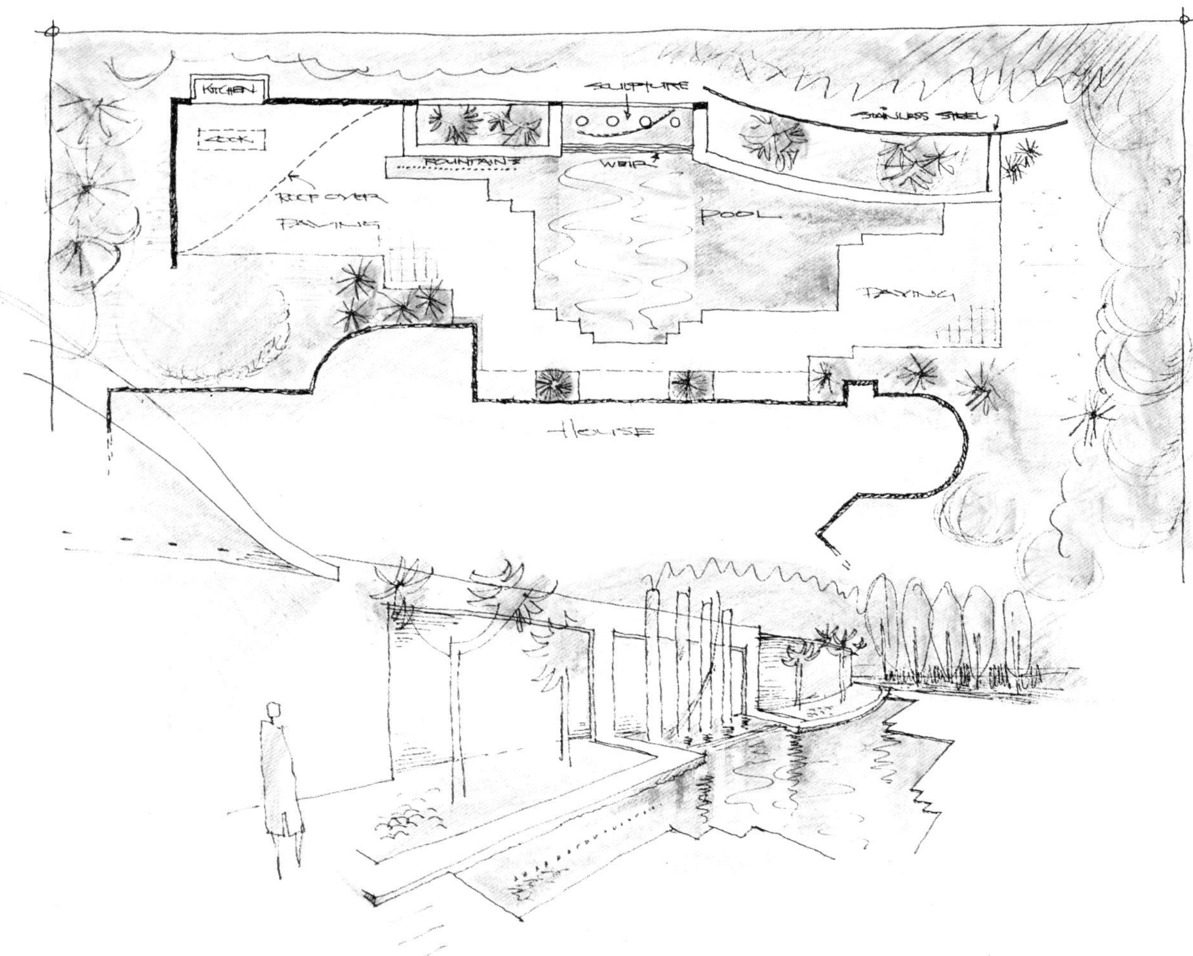

Left *A sketch plan and main view elevation of the Sanders' garden and pool show the imaginative use Smyth has made of a long, narrow strip of land.*

Left and above *At night the pool area is transformed into a mysterious sculptural landscape. Trees which during the day take second place to hard landscaping elements are dramatically uplit and the distinction between horizontal and vertical is blurred by reflections in the pool.*

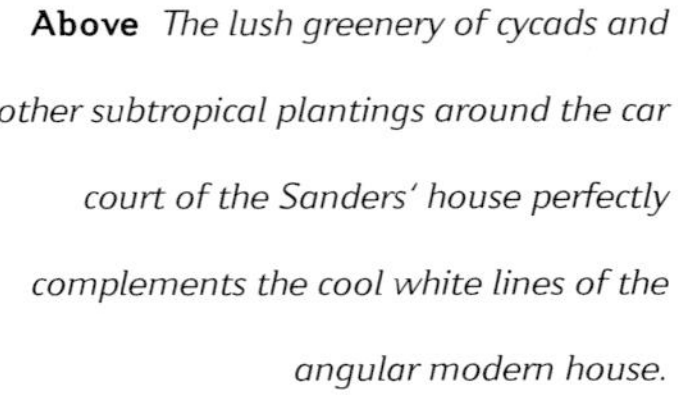

Above *The lush greenery of cycads and other subtropical plantings around the car court of the Sanders' house perfectly complements the cool white lines of the angular modern house.*

plastered boundary wall. A quiet inlet on one side of the pool has a row of water jets 45cm (18in) above the water level. Four low, elegant, steps create waterfalls beneath a dramatic, tubular stainless-steel sculpture on axis with the centre of the house.

The design stroke within the sculpture is a beautiful graceful band, or arc, of thin stainless-steel sections, contrasting with the strong uprights of the stainless-steel tubes. The sculpture highlights another of Smyth's heartfelt beliefs:

> One of my philosophies is that you have to take a risk, rather than sitting in a predictably safe seat. You have to be prepared to put your money where your mouth is. That sculpture, for instance, it could have been an absolute disaster. When you have created something on that scale, you just can't take it down again.

Backing the sculpture and running behind the pool is another splendid perimeter fence, a louvred screen of thin, stainless-steel sections set as horizontal bands.

Textural contrasts abound, the stainless steel is a sleek counterpoint to the pool, white plaster and the dramatic sculptural planting:

> Paring back colours to almost black and white means that what you see is what you get. You can't rely on bright colours to hang it together. If your forms are wrong, you can't rely on the planting to disguise it. There are no crutches or wheelchairs here.

Other landscape designers in New Zealand credit Smyth with having broadened the range of native and foreign sub-tropical plants available there. He likes

to use plants such as *Dracaena draco, Aloe bainesii* and *Cycas revoluta* – specimens that are more likely be to found in select botanic gardens in northern, temperate climates.

Like all the best landscape designers, Smyth places the planting plan himself, but is the first to admit that he didn't always get it right:

> I like structural plants. I planted *Dracaena draco* when no one else knew about them. *Aloe bainesii, A. thraskii* and *A. plicatilis* all have this structural look. And I like strap-leafed plants – clivia are good flowers for the shade. So are scadoxus with their big leaves. I scout around and go to specialist growers. Initially I did some horrific planting, I used to use shrubs – now I don't like them as well. . . . It's important to keep moving on and developing so people can't imitate me, I'm devious in the nicest possible way.

The imaginative use of plants is not an element of Smyth's work that would immediately spring to the minds of many commentators when considering Smyth's gardens. In his own words:

> It has been said about my work that I sacrifice nature on the altar of the contemporary, but I prefer to say that I distil the essence of the spirit of nature.

Above *Ted Smyth's stainless-steel wall sculpture behind the pool of the Sanders' house is a bold masterstroke that demonstrates Smyth's willingness to take risks with a design.*

We have no wish to imitate nature. We are fascinated by . . . sites whose constant and dramatic restructuring cannot be mapped: lagoons, deltas, dunes, river banks, ravines. It is incredible... that there should be a wide gulf between knowledge of nature and the inexplicable survival of picturesque garden stereotypes.

Michel Desvigne and Christine Dalnoky

Desvigne & Dalnoky

Urban Park, Issoudun, France

Desvigne and Dalnoky were trained at L'Ecole Nationale Supérieure du Paysage at Versailles. Since it was founded in 1973, the college has been credited with being a major influence on the new approach to French landscape design. Students are taught that the design should be based on the features of the existing landscape, and should not be seen merely as decoration.

Michel Corajoud and Alexandre Chemetoff, professional landscape architects, theorists and teachers, devised the syllabus to be a combination of 'academic' training in the techniques and theories of landscape architecture along with practical experience. Chemetoff designed some of the plantings for the Parc de la Villette, the former nineteenth-century abattoir and cattle market, reworked as a public park in the north of Paris.

The college's approach can be summed up in these four basic tenets: Anamnesis, Preparation, In-Depth Vision, and Relative Thinking. Anamnesis is the analysis of the layers of signs which a site holds. It is the review of all that has happened there to shape it into a specific landscape. Preparation sees and evaluates the site as process, in the context of all the natural elements of its topology: the cycle of seasons, the climate, the recycling of water, the alternations of day and night, of growth and decline. In-Depth Vision 'reads' a site in all its layers and complexities as a habitat, rather than an open space to be filled with decorative, historical pattern-book designs. Relative Thinking involves the site and the setting beyond its boundaries. This relates to the examination of the relationship between buildings and other, peripheral spaces such as roadsides and the uncultivated areas of 'non-places'. The important contemporary views of the Ecole du Paysage on process in garden and landscape design so-called

Far right *The Park at Issoudun, where the marshy, riverside site has been made accessible by the installation of raised boardwalks designed by Desvigne & Dalnoky.*

GARDEN STATISTICS

Client: City of Issoudun
Budget: FF4 million
Designers: Desvigne & Dalnoky
Area: 3ha (7.5 acres)
Climate: North European
Soil type: Neutral
Aspect: Full sun
Date of completion: 1994
Number of gardeners: 2–5

Below *The designers have 'substituted' a public park for an existing group of allotments. Substitution is an important part of their theory and practice.*

are re-echoed internationally in the work of landscape architects and designers such as Robert Irwin, creator of the Lower Central Garden at the Getty Centre in Los Angeles, George Hargreaves, Chairman of Landscape Architecture at Harvard, West 8 and Adriaan Geuze in Holland and Torres and Lapeña in Spain.

Desvigne & Dalnoky, based in Paris, works mainly in France. It has also completed projects in both Italy and Spain, and is now designing the Greenwich Reach landscape in London for the Millennium Experience in the year 2000. There is also a major, unbuilt scheme in former East Berlin involving the contemporary reworking of the Lustgarten Platz. The great 350-room palace in the Versailles style was destroyed during the Second World War.

The design for this uncharacteristically large site demonstrates the historical awareness, meticulous analysis and simplicity inherent in all of the designs of Desvigne & Dalnoky. Trees on grid plans would cover the entire square as an echo of the dense treescapes in Berlin. In the centre of the square they proposed a large stone, stepped, raised square called the Monument Garden, the site of a group of flowering trees that would be called the Sacred Grove. The square is designed to reflect the grandeur and historical importance of the former palace, and the existing grandeur of the Berlin Cathedral and the Altes Museum, which are nearby. Desvigne & Dalnoky have proposed a very few key design elements to be utilized with their characteristic, elegant simplicity.

The Urban Park is much smaller in scale and is situated on the edge of a provincial town. The site is part of the town of Issoudun in the Indre region on the northern edge of the Massif Centrale. The 3-hectare

Right *Blossoming fruit trees edge the boardwalks that surround the new lines of planting. Some of the trees were already there and some are newly planted. Together they create a reference to medieval strip planting.*

Left *Walking along the River Theol or fishing there has become much easier since the boardwalks were built.*

Below *Plan of the Urban Park, Issoudun. The ground plan of the park emerged from axis lines to main landmarks in the town across the river.*

(7.5-acre) riverside site is the French version of the British allotment. Small gardens and orchards have been tended there for generations. The objective was to create a small urban park on a very limited budget, using a design that not only recognized the history of the patch, but was inspired by it.

Desvigne & Dalnoky have used one of their basic design tenets: to vary the familiar aspects of site content with elements of substitution making the new design. They exploded the original scale of the small allotments into a grid of four large squares, subdivided into four smaller ones. The formality of their skewed, contemporary grid is an expression of the *regulier* style intrinsic to the landscape heritage of France. Think of the four-square grid patterns (both macro and micro) to be seen endlessly in any of the great seventeenth-century French gardens by André Le Nôtre. Another reference to that formal style is the groupings of trees planted in *allées*, some complete and some irregular.

The centre of the entire grid is on axis with the historical buildings in the main part of the town across the river: a medieval bell tower – La Tour Blanche – a church, a bridge, bastions and museums. Two halves of the grid are bounded by rough wooden boardwalks, and the corner of one is cantilevered out over the River Theol. The boardwalks are practical for winter walks, for the ground near the river can become soft during that season. The wooden planks have weathered down to a recessive grey colour. Irises have been planted in long rows, making a pretty display in the early spring.

This part of the design and the straight lines of trees and shrubs in other parts of the grid carry a reference to an earlier time in European history, to the medieval system of strip farming. Here at Issoudun, lines of tall willow trees have been planted close to the houses lying adjacent to the park. In the next section of the grid there are straight lines of shrubs of medium height, and beyond is the grid of iris beds. Desvigne & Dalnoky's design is unique, for they have been inspired to make gentle but elegant design references to both their country's history of peasant agriculture and, using the four-square grid, to the refined apogee of garden design at the court of Louis XIV.

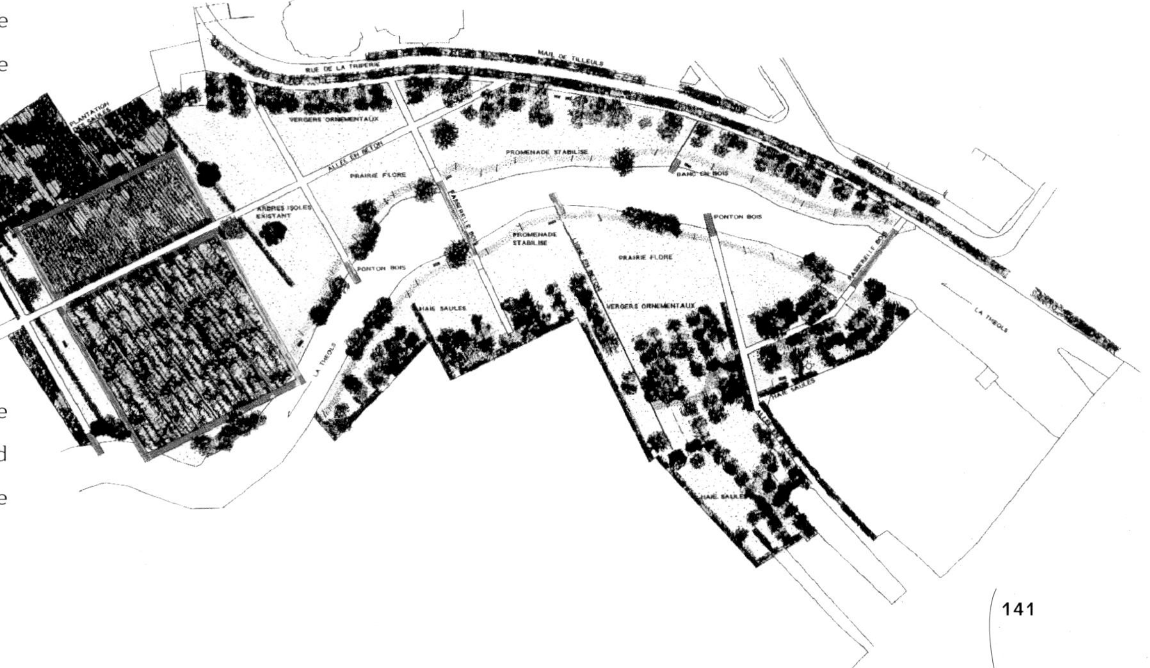

Rios Associates

Satellite Courtyard, Long Beach, California

Integrating technology into the human experience. There's often a fear that goes along with technology, but when you enter this space, you're not afraid of these dishes; you feel connected to them, and realize they are beautiful forms. Technology can be very beautiful.

Mark Rios

In all cultures and over many millennia, humans have used whatever technology and building materials were available to make structures that reach up towards the sky. The pyramids of Egypt, southern India, and Mexico, the spires of the great medieval cathedrals of western Europe, and the 'fingers reaching up to god' of the slender, wooden spires of New England churches, all represent the human yearning to reach upwards, towards the unknown.

Stonehenge on Salisbury Plain and the many stone circles in Ireland, Scotland and Brittany are other examples of man trying to communicate with the all-encompassing heavens. So too are the huge snake and water-spider mounds made by the Indians of the Missouri River basin, and the giant animal shapes drawn out in stone lines by the Indians of the Nazca plain in southern Peru.

Computer-linked communications satellites, the god-like technological toys of man, now spin through the less obviously spiritual skies of the late twentieth century, giving us the capacity to communicate instantly with all parts of the globe. Instead of stone, earth and wood, we see power pylons, radio towers and satellite dishes of metal as the vertical 'marks' on the contemporary landscape.

Mark Rios, a landscape architect with a practice based in Los Angeles, California, has transformed a former parking lot in Long Beach, California, into a sculptural landscape. In the subject of this Case Study, he has used the high-tech signal-receiving antennae satellite dishes as the central design element of the Satellite Courtyard. Rios' client can be located at 118°11'W longitude and 33°46'N latitude. These are the map co-ordinates which exactly locate Hughes Communications Inc.,a major supplier of high-tech satellite-dish receiving antennae. They also have a street address in Long

Far right *'Saucer pots' are a witty, practical variation on the high-tech dishes in the Satellite Courtyard. The pots are planted with dwarf forms of white-flowered plumbago, Australian bluebell creeper and evergreen star jasmine.*

GARDEN STATISTICS

Client: Hughes Communications Corporation Inc.

Budget: N/A

Designer: Rios Associates

Area: 0.6ha (1.5 acres)

Climate: Sunny and dry

Soil type: Sandy

Aspect: West

Date of completion: 1996

Number of gardeners: 2–3

Beach, California! Many late twentieth-century, high-tech industries with main headquarters in the silicone valleys near San Francisco have outposts down in the southern part of the state.

The Satellite Courtyard has been placed at the front of the company's building to mark it for new visitors and potential clients. It also serves as a place for employees to sit and take a break. The satellite dishes here bring to mind the three-dimensional or bas-relief signs that used to hang from shop fronts: the three golden balls of a pawn shop, the cigar-store Indian or even the painted barber shop pole used in nineteenth-century America. Mark Rios has updated this traditional, artisan concept to create a high-profile corporate identity in front of Hughes Communications' headquarters.

The Satellite Courtyard is the starting point for a tour of the Hughes Building. Visitors and new clients are stunned to learn that the satellite dishes are not just obsolescent hardware, but antennae taking signals from satellites out in space. These signals are converted into video images for the home television screens of America, controlled by the television networks that are Hughes Communications' principal clients.

The notion of using the satellite dishes as landmarks to signpost the Hughes headquarters originally came from Andrea Cohen Gehring, AIA, the design director at Widom Wein Cohen in Los Angeles. The satellites in the courtyard provide the opening beat to the two-storey rotunda in the centre of the building. Here models of satellites are displayed in front of a *trompe-l'oeil* painting of outer space.

Generally, architects ask landscape designers to 'shrub up' the area around their buildings, although the more sight-challenged ones tend to think of the planting around their 'amazing' structures as 'green slime'. Gehring was looking for something more elaborate and Rios Associates were called in to implement the broad concept.

Rios began by investigating not only the subject of satellite dishes, but also material from ancient civilizations, such as the artefacts associated with man's

Above *An aerial view of the Satellite Courtyard, showing the communication dishes set in a robust grid of stone and gravel.*

Below *A plan of the Satellite Courtyard.*

Right *The stainless-steel mesh of the courtyard fence is repeated on frames covered in white Brazilian nightshade,* Solanum jasminoides *'Album'. Rios placed an emphasis on white-flowering plants throughout design.*

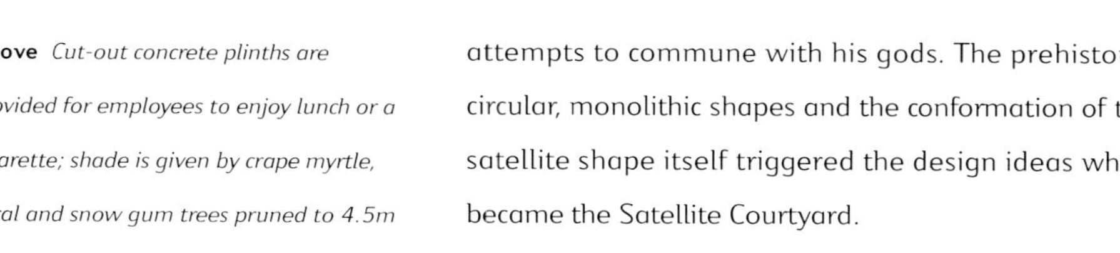

Above *Cut-out concrete plinths are provided for employees to enjoy lunch or a cigarette; shade is given by crape myrtle, coral and snow gum trees pruned to 4.5m (15ft) so as not to block the satellite dishes.*

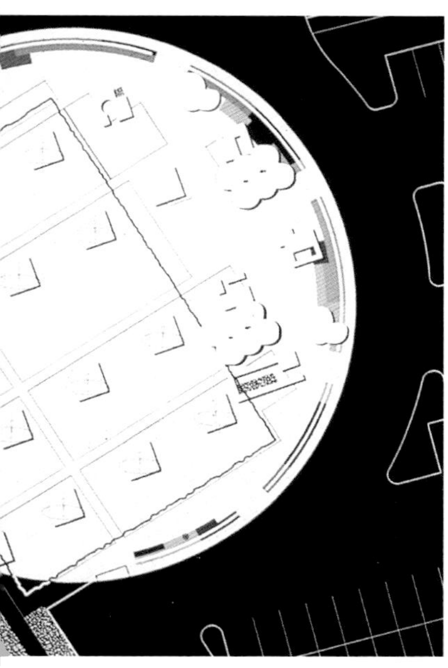

attempts to commune with his gods. The prehistoric, circular, monolithic shapes and the conformation of the satellite shape itself triggered the design ideas which became the Satellite Courtyard.

The dishes were perceived by Rios and his project designer, Corinne Capiaux, as beautiful, sculptural objects. Each of the 12 dishes measures 3–5m (10–17ft) in diameter. They were placed on square concrete plinths, 45cm (18in) high. These were set out on a 3 x 4 grid, bounded by a high, black, chain link fence. Black was chosen to make the fence recede into the background. It also made the white satellite dishes even more striking. A circular 4.2m-high (14ft-high), silver, stainless-steel mesh fence, with a diameter of 27m (90ft), surrounded the entire site, providing maximum security.

The ground plan of the design is a square in a circle, the reverse of that other, endlessly pleasing and ancient pairing: the circle in the square (the magnificent floor in the Pantheon, Rome, being the most perfect example from antiquity).

In an area between the two fences, Rios has placed other concrete plinths of varying cut-out shapes, to encourage different-sized groups of people to sit there. These seating plinths continue the central grid pattern of the satellite bases. Rios thinks of them as

> huge, raised-up blankets that you can lie down on or spread out a picnic lunch on, or, you can sit with your feet in the holes in the middle, almost like sitting at a Japanese table'.

The planting near other buildings in the area is fairly business-park-standard. There are tall trees, grass-covered earth mounds and an underplanting of shrubs. Rios wanted the Satellite Courtyard to be a complete contrast to its surroundings. He wanted to create something very minimal and Zen-like, so visitors would feel that they had arrived at a special place.

The company is pleased with the Satellite Courtyard. It is a dramatic signal of their location and products, a relaxing area for employees, and having the satellites nearby has proved more cost-effective.

Nature is basically curved, warped, undulating, jagged, zigzagged and sometimes beautifully crinkly. It never looks like a Platonic temple.

Charles Jencks

Charles Jencks

The DNA and Physics Garden of the Garden of Cosmic Speculation, Borders area, Scotland

Is this extraordinary twentieth-century landscape a return to the design philosophy of William Kent, and his belief that 'nature abhors a straight line'?

Charles Jencks is the leading thinker and guru of Post-Modernism. In 1990, Jencks and his late wife Maggie Keswick, an authority on Chinese gardens, began to create a stupendous and influential late twentieth-century landscape. It consists of several gardens of varying sizes on 16 hectares (40 acres) of an estate among the low, rolling hills of southern Scotland.

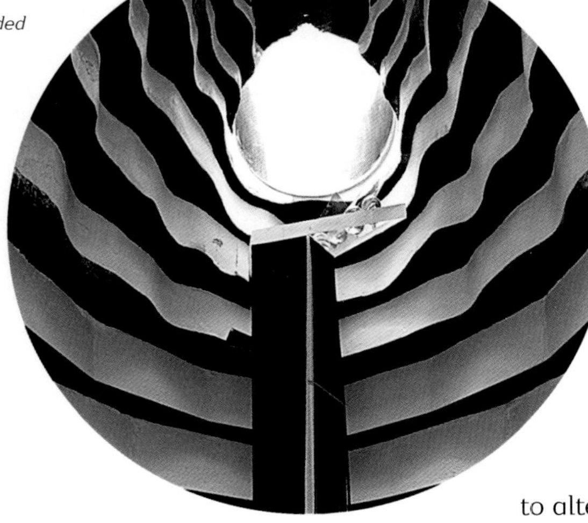

Far right *DNA sculpture of the Sense of Taste, the giant mouth suspended above two species of wild strawberry, in the DNA and Physics Garden.*

Chaos and Complexity Theory combined with Feng Shui, ancient Chinese geomancy, are the two philosophical strands of thinking, practice and inspiration. These elements were combined with the skills of master craftsmen: a mason, a carpenter and metalworkers. There have also been many close encounters with massive diggers and earth-moving equipment. Charles Jencks continues to alter, add to and improve this extraordinary concept.

GARDEN STATISTICS
Client: Lady Keswick
Budget: Materials £15,000 Sculpture £25,000
Designer: Charles Jencks
Area: 16ha (40 acres)
Climate: Southwestern Scotland
Soil type: Neutral
Aspect: South
Date of completion: 2000
Number of gardeners: 2+1 helper

Chinese geomancy is derived from the Taoist tradition of seeing what monks and philosophers following the great teacher, Lao-Tzu, called the 'bones of the earth' in its waters, valleys, hills and mountains. All these features contain the currents of invisible energy, *ch'i*, the vital spirit of earth, the cosmic breath of subterranean dragons. Today, the Hong Kong businessman brings in the geomancer to divine where his Post-Modern skyscraper should be built. With high land values and limited space, today's geomancer has little choice but to get it very right indeed. Jencks, a qualified architect and teacher, documented the Post-Modern in contemporary architecture. He continues to identify new trends, some of which are set out in his book *The Architecture of the Jumping Universe*. The book includes a straightforward exposition of the philosophy behind these gardens:

Above right *In consultation with Charles Jencks, this superb symbolic, axonometric, computer-generated drawing was made by Liane Wilcher from the scanned photographic images that she took in the DNA and Physics Garden.*

Far right *Double helix sculptures of the five Senses: (top to bottom)* Touch, Hearing, Taste, Sight *and* Smell. *Jencks'* sixth sense *is on the next page.*

Right *An overview of the DNA and Physics Garden, Jencks' visionary, complex, unique and witty contemporary adaptation of the traditional vegetable patch.*

Our first assumption was that nature's forms are continuously changing and curved, as we applied this notion to drawing together the hills, streams, hedges and walls. During this time I was researching developments in recent science and cosmology – what is called 'non-linear dynamics', or, more popularly, Chaos Theory. I was working on [*Architecture in a Jumping Universe*] which argues that design must look to science and contemporary cosmology if it is to recapture the depth and conviction it had in previous eras. Furthermore, these disciplines are telling us something surprising, positive.

The universe, it now appears, is much more creative, self-organizing and unpredictable than anyone had thought 20 years ago, when it was

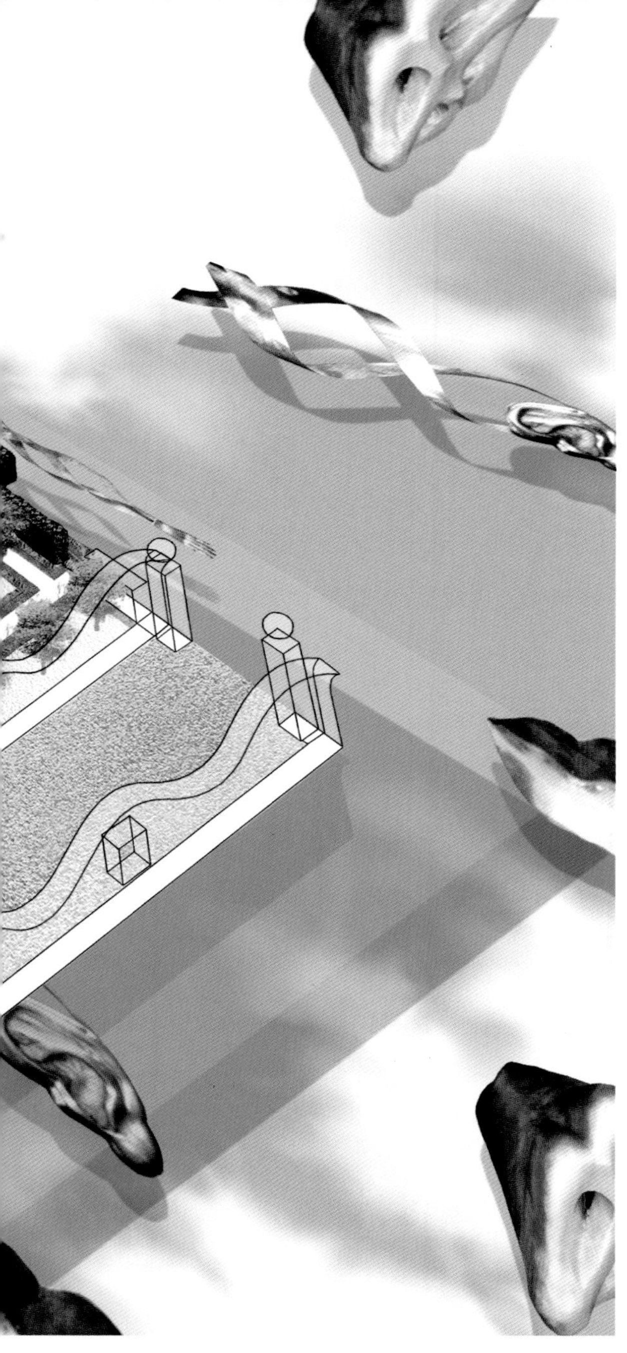

most commonly thought of as a complex machine. Contrary to the Newtonian view of scientific determinism and the Christian view of Genesis, the universe is, in fact, cosmogenic, meaning that it jumps all of the time to new levels of organization. . . . The new sciences of Complexity, of which Chaos is just one of 20, show the omnipresence of these sudden leaps at all scales.

Jencks' 'jump' here is an enormous one within the context of contemporary landscape architecture and design. Frank Gehry has this to say about Jencks' cosmogenesis theories:

> Charles is the only architectural writer I know who will go way out on a limb, saw the limb off, fall through the air, grab another limb, and start all over again. That's what I love about him. He's willing to stick his neck out.

Jencks says that the starting point for the Garden of Cosmic Speculation was the dining room of his house. He and Keswick called it the Dragon Dance Room, for it is used for Scottish reels, as well as cooking and dining. The decoration there is non-linear, patterns and shapes are emphasized with curving folds and waves.

The axis of the gardens begins below the house and moves down the slope. Jencks has given them witty and wonderful names. First comes the Dry Cascade and then the Maze Brain. The Garden of Fair Play is the tennis court, beyond it is the DNA and Physics Garden and, finally, the largest and most dramatic incident: the 15m (50ft) spiral mound. Jencks says that this has several names, all denoting a similar shape – snail, ziggurat, mound. It is bounded by two different spirals, which only meet at the top. As they ascend, the paths rise and fall. As a result, in order to go up the mound, you sometimes have to go down, and vice versa. Nearby is the 120m-long (400ft-long) double-wave earthwork, which is called the snake or S-shaped earthwork.

These earthworks and the self-similar pair of lakes in which the exquisite grassed spiral – or paisley shape – is sited are the largest parts of this grand design. The

grass mound and double-wave require one gardener cutting full-time April to September to mow them, supervised by the head gardener, Alistair Clark.

It is the DNA and Physics Garden that is the focus of this Case Study. The formal beds are planted in waving lines which follow the curves and lines of the unfolding DNA. This linear pattern of waves underlines the whole garden, and in this area it is miniaturized and planted with vegetables, flowers, fruit and healing herbs, just as they would have been in the traditional *physick* garden of a monastery or manor house. Local red sandstone rubble makes the Dragon Walls, a pair of superb, gently hump-backed enclosures. In one there are three openings to view the DNA and Physics Garden. (The stone grills covering these openings are reminiscent of similar features in the traditional gardens of Soochow, China). Through the grills the circle for Edible Harmony, the square for Physical Reason and the triangle for Kitchen Justice are visible. These witty word-plays are carved under each of the openings. All of the stonework is by a local master mason, Hugh Drysdale.

Above *A lady with her brain exposed symbolizes female intuition. She is sitting beside a double helix sculpture. This is Jencks' design for the sixth sense:* Anticipation.

The DNA and Physics Garden is altered and improved annually by Jencks but the basic grid plan of its formal parterre is constant and based on the five human senses plus the sixth sense, the female sense of intuition or anticipation. Each area is centred around a sculptural version of the DNA double helix. *Sight* is perhaps the most dramatic of these. It contains a miniature version of the 15m-high (50ft-high) spiral mound in the shape of a double helix. Inside the mound is a grotto-like room, with crinkly black and white fractal-banded wall patterns. At the top is an aperture in the shape of an 'M'. On bright days this casts the form of the letter inside the room, as a commemoration of Jenck's late wife, Maggie. *Smell* is represented by fragrant thyme plants which encircle the flared nostrils of a nose from which Jencks wants the smell of rotten vegetables to exude. *Hearing* is an ear trumpet finial which pivots in the wind activating chimes and bells. *Touch* is a sculpted hand rising above thistles and nettles, enclosed by a DNA double helix built of blocks. *Taste* has an aluminium mouth and thyme suspended above two species of wild strawberry. Finally, *Anticipation* is a woman looking at her open brain as it receives impulses from her fingers which wave in the breeze – the sense of intuiting the future by picking up and interpreting vibrations.

Jencks' three-dimensional realizations of historical and current concepts of the universe are playful and wacky, but also visionary, brilliant and extremely serious. The stone gate piers at entrances to the DNA

Left *Jenck's galactic seat of seven galactic spirals. It is cast concrete and the lead finish is from blue-grey paint.*

and Physics Garden put a contemporary 'spin' on the traditional pineapple or eagle finials of the seventeenth and eighteenth centuries: on the left, the old view of the universe in bronze, on the right, the new in aluminium. These unique metal spheres represent a model of the major theories propounded about the universe: Ptolemaic, Constellational, Armillary, Atomic, the Gaia Hypothesis, and the Universe as a whole.

We think of the DNA and Physics Garden as the 'micro' versions of the theories played out by Jencks in the 'macro' shapes of the grassed mound and the double-wave earthworks. The miniature grassed mound with its grotto is the best example.

In its totality, the Garden of Cosmic Speculation is not only a grand, amusing and serious creation, it also engages a wide audience from all backgrounds. An expert on Tudor gardens 'read' the mound as castle look-out, a hold-over from medieval times. An expert on eighteenth-century gardens was reminded of the enormous, grassed verges of the Moon Ponds at Studley Royal in Yorkshire. The sculpted, grass theatre at Claremont in Surrey also comes to mind, as does Hogarth's Line of Beauty. To others, it evokes images of Land Art in the United States in the 1960s, and prehistoric earthworks in many other parts of the world. The range of these reactions must show the power of the garden's rhythm and beauty as a visionary landscape, theories of the universe notwithstanding.

Below left *The sense of Sight: a micro spiral 'eye' mount in the DNA and Physics Garden is a miniaturized version of the double spiral mount in the larger, cosmological landscape nearby. Inset is the fantastic interior of the eye mount with the oculus, surmounting a metamorphosis of black optically vibrating waves from thin straight ones to thick curves, eye to inner eye, illusions to seeing.*

The drawings of other designers often surprise me. Such good graphics, but they seem to work without knowing about plants. I cannot really believe in a designer who does not live in a garden.

Jacques Wirtz

Jacques Wirtz

Parterre du Carrousel, Tuileries, Grand Louvre, Paris, France

Inexorably, time and history move on, bringing change and destruction to our landscapes and gardens, which are some of the most ephemeral products of civilization. In France, 300 years of garden history separate two major re-creations of the formal gardens of the Tuileries in Paris.

The existing Tuileries gardens were originally created for Catherine de Medici in the sixteenth century. Since the early seventeenth century they have been open to the public. André Le Nôtre (1613–1698) was the third generation of the family of head gardeners to the French royal household and he grew up in the Tuileries. In 1664 he was given the job of transforming the site. His new design included the main stone terraces adjacent to the Place du Carrousel.

In France, the arts establishment threw up their hands in *horreur* when a Belgian landscape design practice was commissioned to redesign part of the Tuileries. Wirtz International, headed by Jacques Wirtz and his two sons Peter and Martin, won the competition for the redesign of the Parterre du Carrousel on the east side of the gardens. The French call the reworking and restoration of historical gardens a *continuation*. The Wirtz design is but another layer in the long history of the gardens. In the past, Wirtz's work has been described by one critic as 'a modern reflection on well-known tradition . . . uniting in his gardens as much beauty of the past as visionary force of the future.' The design for the Place du Carrousel confirms this judgement. The Arc du Carrousel dates from Napoleonic times. It is set on the grand axial vista of Paris that starts from the glass pyramid by I.M. Pei in the Louvre courtyard, goes through the centre of the Tuileries, up the Avenue de Champs-Elysées, and finally centres on the Arc de Triomphe de l'Etoile, and the Grande Arch de Défense. This is

Far right *A down-view of a single, raised parterre of yew hedges and lime trees. Its pair is across the Grand Louvre courtyard, both frame the Arc du Carrousel, the centre of the design by Wirtz International.*

GARDEN STATISTICS
Client: Etablissement du Grand Louvre
Budget: FF65 million
Designer: Wirtz International
Area: 4.3ha (10.75 acres)
Climate: Temperate
Soil type: Sandy loam
Aspect: West
Date of completion: 2001
Number of gardeners: 6

the western end of the arc of *grands projets* for Paris, commanded by François Mitterand. On the eastern point of the arc is the new opera house in the Bastille and the large public park, Parc de la Villette.

Some commentators say that the Mitterand government was able to get away with the contemporary designers' competition for the new Tuileries gardens because the works were within the package of national garden restoration. This included the 20-year renovation of the gardens at Versailles – the model of the formal garden style of Louis XIV, interpreted, clarified and codified by Le Nôtre. In creating their design, the Wirtz team had to honour France's tradition of formal design while also acknowledging the contemporary.

Wirtz refers to the classical influence on his work as 'the wisdom of our ancestors'. His son Peter attributes much to their nationality:

> Belgium has always been strongly influenced by French gardens with their formality (and England with its loose romantic tradition), and by Germany too; it's the same in music, art and cuisine. We're a country where the cultures come together. In garden design here, there is a great mix and many styles exist side by side.

Wirtz's design for the Grand Louvre project is centred on the Arc du Carrousel. Peter Wirtz gave the following explanation of the intention of their design:

> We wanted not only to create a buffer, but part of a green world between the hard glass and stone surfaces of Mr Pei's pyramid of glass and the Louvre courtyard, and make the Arc du Carrousel a true gate. It formerly seemed too small in that desert of stone. Now, it's like a keyhole to the rest of the gardens. Go through it and you find radials – rows of clipped yew hedges like projecting fingers.

The radial hedges recall the box hedges in the Wirtz's private garden in Schoten. They edge the paths of the former kitchen garden of the nearby château. They have lost their knife-edge geometry and changed into low, organic billows of green. Over the past 45 years, the hedge has become a Wirtz trademark:

> I use it as a readable element, to provide equilibrium. I gained a certain reputation and indeed made à la mode – a term I detest – the use of box. But not in the style of Le Nôtre, in my own style.

Framing the Place du Carrousel and its arch are a pair of raised parterres in the classical, formal language of geometric shapes. Squares, rectangles, a circle and an oval lead up to the middle of each parterre and in the centre is a clipped, square palisade of lime tree canopies on clear trunks. Within the hedge patterns and the lime tree squares, and asymmetrically placed among the radial yew hedges, is the national collection of 18 bronze statues by Artistide Maillol. They were given to the country by Dina Vierny – the artist's model. André Malraux, then Minister of Culture, had them placed here in 1964 to create a sculpture garden.

Right *The national collection of sculptures by Aristide Maillol is arranged among the yew hedges radiating from the centre point of the Arc du Carrousel and on raised parterres to the right of the arch and behind it to the left.*

Above *Stone paving lines diverge from the Arc du Carrousel and then connect to radiating yew hedges, making visual and physical links to the redesigned Tuileries gardens.*

Right *The plan by Wirtz International is so large that only half of it can be shown.*

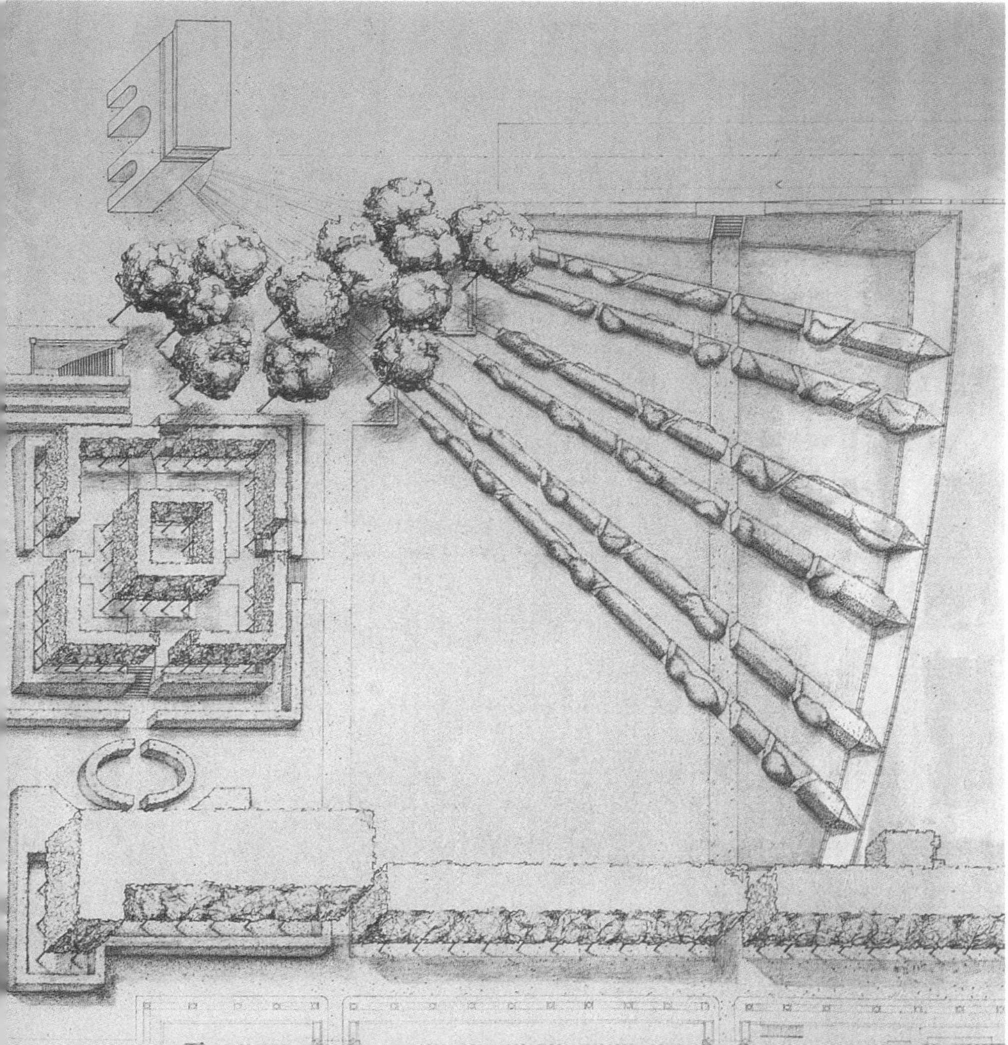

Jacques Wirtz balks at labels, preferring not to talk about a particular garden style. To him, trying to explain a garden is a kind of betrayal: 'A garden is like a painting or piece of music, it should speak for itself.'

The installation of the Tuileries garden was not an easy project. The historic significance of the site combined with the Wirtz practice's foreign nationality and high levels of bureaucracy meant that each and every trip to Paris was *une grande battaille* to realize the approved design.

Contemporary innovation in Wirtz's classical designs will reach another high point when the extraordinary fire, water and air (artificial fog) elements are installed to celebrate the millennium on 3.6 hectares (9 acres) at Alnwick Castle for the Duchess of Northumberland.

'I would be a very bad professor at a school of horticulture', says Jacques Wirtz, 'once an interviewer for a German magazine asked me about my theory of design. I said, "Give me a plan and I'll make you a garden. But, don't ask me about theories."'

Gardening appeals to us all the more when we are caught up in the whirlwind beyond ourselves, in the great, natural life cycle. There dwells an underlying faith, a certainty that this season's planting, pruning and nourishing will be rewarded.

Jack Lenor Larsen

Jack Lenor Larsen

LongHouse Garden, East Hampton, Long Island, New York.

Jack Lenor Larsen was already emerging as an icon in the design world during the 1960s. He had studied architecture at the Cranbrook Academy in Bloomfield Hills, Michigan, with its many design associations from the 1930s. Other notable designers and architects attending the Academy included Charles Eames, Florence Knoll, Benjamin Baldwin and the Saarinen family. Larsen is widely considered to be one of the most creative and inspired textile and fabric designers of this period in the United States and elsewhere.

Far right *Larsen plays brilliantly with perspective and a single colour in his Red Garden: Japanese ceremonial red for bark-stripped cedar posts and the blue-red of azaleas. The focal point is a stoneware jar by Toshiko Takaezu.*

For over 50 years his fabrics have been sought after by designers all over the world. When Larsen founded his own company it produced hand-woven textiles of diverse natural yarns in random repeats. Over the years, these fabrics were developed until they came to represent the height of style and sophistication in contemporary, twentieth-century, domestic and commercial interior design.

In the late 1950s and during the 1960s, the US State Department sent Larsen to south-east Asia where he worked on a project designed to encourage local crafts. Since then, Larsen's work has continued to be informed and inspired by many trips within Asia and to India, Africa, Europe and South America. As a result, he has become one of the world's foremost authorities on traditional and contemporary crafts. Having gained his reputation for innovation in fabric design, Larsen is one of only two designers to have been given the ultimate accolade of an exhibition at the Palais du Louvre. He is the author of nine books written over 30 years, a scholar and curator, with exhibitions on textiles and fabrics in museums in America and abroad, a world traveller and a gardener. Larsen's extraordinary and wide-ranging career has brought him into contact with leading twentieth-century architects such as Edward Larrabee Barnes,

GARDEN STATISTICS

Designer: Jack Lenor Larsen

Area: 6.4ha (16 acres)

Climate: Zones 4–5

Soil type: Sandy

Aspect: South/north and west

Date of completion: Ongoing

Number of gardeners: 1 full-time plus contractors

Charles Forberg, Louis Kahn, I.M. Pei, Minoru Yamasaki, and Skidmore, Owings and Merrill. His work is in permanent collections in New York, Chicago, Philadelphia, Amsterdam, Copenhagen, Edinburgh, London, Paris and Zurich.

A few years ago, we began to hear about an unusual and brilliant garden on Long Island. It was on a very overcast day in 1995 that we saw Larsen's garden at the LongHouse. His design shows what can happen to a fairly unpromising piece of east coast American woodland when the designer has knowledge, verve, a superb 'eye' and experience of a locale. Before buying the LongHouse, Larsen had owned an adjacent property called the Round House. This was his first house and garden. It taught him what would flourish in the dry, sandy soil.

Below *The master plan by Larsen of the LongHouse and its gardens.*

When making his new garden, Larsen incorporated the Red Garden, one of the most striking features from the earlier property. It consists of an *allée* of parallel cedar posts painted a fiery red reminiscent of the *torii* gates of Japan. The posts are underplanted with various red azaleas chosen for their vibrant, clashing colours. Purple plum and red barberry complete the design. The focal point of the *allée* is a large, exquisite stoneware jar by the potter, Toshiko Takaezu. The arrangement of the posts creates a heightened perspective, making the jar appear much farther away than it really is.

The entry to the LongHouse and its gardens is through an *allée* of impressive *Cryptomeria japonica*, running from the roadside verge to the turning circle at the gatehouse. The extended, crossed wood posts of the gatehouse, as well as the gable ends of the house, call up images of the wooden structures in the seventh-century Shinto temple precinct at Ise, Japan. Larsen's architectural use of them here is but another reflection of his aesthetic of simplicity and restraint, whether in his textile designs, houses or gardens.

The patch of land Larsen bought for the LongHouse was former farmland which had been left fallow for 50 years. Bittersweet, poison ivy and wild grape vines 12–15cm (5–6in) in diameter had rollicked up the bare trunks of sad-looking pine trees, with their tall heads pointing downwards from lack of sun. On the credit side of the 'garden-potential ledger', there were some old oaks, groves of beech and some plantations of indigenous dogwood, a hectare (2.5 acres) or so of blueberries and, within a shady area, a large plot of native ginseng. A usable depth of leaf mould had formed over the sandy soil as the land had not been worked for many years. Larsen thought that the most positive existing features were the dead-straight banks which had evolved as a result of the farmer piling up the earth as field borders when the land had been actively farmed. Another advantage was the site of the house, which is 300m (1,000ft) from the road.

Left *The lawn amphitheatre with its simple, rough wood seats where Larsen organizes performances.*

Below *Stucco pillars frame a square pool and pond. The pillars support finials of a horizontal variation on the ends of the LongHouse roof. The extended gable beam design of the Ise Shrine was Larsen's inspiration for the design of the house.*

Further basic planting and ground preparation for the new garden included clearing saplings, vines and fallen trees and opening up the woodland paths and a couple of grassy meadows with the ever-useful JCB backhoe. Larsen planted several thousand Canadian hemlocks, bare-rooted and cheaply priced, on the banks. He then ordered hundreds of small beech, birch, dogwood and winterberry to the same specification. To counter drought conditions, he installed 0.5km (⅓ mile) of irrigation piping. The gypsy moth attacked twice in as many years, but he was able to save the very young beech trees. Larsen was still maintaining his garden at the nearby Round House, which was time consuming in terms of the new project. Bamboo, cryptomeria, western cedars and Pfitzer junipers were all moved from the Round House to the new LongHouse garden. Being a practical person, he collected mountain laurels from new housing developments.

Larsen had wanted a large pond in a spot about 1.5m (5ft) lower than the ground level. A conservation team advised him that there would be insufficient run-off, so – ever creative and adaptable – he turned the area into a bowl-shaped amphitheatre, inspired by the ancient ring forts he had seen in western Ireland. The grassed ring is not only an amphitheatre: the lower side of the bowl has an outer earth ring to stop both the view of the road and the sounds resonating from it. He has planted thousands of snowdrops and crocuses inspired by what he calls the '*millefleur* spring plantings' at Hidcote in Gloucestershire. Sadly, the bowl looked wonderful the first spring, but then the bulbs became a banquet for the voles in the second year. By contrast, the grass bowl's acoustics were fine and the first concert to take place in it featured a jazz combo led by Larry Rivers. The amphitheatre has also been used for dance performances, readings and installations of contemporary sculpture. When the tough zoysia grass finally covers it, then there will be no need to water, mow or weed.

raised garden. Mat-forming plants, including four varieties of a low-growing and spreading juniper, beach plums and dune grass, cover the sand-covered slopes. There is a wide section on the top of the bank reserved for santolina, lavender and other drought-resistant plants.

The LongHouse covers an area of 1,210 sq m (13,000 sq ft). It has a total of 18 spaces on four levels. The raised main floor of the house has another advantage (Le Corbusier's term 'piloti' would work as

Below *Ornamental grasses edging the pond at the LongHouse*

On arrival at the house the visitor is confronted with the sand hillocks that form the Dune Garden – considered a necessity by Larsen since he rarely goes now to the nearby beaches. Here he has planted a range of maritime plants and grasses. The dunes and the plantings together constitute a superb reference to the Long Island Sound and the proximity of the Atlantic Ocean. Even more exciting than the Dune Garden is the Raised Bank Garden which is on a level with the first-floor rooms of the house. A bridge connects the conservatory and dining room to this

a definition for the pillars). It creates a large, free undercroft space that can be used as an extension to the living space provided by the main house – as an outdoor dining room perhaps, or simply as a shady space on a hot, summer's day.

The undercroft gives a view of the two main axes of the garden. Perpendicular to the house is a 15m (50ft) black lap pool, and in line with the house is more water, in the form of a large pond. From the upper floor of the house, the pink garden can be seen on the other side of the water: the pale birch trunks, a group of maples specially selected for their splendid autumn colour and, perhaps most attractive of all, the masonry and bronze forms of Grace Knowlton's giant spherical sculptural shapes wonderfully spaced on the lawn by the pond.

When we first saw the LongHouse garden, Larsen had just finished creating an incredibly imaginative maze out of sunflowers. In late spring, a rabbit could have looked over the tops of the young plants. By early autumn, when the mature plants had reached their full height of 2.4m (8ft) he would have been well and truly dwarfed.

Below centre *Blown glass balls by Dale Chihuly, 1995. On the left is* Opaque Float with Gold Leaf and Green Lines, 1995. *The ball on the right is* Midnight Blue Float, *1992. The wood and bronze construction in the background is* Gateway Bell, *1993, by Toshiko Takaezu.*

Below Untitled, *1989, by Pavel Opocensky, Pennsylvania granite.*

Edgar J. Kaufmann Jr. is a knowledgeable and enthusiastic supporter of the arts in the United States. His father commissioned Frank Lloyd Wright to envision the magnificent family house in Pennsylvania, Fallingwater. Kaufmann comments on Larsen:

> Jack Lenor Larsen's career is a stupendous success story, spreading to the corners of the earth, integrated with modern society, and amply recognized.

[Michelangelo's] Campidoglio in Rome is a demonstration far beyond the resources of painting or what architecture and sculpture fundamentally, unequivocally, are. He affirms that architecture is a space, an environment . . . It says that the human act creates the environment, shapes the human world.

Vincent Scully

Arata Isosaki

Tsukuba Civic Centre, Tsukuba Science City, Ibaragi Prefecture, Japan

Tsukuba Scientific New Town was part of a comprehensive plan, one of several of its kind, aimed at drawing away areas of activity and population from the dense conurbation of approximately 12 million residents in Tokyo, one of the largest cities in the world. Tsukuba is a 2,700-hectare (6,750-acre) site for a community of 120,000, some 64km (40 miles) to the north-east of Tokyo. As with so many new towns, it was intended to be culturally and economically self-sufficient.

Far right *Traditional Japanese garden elements of stone and water employed in a splendidly artificial, Post-Modern design by Arata Isosaki, one of Japan's greatest contemporary architects.*

Development work began in 1966. By the late 1970s, it was clear that the plans for the new town had not been properly realized, despite a new university on the site. The large university buildings and high-rise apartment blocks of 'the academic new town' appeared to be abandoned and the Le Corbusier-inspired buildings looked inhumane and shabby. Furthermore, a population of only 30,000 had been attracted to Tsukuba – a quarter of the projected figure. Many university and research institute employees preferred to make the two-hour commute to work from Tokyo each day.

In an attempt to improve this situation, the Housing and Urban Development Corporation of Japan asked ten architectural practices to submit plans for a new civic centre. They were asked not to submit designs for the development, but to respond to the corporation's brief with written analyses. In his report, Arata Isosaki emphasized the site's many problems and suggested improvements. By attacking the difficulties openly and frankly, he won the commission. *Time* magazine refers to Isosaki as the international 'star' of Japanese architecture, an opinion supported by many projects including: an Olympic gymnasium in Barcelona; the Museum of Contemporary Art in Los Angeles; the University of Art and Design in Tokyo;

GARDEN STATISTICS

Client: Housing & Urban Development Corporation of Japan

Budget: $54 million

Designer: Arata Isosaki

Area: 8,000sq m (86,112sq ft)

Climate: Northern temperate

Soil type: Sandy clay

Aspect: South

Date of completion: 1983

Number of gardeners: Contractors

an arts centre in Minnesota and in Orlando, Florida, the Walt Disney corporate headquarters.

In the late 1980s, Isosaki submitted his innovative master plan for the Paternoster Square project near St Paul's in London, but Prince Charles wanted, and is getting. . . his neo-Georgian way. Isosaki acknowledges that the influence of the West on his work is as important as that of the traditions of his native Japan:

> You must understand our values. Our values, the first cultural things, when we were very young, came from the United States. Every kind of cultural high standard – rock music, architecture, technology, computers, cars, everything – came from the United States. Today, Japan makes cars and everything much better, but it doesn't matter. The first things we learned were western. Even the books in the college libraries were western.

In the design for Tsukuba, as in that for the Los Angeles Museum of Contemporary Art, Isosaki 'quotes' from earlier historical styles of both Japan and the West. This is a major function of Post-Modernism and a notable characteristic of Isosaki's work.

When he was interviewed in 1987, Isosaki referred to two types of quotation: '. . . just copying traditional elements on the surface of a building. This is a method which is fashionable in Tokyo and Japan. They copy tradition.' He prefers to use 'a transformed quotation', which he describes as a parody:

> Parody is not directly using the patterns of the past, but using the ideas, the same ideas with a different means. Pastiche is just transporting the past style to the present, but if we can use those quoted elements in some very different ways, it makes something more interesting.

Isosaki admits to having quoted a long list of architects, both historical and contemporary: Giulio Romano, Michelangelo, Claude-Nicolas Ledoux, Otto Wagner, Richard Meier, Michael Graves, Charles Moore, Aldo Rossi, Hans Hollein, Peter Cook, Adalberto Libera, Philip Johnson, Leon Krier, Lawrence Halprin, Ettore Sottsass and many others.

The Tsukuba Civic Centre was finally completed in 1983. At its centre is the totally artificial, hard landscape of the sunken forum. Here, Isosaki quotes from the paving patterns created by Michelangelo in the Campidoglio on the Capitoline Hill in Rome:

> I quoted Michelangelo, but with everything completely reversed. For example, the black and white of the pattern is reversed, and levels are opposite. The Campidoglio is on a hilltop, but at Tsukuba, it's the lowest point. Convex becomes concave. It is a quotation, but not direct.

An overlapping, layered, Modernist grid of walkways embraces the forum. It also creates a contrast with the other elements leading down into the space. Naturalistic boulders edge wide stairs which

Below *Humanizing allées of trees edge the layered stone grids in the oval, sunken forum in the centre of Tsukuba.*

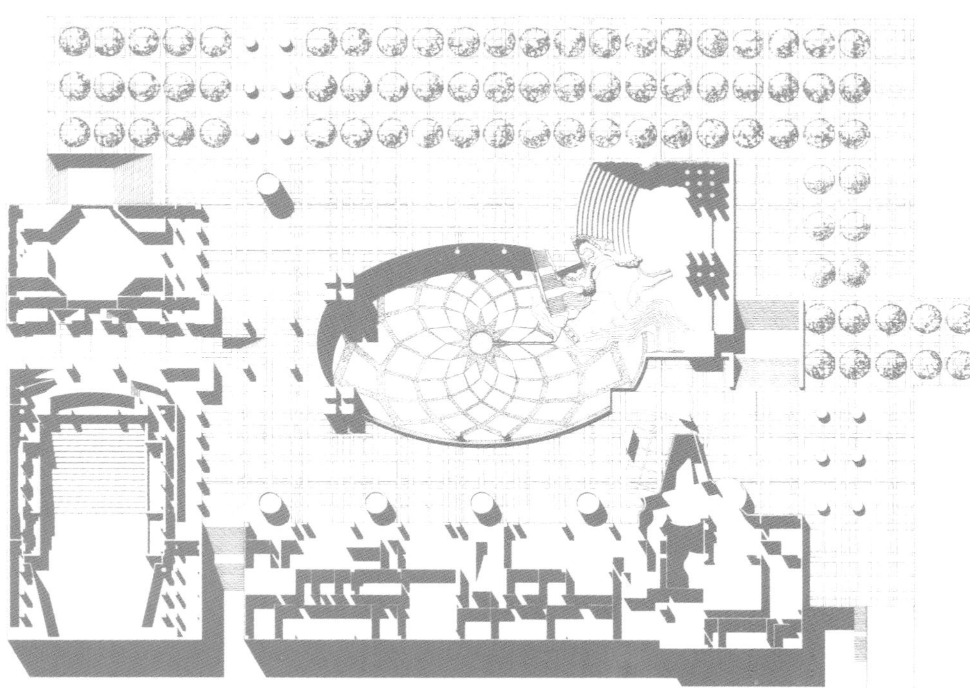

Left *The Tsukuba master plan with the central forum. It shows Isosaki's quotation from historical architecture: a homage to Michelangelo. Isosaki has reversed the superb oval paving pattern from the Campidoglio in Rome.*

Below *A reference to the ancient Greeks' worship of Daphne as a bay tree. This magnificent bronze version with its gilded bronze drape is by Hidetoshi Nagasawa. It stands at the source of the forum's water course.*

connect the forum with the upper areas and also serve as an amphitheatre. The boulders also frame the rushing cascade of water which falls down from a large upper pool. Isosaki has reduced the torrent to a narrow rill as it passes through the Campidoglio paving pattern. At the exact centre of this pattern, it disappears from sight into an opening. This corresponds to the central point of the Campidoglio, the site of one of the few bronze equestrian statues which has survived from Roman times, that of the Emperor Marcus Aurelius.

When he was asked about his use of space in the forum, Isosaki said:

> I made the centre space simply a space – a void; I portrayed a metaphor in which all the usual spatial arrangements are reversed or inverted. Everything is situated around a void, descending and then vanishing into the oblivion at the centre.

The more plant-orientated readers of this book will be pleased to know that in this development Isosaki has included for them *allées* of trees which march through the layered grid of thoroughfares above the sunken forum. The trees have begun to provide a soft, green ribbon of leaf, which contrasts with the rigorous architecture.

Raymond Jungles

Garden of 'The Colourful Corporate Headquarters', Boca Raton, Florida

The plant is, to the landscape artist, not only a plant – rare, unusual, ordinary, or doomed to disappearance – but it is also a colour, a shape, a volume or an arabesque in itself.

Roberto Burle Marx

The splendid statement above was made by Roberto Burle Marx, the Brazilian artist and landscape designer, considered one of the most important influences on landscape architecture this century. A wonderful ceramic mural by Burle Marx is on the far side of the swimming pool in the garden of the Jungles-Yates house in Key West, Florida. We first saw this garden in January 1998 and it was a stunning introduction to the tropical landscape designs of Raymond Jungles and his wife and collaborator, the artist-muralist Debra Lynn Yates.

Far right *Giant, variegated, yellow bamboo is a counterpoint to the mural by Debra Lynn Yates, who describes Miami as the place '. . . where the US meets the Third World, more than anywhere else in America.'*

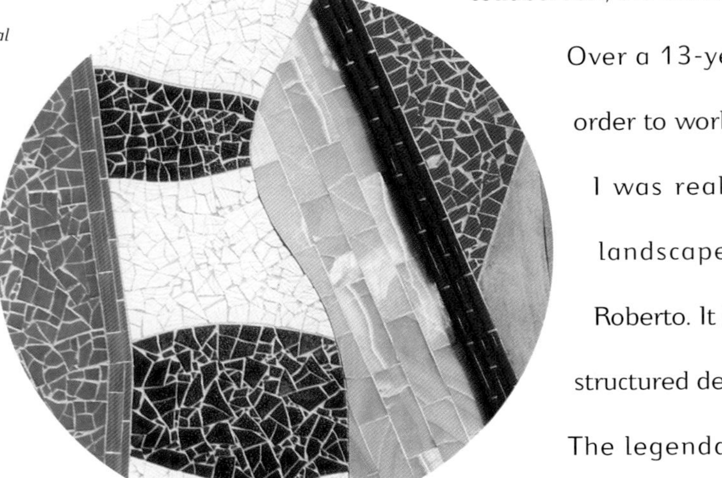

Over a 13-year period they had both visited Brazil in order to work and study with Burle Marx. Jungles recalls' I was really struggling between architecture and landscape architecture when I read a book about Roberto. It blew me away. He seemed to be able to fuse structured design and nature.'

The legendary Brazilian has been credited by some academic pundits on the landscape as *the* prime mover of the modern garden in the twentieth century. He always thought of himself as primarily a painter, just as Noguchi viewed himself as a sculptor and Barragan an architect, but like them, he became obsessed by landscape design. In his youth during the 1920s, Burle Marx was a student painter in Berlin. Here he visited the Dahlem Botanical Gardens, where he discovered the native plants of Brazil that were to became his lifelong passion. The plants that Burle Marx used in his designs were chosen from indigenous tropical species. His selection was shaped and defined by his vision as a painter. The influence of artists such Arp, Miró and Gorky can all be seen in his designs.

Burle Marx's twentieth-century architect collaborators were Le Corbusier, Lucio Costa and Oscar Niemeyer. With the latter he designed landscapes in their country's enormous, purpose-built capital,

GARDEN STATISTICS

Client: Withheld at client's request
Budget: $200,000
Designer: Raymond Jungles
Artist: Debra Lynn Yates
Concrete patinater: David Shankman
Area: 2,880 q. m (30,420sq ft)
Climate: Zone 11
Soil type: Sand on rock
Aspect: East
Date of completion: 1993

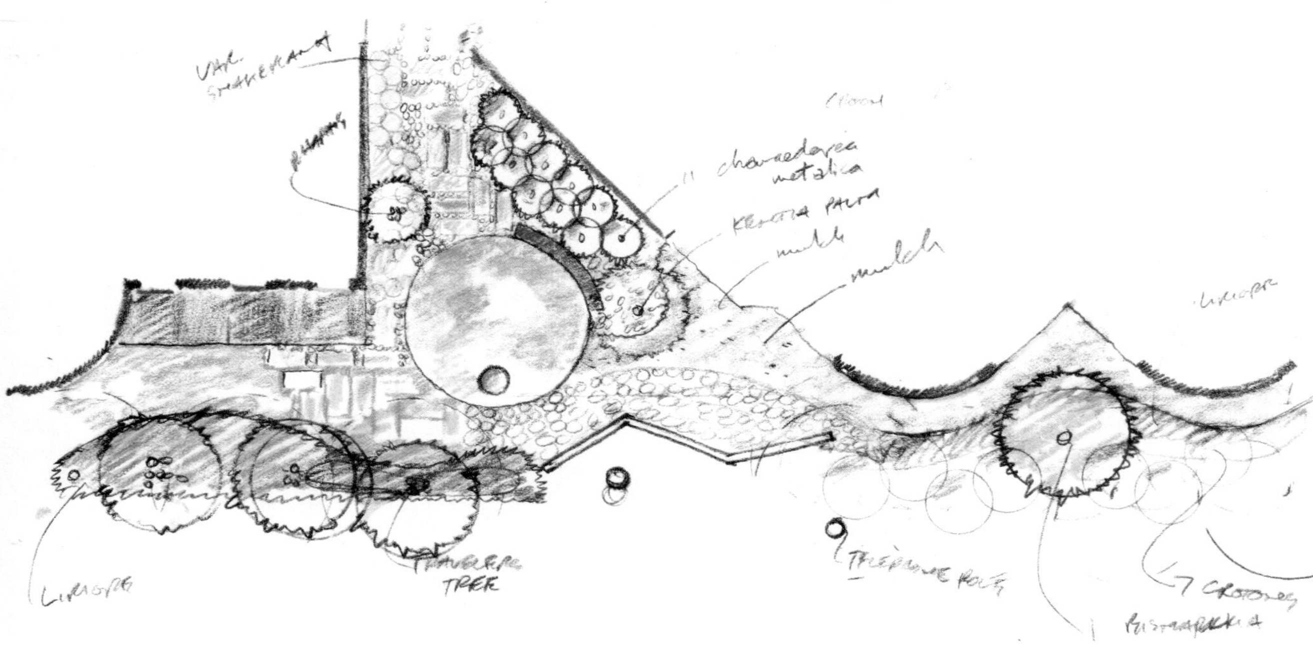

Left *An early sketch plan by Jungles for his landscape design at 'The Colourful Corporate Headquarters'.*

Brasilia. Other creations from his multi-faceted range of designs are the abstract sculptural parkways and wave-shaped patterns of the promenade of Copacabana; further evidence that a good designer can design anything?

In his garden designs, Burle Marx planted large drifts, swathes and massings of native Brazilian plants in bold curves, free-form biomorphic shapes that make a great visual impact. The planting often contrasts with the precise, geometric plan and paths of his gardens, as well as the modern architecture to which they were pendant. Burle Marx said that 'a garden is the result of an arrangement of natural materials according to aesthetic laws, interwoven throughout are the artist's outlook on life, his past experiences, his affections, his attempts, his mistakes, and his successes.'

Both Burle Marx and Jungles have been obsessed by the dramatic 'palette' of tropical plants. Plants which are classified as hot, glasshouse or conservatory subjects in the temperate climates of North America and Europe 'rollick away' in Jungles' designs. Architectural leaf shapes and the hot colours of tropical flowers make his gardens singular. 'Plants are the stars in my landscapes' says Jungles. Some of the plants that he most commonly uses are saw palmetto, sabal, fishtail, coconut, fan and *veitchii* palms, many types and sizes of bamboo, leather and firecracker ferns, cycads, oleanders and bananas, orchids, all sorts of bromeliads, purple, coral and pink bouganvillea, many colours of lantana, multicoloured birds-of-paradise, white and pink crinum lilies, single and double-flowered hibiscus and silk floss trees.

Below *A strong, abstract, mosaic wall by Debra Lynn Yates, who has been influenced by Gaudì and the vibrant colours of Florida and the Caribbean.*

From Brazil, Jungles has imported species to grow on in his Key West garden and then be planted in his Florida projects: drunken sailor tree, bismarckia palms and traveller's tree are but a few examples.

Raymond Jungles and Debra Lynn Yates were commissioned as a team to work on 'The Colourful Corporate Headquarters', the subject of this Case Study, referred to hereafter as Colourful HQ! Some of the main objectives of the garden were to create a design for corporation offices which reflected the owner's commitment to the arts, to make areas where the employees could eat, smoke and relax on their breaks from work, to create a more distinctive and noticeable entry point to the building and to lead the visitors to elevators which would take them to second-floor offices. There were to be garden views from all of the offices and the design had to integrate the highly coloured art pieces inside the building with the garden, creating a cohesive experience. Finally, the HQ was to be a distinctive presence on the busy highway, the adjacent US 1, the Dixie Highway.

Jungles and Yates worked closely with each other and with the owner, his architect and design consultant on all of the hard landscape elements: the owner's garden, the employee garden, the water garden, the serpentine wall, the walkways and built-in benches, plus the planting, lighting, address graphics and the all-important irrigation.

There were special problems relating to the existing site. The first was the 4.5m (15ft) projection of the building's second floor. On the first site visit the half-dead plants and mundane paving beneath the overhang were immediately striking. The relation between building and parking lot had to be improved, and space for a water garden and palm trees found from it. The undistinguished, multi-tenant architecture of the building also had to be improved and made more memorable by the new design. Jungles and Yates took their cue for the exterior from the art collection inside, designing colourful murals and bold planting.

Jungles and Yates were extremely pleased with their revamp of the Colourful HQ. The employees make full use of the redesigned outdoor space and, perhaps, highest praise of all, even the building inspectors became very complimentary on their various visits to the gardens.

Below *The once dark and dreary under croft of a company headquarters transformed with robust planting and mosaic walls.*

My hope is that my intuitive method of working manifests so that people will connect viscerally with the work in a way that makes it their own, and provides a lens for their own vision. I cannot define what that will be exactly. Each person has an individual response.

Kathryn Gustafson

Kathryn Gustafson

Fragments of Garden History, Terrasson-La-Villedieu, Dordogne, France

During the spring of 1992, in the region of Perigord, France, the unusually visionary town fathers of Terrasson-La-Villedieu decided to organize a competition for the design of a new public park and gardens. They invited Kathryn Gustafson, the American landscape architect with practices in Paris, Seattle and London, to participate in a competition for a public garden. The site was a beautiful, forested hillside overlooking the town. *Continent Imaginaire* was the title of the brief. It specified a series of designs to be based on various historic gardens of the world, with a greenhouse information centre as its main public focus.

Far right: *This spectacular, 900m-long (2,952ft-long), gilded aluminium ribbon leads visitors through the oak grove of Fragments of Garden History.*

The 6-hectare (15-acre) site has spectacular views over the town and the valley of the River Vézère. The slope is on a 1 in 4 gradient and there is a network of caves in the ancient oak forest. Maple and acacia have colonized the forest edge and in the open field areas there is a diversity of indigenous plants. Water from a group of cistern wells and an intricate and historic drainage system serve the central fountain and hospital of the town.

The town of Terrasson, which has 6,000 citizens, financed the initial phase of the competition. The later phases were underwritten by a broad-based group of sponsors: Terrasson, the province of Dordogne, the Region of Aquitaine, the nearby town of Brive-la-Gaillard, the Ministry of Culture, the Ministry of Tourism and the European Community. The initial budget was FF10 million, (£1 million / $1.6 million) for the garden, and FF4 million (£400,000/$640,000) for the buildings. Kathryn Gustafson, the leading landscape architect on the project, worked with Ian Ritchie, an English architect. The complexity and richness of the garden is the result of collaboration between Gustafson, Ritchie and

GARDEN STATISTICS

Client: Municipality of Terrasson-La-Villedieu, France

Budget: FF10 million

Designer: Kathryn Gustafson

Area: 6ha (15 acres)

Climate: Temperate

Soil type: Alkaline mixed

Aspect: North

Date of completion: 1995

Number of gardeners: 4 + 1 part-time

other landscape architects, artists and garden historians from Australia and France. A better, more specific and poetic name evolved for the project, its title was changed to: 'Fragments of Garden History'.

Despite the diversity of its members, the group agreed that history cannot be, nor should be, re-created. Basic elements of garden history were to be translated into contemporary forms. Think of a book on classical architecture – Vitruvius perhaps – with façades, floor plans and orders of columns. Having studied the elements, buildings in the classical style have even more meaning and coherence for us. At Terrasson, we see contemporary design concepts inspired by the high points in many centuries of garden history. The fragmented presentation enhances visitors' interest regarding gardens of the past. Imagine grass-covered, earth-form amphitheatre terraces reminiscent of Claremont in eighteenth-century Britain, add the long canals and serial water jets of the *regulier* style of seventeenth-century France and the slanting, stone water slides of the sixteenth-century Mogul summer palace in Kashmir. All of these images and many others are brought from the depths of visitors' memories and into the foreground of their immediate experience while they explore this new garden.

The opening design note of the gardens is the Axis of the Wind. It is a line of wind vanes on slender, 15m (50ft) metal masts. Omni-directional ball joints connect the vanes to the masts, showing not only wind direction but also wind turbulence. On each mast there is a bell. The visitor not only sees, but hears the wind.

The sonorous, 'singing' wind masts lead from the car park and entrance path. At the entrance to the garden the visitor catches a first glimpse of the *trompe-l'oeil* of parallel land forms running across the main clearing at the top of the site. The area is planted with high grasses and white roses. The main path, edged with clipped box, slopes up to the Elements Garden and the Glasshouse Fragment. This is an extremely simple, innovative glasshouse with a flat, high-tech glass roof which, when viewed from above in certain lights, appears to be a small lake. The laminated, toughened glass is secured with 'phantom fixings' developed by the Ritchie team. The sturdy walls are made from stacked *gabions*, wire mesh boxes filled with stones stacked up to form the walls. The glasshouse is an exhibition space, a book shop and a café-bar. It serves as a landscape interpretation centre for the gardens, providing visitors with a historical background and visual images of the designers' sources of inspiration.

Adjacent to the glasshouse is another large clearing. Here the land has been modelled into an amphitheatre of grass and steel. The area provides spectacular views of the town, the river valley and the Rose and Water Gardens. The roses are planted to grow up, over and down a 1,000m (3,280ft) steel pergola, creating a suspended tapestry of flowers that floats down the hill towards the Water Garden.

The pools in the Water Garden represent the moment in which water, formerly used for agricultural irrigation, became a source of sensuous pleasure in

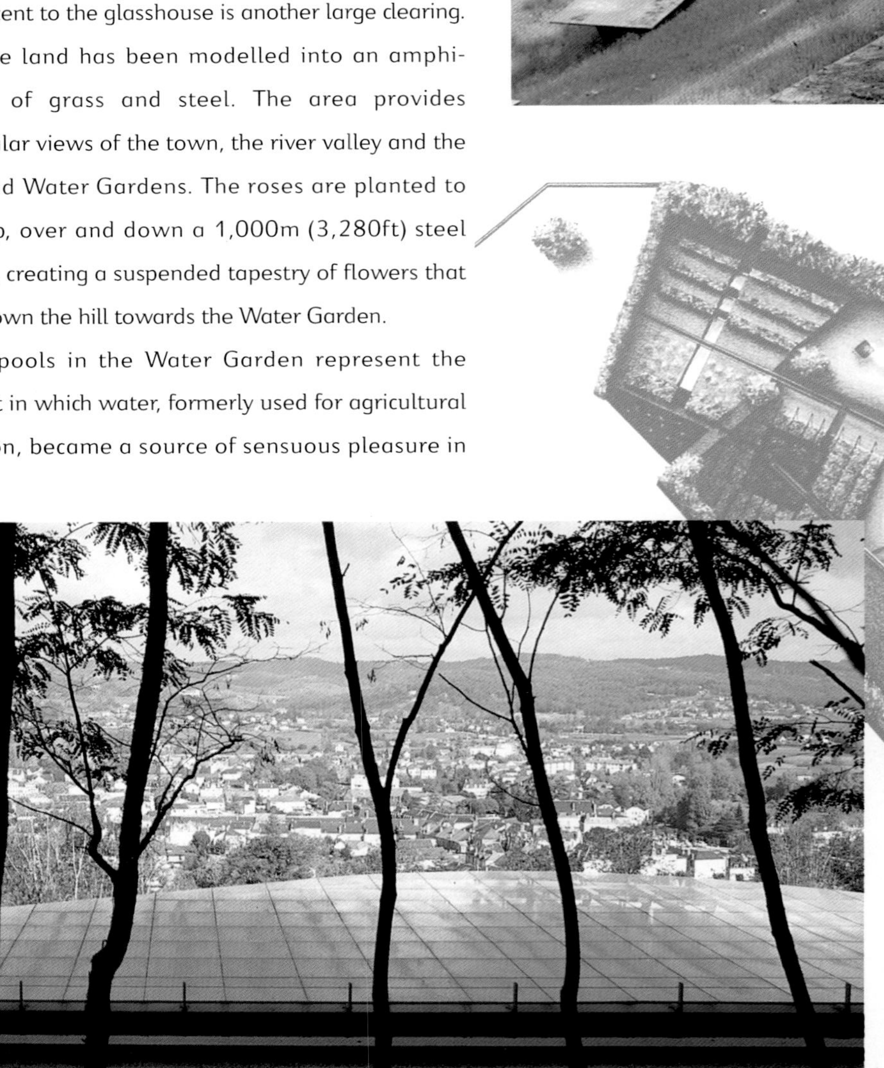

Right *A view of Terrasson-La-Villedieu. The glasshouse in the foreground was designed by Ian Ritchie, the noted contemporary British architect.*

Above *The wind mast is 15m (50ft) high. Changes in the direction of the wind are reflected by the action of an omni-directional ball joint, and by the ringing of the bell attached to each mast.*

Above *Grassed earth tiers and steel benches form an amphitheatre set among a grove of existing and newly planted trees with views of the town of Terrasson.*

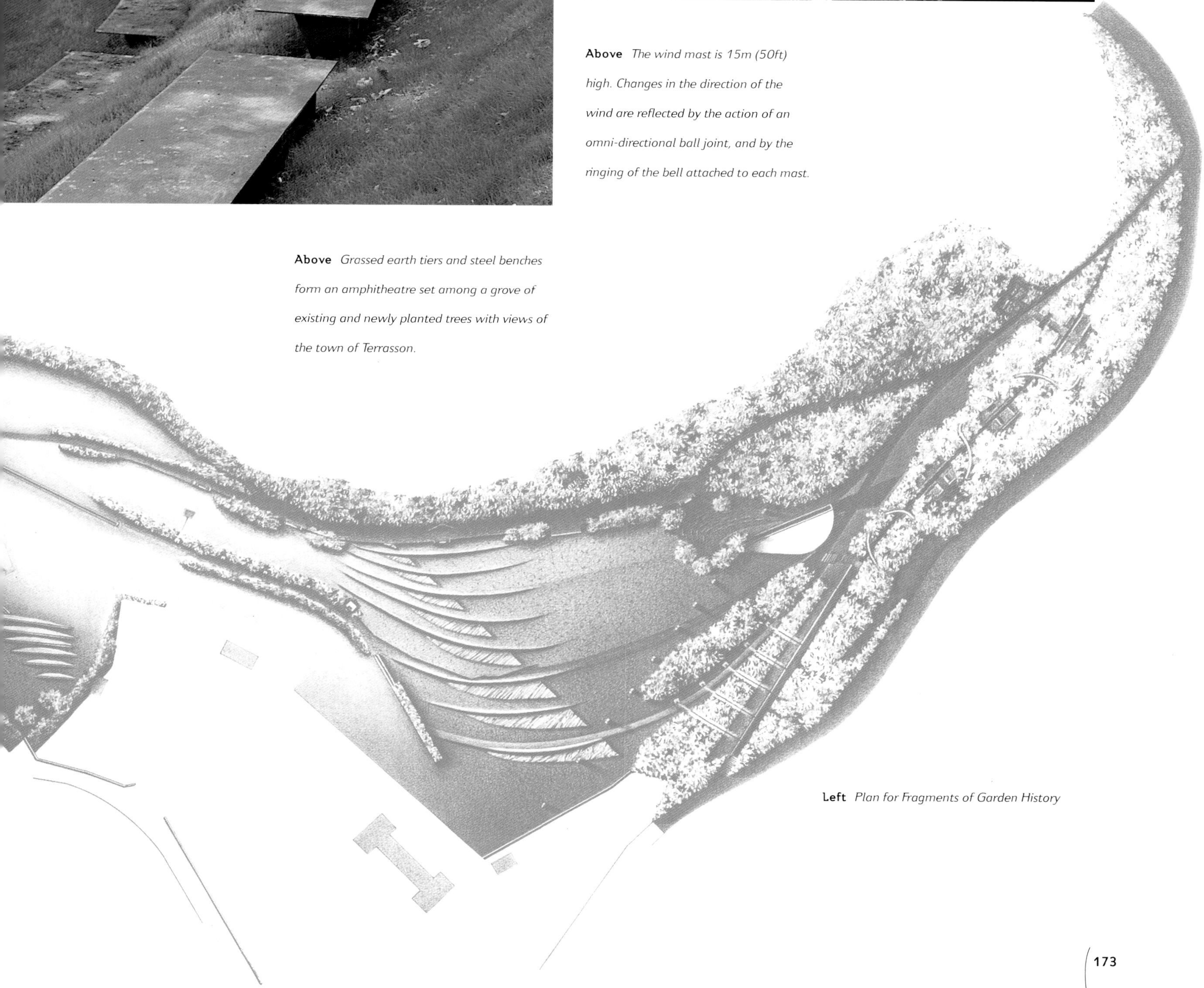

Left *Plan for Fragments of Garden History*

the garden. The Pathway of Fountains leads to a cruciform, four-square design – the most ancient form of garden ground plan. On a sunny day, rainbows play in the water which shoots out from 15 randomly placed jets rising from the large, rectangular pool.

Beyond the Water Garden is an enclosed vault of flowering trees leading towards the Topiary Room. Nearby is a large square of grass used for temporary landscape designs. A designer or artist will create a new pattern or design in the area each year. The design for the first year was a painted garden called 'Ephemeral Tracing'. Low lights in a grid pattern illuminate the area at night.

The return path leads through a large, abstract topiary into the Sacred Forest of the oak grove. Leading the visitor through the oak grove is a 900m-long (2,952ft-long) thin, aluminium, gold-leafed ribbon, weaving in and out of the tree canopy 5m (16ft) above the path. Set alongside the gilded ribbon are four small gardens which explore the role of particular plants chosen from the

indigenous vegetation. These gardens show their transformation through hybridization; the species found here are the Montpelier maple, rhododendron, azalea, and ferns and mosses.

Gustafson came to landscape from fashion design: the moulding of wool jersey versus the moulding of clay. The very important first sketches for a landscape design are made in clay and the resultant bas-relief is the inspiration for the project. Large-scale landscapes for the Shell and L'Oréal headquarters, and the Plaza of Human Rights, adjacent to the new cathedral by Mario Botta at Evry near Paris, are three other major achievements. Gustafson has collaborated with Neil Porter and John Lyall on the New Crystal Palace Park Project near Bromley, London; they have received partial funding for phase 1 of the park – the restoration section. Gustafson and her collaborators worked on this project against huge opposition. The designs respect the nineteenth-century remnants of the park while bringing to a partly derelict site exciting, contemporary twentieth-century buildings and a landscape for the public to enjoy.

Far left *A dramatic variety of water designs. The water steps in the foreground evoke a sixteenth-century Mogul garden in Kashmir or Lahore.*

Centre *An apparently endless formal canal echoes the seventeenth-century château gardens of André Le Nôtre.*

Above *Gustafson's brilliant field of water jets in the Water Garden.*

In order to travel into the future, it is necessary to walk towards the pure clarity of the past.

Fernando Caruncho, inspired by Petrarch

Fernando Caruncho

The Wheat Parterre, Mas de les Voltes, Ampurdan, Catalonia, Spain

Ancient agriculture meets formal contemporary garden design in the late twentieth century. Wheat, olive trees, cypresses, water and grass are the elements of this astonishing and original Case Study.

Caruncho is classically educated, as can be seen from any of his designs, which combine profound simplicity with extraordinary sophistication. He came to garden design while studying classical philosophy at the University of Madrid. He thinks of himself as a gardener, not a landscape architect or a designer. He made his first garden for an uncle (in a house by Richard Neutra) when he was 21, and he knew then that he had found his vocation.

In additional to the classical philosophers, Caruncho also venerates Descartes and Goethe. Rousseau – from the same period but on the opposite side of the philosophical equation – is an anathema, as are the unnaturally 'natural' English park lands of Capability Brown. And, of course, he finds particularly loathsome and boring the flowery, English, cottage and manor house garden style, as typified by those 'good taste', book-writing, sub-Gertrude-Jekyll, English granny gardeners.

Caruncho says that his designs are a constant attempt 'to capture the light (*vibration lumineuse*)' in the garden space, through a formal setting of the simplest elements: 'Everything in a Spanish garden is founded on how you deal with the light.' The rich history of Spanish gardens, which display the combined influence of the Moors and the Italian Renaissance, also informs his design. Caruncho's favourite historic gardens are the Alhambra Palace gardens in Granada; the Boboli gardens of the Pitti Palace, Florence, and André Le Nôtre's Château Vaux-le-Vicomte, south of Paris. Contemporary aesthetic heroes of his are the Minimalist architects Louis Kahn, Tadao Ando and Luis Barragan.

Far right *Caruncho's design is a formal masterpiece using vines, olives and wheat, the plants that were fundamental to the economy of the ancient Mediterranean. A huge circular pool is the focal point within a wheat parterre.*

GARDEN STATISTICS

Client: Finca Mas de les Voltes
Budget: N/A
Designer: Fernando Caruncho
Area: 9,500sq m (102,345sq ft)
Climate: Northern Mediterranean
Soil type: Clay neutral
Aspect: North/south
Date of completion: 1995
Number of gardeners: 3

Right *The geometry of alternating olive and cypress trees casts dark shadows in the summer sun of a late afternoon. This view embodies Caruncho's late twentieth-century ode to the idyllic Roman* rus *of Horace and Virgil.*

Until last year, when he was commissioned by Ricardo Legorreta to make a garden in Florida, Caruncho had worked principally in Spain and France. Recently, he has been commissioned to design the garden of the new Spanish Embassy in Tokyo.

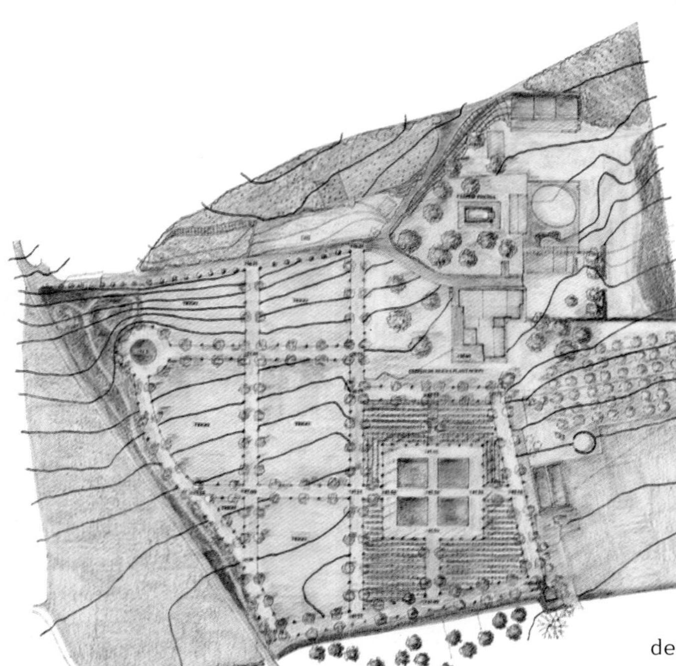

Above *Note the contour lines in the master plan of the Wheat Parterre. The subtle grading of the slope means that the parterres disappear, becoming one field of wheat from the bottom of the plan.*

Caruncho's design concept for this project was wheat, one of man's most ancient cereal crops, used as the basis of a simplified, formal parterre of soil and water, to be built on a farm in northern Spain. The Parterre contains echoes of both the agricultural and the architectural history of Spain which were both primary influences. Among the highly-developed Islamic arts and sciences which were brought to the country by the Moors in the eighth century were advanced agricultural methods and irrigation techniques.

These innovations also made possible the creation of the great gardens of Cordoba and Granada, such as the Alhambra, their designs based on the formal style that had originated in Persia. The parterres of the seventeenth century were also a source of inspiration. The Wheat Parterre in early spring resembles the *parterre à l'anglaise* or. *gazon coupé*, which was formed from designs made in cut turf.

When asked about his spiritual home, Caruncho replies that it is in Tuscany. He now realizes that the Wheat Parterre, with its Italianate qualities, has been unconsciously inspired by the paintings of Piero della Francesca. Just think of the coffered squares of the ceiling in the cool, geometric, painting *The Flagellation of Christ*. Late in life, della Francesca became so obsessed with linear and mathematical theory that he gave up painting altogether.

Caruncho sees the garden as a mirror of the universe: 'I strive to arrange a space that invites reflection and inquiry by allowing the light to delineate geometries, perspectives and symmetries.' In his gardens, the harmonies of the enclosure express for the spectator a sense of order and balance. He thinks that gardens can also narrate some sense of the history of ideas, arousing rather the same feeling as a rose window in a Gothic cathedral; the cathedral in Ghent is a particular inspiration.

The Wheat Parterre was conceived as the quintessential landscape of the Mediterranean, since wheat, olives and wine have been produced on this land since ancient times. He wanted the garden to be connected with the context of the farm land and to be faithful to the ancient culture. The brilliance lies in the simple minimalism of his late twentieth-century concept.

When Caruncho arrived on the site in northern spain, the large, stone farmhouse or *masia*, with its ancient tile roof and splendid strong-arched loggia, had

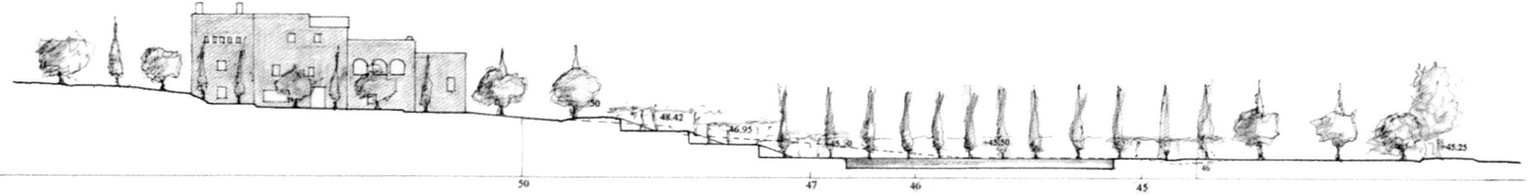

been completely restored, but the land was exhausted:

> The soil had been depleted by centuries of overwork until nothing would grow here. It was a monumental task to replenish the land. We had to bring in 16,000cu m (565,000 cu ft) of new soil, but we knew we were not only creating a garden but restoring a millennia-old landscape.

To enclose the wonderful wheat and carp pond parterres and the rest of the garden, Caruncho has planted stands of bamboo, groves of evergreen oaks, and orchards of cherry, apple, pomegranate and fig. The four, square carp ponds are set in grass and enclosed by shallow terraces of grape vines. Screened by a terrace wall is a kitchen garden and a rose garden for cutting, and nearby the only other colour is from water lilies in a raised pool at the base of a ruined watch tower. These are the only flowers Caruncho has included anywhere in the design. He maintains firmly:

> 'This is an agricultural garden...here a flower – any flower – would look out of place. For flower-filled borders one can go to Sissinghurst, but the landscape of the Mediterranean needs something quite different. This is a garden of forms, geometry and light.'

This is borne out by the seasons and the work that has been completed in the gardens. Caruncho is at his most poetic on this subject:

> In the summer, the wheat is tall and golden and the great plots sway gently in the wind. There is fruit in the orchard. Autumn brings the grape harvest and the cutting of the wheat. In winter the earth is ploughed and sown and marked by wonderful patterns. And in the spring, once again, all is a sea of green. What could be more beautiful or ennobling than producing flour from wheat, wine from the vines, oil from the olives and fruit from the trees? In a sense this is the first garden, a garden with all the purity of a Platonic ideal.

Late afternoon in this garden in any season, when the western sun is low in the clear Mediterranean sky, the carp ponds shimmer darkly or reflect a passing cloud.

Above *A cross section of the Mas de les Voltes design reveals the relationship between the imposing farmhouse, the parterres of wheat and water and the verticals of the olives and cypresses.*

The olive trees tremble with the silvery underside of their leaves catching the light, the wheat is golden, and the cypresses cast strong, dark shadows across the immaculate lawns of the paths. All these elements are caught in the light-filled space that Caruncho describes in all of his gardens – *caja de luz* – 'box of light', and here, it is a wondrous illumination.

Above *A line of tall cypress trees along the main drive gives onto a view of the wheat parterre. The parterre is bounded by lawn paths and ancient olive trees imported from Italy.*

I will arise and go now,
and go to Innisfree,
And a small cabin build there,
of clay and wattles made...

W.B. Yeats, *'The Lake Isle of Innisfree'*

Walter Beck & Lester Collins

Innisfree Gardens, Millbrook, New York

When it was first built, Innisfree had a 'cup garden' which demanded the attention of two full-time gardeners just to maintain the moss steps which could be walked on only once a week. The steps led to an exquisite Chinese tea house, a construction hardly congruent to the small cabin of clay and wattle which is descibed in Yeats' beautiful poem.

Marion and Walter Beck, who created this amazingly spiritual garden, tried out various names for it, all Chinese-inspired: Garden of the Seven Gates and Way to the Clouds were both contenders. To friends and the locals of Millbrook, however, it has always been Innisfree, the name inspired by W.B. Yeats' famous poem.

Far right *An autumn view of the lake at Innisfree which is bounded by a series of traditional, Chinese-inspired cup gardens. Regarding her late husband's work, Petronella Collins said, 'The lake is natural, but please be assured that everything else is not. Lester fiddled with everything.'*

The garden was created over a period of about 50 years. It is included as a Case Study on account of its use of the 'stuff' landscape architects and designers shape, improve and make more expressive: earth, rocks, water, trees and shrubs. Innisfree is an object lesson in the timelessness of the appeal of simplicity in the landscape.

The 80-hectare (200-acre) site, with its 16-hectare (40-acre) lake, was found by the Becks in the mid-1920s. She was heiress to an iron fortune and he was a painter obsessed by the design principles of Chinese painting. They started to make the garden in 1930. After Beck's death in 1954, the garden continued to evolve under the care of Lester Collins, a friend of Beck's and a landscape architect captivated by the gardens of China and Japan.

Both Beck and Collins were drawn to the notion of a garden created from a piece of the natural landscape. They believed that the viewer should be led to experience the moment, the now, of particular parts of it. Their credo was to build the essence rather than the copy.

GARDEN STATISTICS

Designer: W. Beck & L. Collins

Area: 73.6ha (182 acres)

Climate: Zone 5

Soil type: Neutral to acid

Aspect: Southeast

Date of completion: Never

Number of gardeners: 5

Right *The Point, the southernmost promontory on the lake, with stone seats designed by Beck. He created the main path around the lake to connect the cup gardens.*

Below *A hilltop reservoir feeds this serpentine stream in one of the many cup gardens edging the lake.*

Water, rocks and trees were the basic elements of the traditional Chinese garden, and later the gardens of Japan. Linguistically, the combination of the two words, water and rocks, are the Chinese characters for a landscape designer. Beck coined the term 'cup garden' after a trip to London, where he discovered the landscape paintings of the eighth-century, Tang Dynasty poet, painter and garden-builder Wang Wei. He is said by art historians to be one of the greatest landscape painters, and is also credited with the 'invention' of the Chinese style of monochrome landscape painting. This style would emerge later in Japan as *sumi-e*, with the masterpieces of black ink landscapes by the painter, Sesshu. In this style of painted landscape, there are defined and enclosed areas of rock and water.

Beck was also inspired by Wang Wei's poems, such as this one, which is called 'Drifting on the Lake':

The autumn sky is clear into the distance
The clearer so far from human habitation
On a sandy shore a crane, or beyond clouds
A mountain top makes my content.
The limpid ripples calm and evening comes
The moon shines out and I relax
Tonight my single oar takes over
As I drift without thought of going back.

Unrolling along the horizontal plane of a scroll the viewer sees water in the foreground and behind it, within a series of rocky inlets, perhaps a bridge, a philosopher's tea house, a grove of trees, an unusual rock formation or a waterfall. These were the images that inspired Beck's Innisfree cup garden designs. Petronella Collins, widow of Lester Collins, gave an insight into the personalities of Beck and her husband:

> Walter Beck was a mystical man, no doubt about it, and he and Lester had a tremendous rapport. However, my husband was a forthright Quaker, and there were no spirits in any rocks.

Beck designed more than a dozen cup gardens around the Innisfree lake. The focal points of a Chinese painting are asymmetric and three-dimensional. The visitor walking the circuit of Innisfree experiences a constant shifting of focal points that cannot be conveyed though the static rocks and water in a Chinese black ink scroll. The circuit of changing views and perspectives reminded us of our visit to the great stroll garden of the Imperial Villa, Katsura, Kyoto.

Beck managed to capture the mystical atmosphere of Chinese landscape design on an American lake shore. He made his cup gardens by framing an area with earthworks, fences, large rocks or trees. At 90, overseeing works from a wheelchair, Beck completed his last cup garden. He died in 1954 and his ashes were buried near one of his waterfalls.

Beck's design approach to the garden could be summed up by a passage in the book that he wrote about painting:

> One does not think in dimensions or restrictions; one is swayed by rhythms, and there is a willingness to follow wherever the experiment leads.

After his death, Beck's widow asked Collins to help her with the garden. Collins preserved the spirit of the place. The individual cup gardens had been built by Beck with no real relationship between them. Collins applied the full force of his energy and vision to making interconnections. He created new cup garden incidents and a path for visitors to walk on between the gardens. Collins had long thought of Wang Wei's concept of a total landscape. At Innisfree he perceived the lake, the surrounding hills and the three cliffs as one large cup encompassing many smaller ones. Like the great Chinese masters of the landscape, he listened to the garden itself when making his improvements, creating berms and hillocks to draw the visitor on seamlessly from area to area within it. A serpentine stream sculpted in a meadow now looks as though it was hewn from the earth by a glacier many aeons ago.

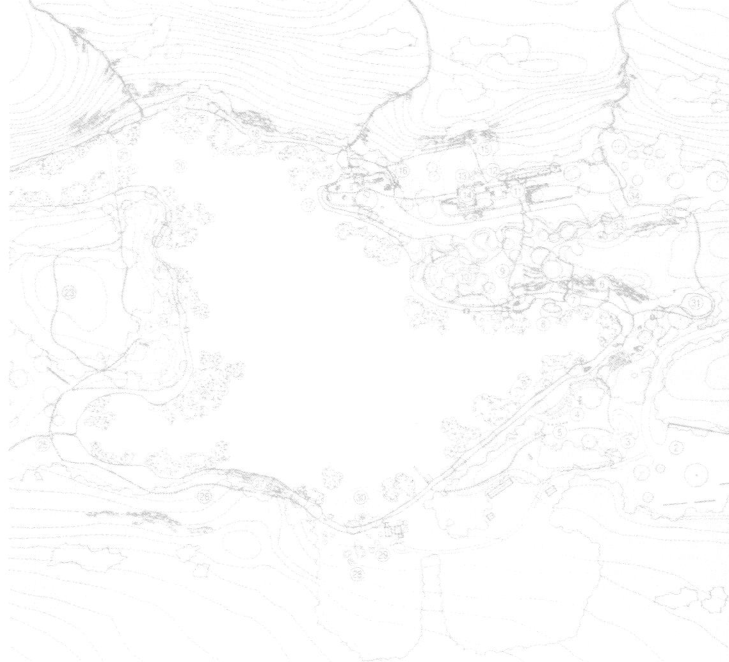

Right *A master plan of Innisfree Gardens.*

Below *Almost 0.4ha (1 acre) of hardy pink lotus in Innisfree lake makes a spectacular sight in July. Here they provide a backdrop for standing stones evoking traditional Taoist stone-worship.*

This is a garden about passion, yours, mine and the passion of the community.

Topher Delaney

T. Delaney & Co.

The Leichtag Family Healing Garden, San Diego Children's Hospital, San Diego, California

The designs for private gardens created by T. Delaney & Co have often emerged from the past lives of its clients. Topher Delaney calls this part of the client brief 'the personal narrative', and it is a key element in the evolving design. The result of this approach is a personalized or 'client-specific' design, a variation on the unique, late-twentieth century concept of the 'site-specific' or site-generated in both landscape sculpture and architecture. Delaney and her colleagues closely question a client's past and likes and dislikes, current preoccupations, and any specific interests or obsessions.

Often the designers will include in the planting plan trees, shrubs or flowers which remind the client of a garden they have known in the past for various reasons. They become living reminders of happy times, pleasures and events that the client has experienced. One client wanted blue lupins to rekindle memories of her last garden in Idaho. The most dramatic composition has emerged in a San Francisco hillside plot, where shattered pieces of a terrace were set asymmetrically as low-standing stones with an interplanting of blood grass. This, the 'Garden of Divorce', became a daily reminder of the lady's recent separation and her own new life. The original terrace had been laid down by her ex-husband.

Far right *Sheltering walls enclose the Healing Garden. The rainbow-coloured blades of this fantasy windmill turn to enliven the wooden birds 'caged' within its supporting struts.*

GARDEN STATISTICS
Client: San Diego Children's Hospital
Budget: $400,000
Designers: T. Delaney & Co
Area: 464.6sq. m (5,000sq ft)
Climate: Sunny and dry
Soil type: Clay
Aspect: West
Date of completion: 1997
Number of gardeners: 2

Delaney has designed three other healing gardens in California. One is at the Highland Hospital, East Oakland, in an extremely poor Afro-American section of the Bay Area. Another, in Palo Alto, is specifically designed for Alzheimer Syndrome patients. Delaney has just installed a large healing garden at the Beth-Israel Hospital in New York. The first of these healing gardens had its genesis in Delaney's own life – an aspect of her own personal narrative. She fought and won the battle with

Above *Delaney designed private spaces for the children and their families within the brightly coloured perimeter walls. Palm, magnolia and eucalyptus trees provide shade in the garden.*

Below *A presentation plan shows the final design development of the healing garden.*

cancer while in the Marin Cancer centre near San Francisco. At the centre of the building was a courtyard, a dull, soulless, concrete-walled, open space where she decided to make a perfect interior garden. Climbing plants furnished the walls, raised planters made scented plants more accessible to patients. The centre-piece is a beautiful, Japanese-inspired fountain reflecting the influence of the Orient on Californian culture. The fountain consists of two large, natural stones, one which acts as a support and one which is angled down to a round, carved bowl to contain the water. Over time, the fountain has taken on a symbolic significance. Many of the patients fill their cups and glasses there, hoping that the gently flowing water will help in some way with their cure.

Healing gardens are an ancient phenomenon. In the fourth century BC, Greece had healing centres or *aesclapia* devoted to the god of medicine and healing – Aesclapius. Many temples were erected to him on high mountains and near healing springs all over Greece. Three major shrines were dedicated to him. They were on the island of Kos, in the city of Pergamon, and at the temple and theatre of Epidaurus, in the eastern Peloponnese south of Athens. Vincent Scully, the great American architectural historian, has made the following comment about Epidaurus and the relationship between the natural landscape of the site and its buildings:

> The whole of the universe of men and nature [came] together in a single quiet order to be (healed).

In the third century BC Aesclapius 'emigrated' to Rome. Here his shrine was consecrated on the Tiber Island. There, in the tenth century, relics of Saint Bartholomew endowed a church and a hospice for healing. During the twelfth century, while staying at this hospice in Rome, King Henry II of England's jester, Rahere, had a vision that the king must return home and found a sister healing centre there. As a result of the vision, a hospice was founded in England in 1132. Over the centuries this healing centre has become Saint Bartholomew's Hospital, London.

Solitude is also a vital part of the healing process. There is a need to be alone in a garden or landscape and this is especially true of those whose lives are devoted to healing. Contact with nature and the processes of growth and renewal provide spiritual refreshment of the body and mind.

'When the doctors can't heal anymore, your heart and your soul still need to be healed, and this is the place for it.' This is the deeply felt response of Deborah Burt to the San Diego Children's Hospital. She is the mother of Sam who has had intensive treatment there. The garden is designed to offer a safe, imaginative, uplifting and above all meaningful environment for convalescent and terminally ill children and their families. Periodically, the hospital staff and the families gather in the garden for a ceremony that they call 'The Celebration of Life'. It is an opportunity to praise the children who have died and those who are still convalescing in the hospital.

Delaney's garden is on the site of a former car park of the hospital. She explains the garden:

> It's a place to imagine life being larger than what's existing at the moment. Most gardens are about miracles of life, but this one deviates from the traditional.

The designers have approached the elements of the garden – the colours, shapes, textures and, above all, the scale of the features – from the viewpoint of a child. The children feel an immediate rapport with the cartoon and computer-game colours of lemon-yellow, deep blue, lilac and burnt orange which wash the sinuous, undulating walls surrounding and intersecting the garden space. The walls form a series of garden rooms with nooks and crannies where families and staff can gather in privacy.

The child's view of this fantasy world is expressed in the garden in many ways. The entrance, which establishes privacy and sanctuary, is through the giant, open-work, painted metal legs of Sam the Dinosaur. Sam is 12m (40ft) long and 6.5m (21ft) high. He is clad with the vigorous, purple-red *Bougainvillea spectabilis* cultivar aptly named 'San Diego'.

Left *A jolly, mosaic sea-horse fountain adds the magic of splashing water to hot, southern Californian summer days.*

Below *The entrance to the garden is a giant, 12m-long (40ft-long) climbing frame for bougainvillea called 'Sam the Dinosaur'.*

Above *This stalking mountain lion silhouette is one of many animal cut-outs in the metal wall sections among the bright concrete perimeter walls. The animals cast shadows onto the swirling cement ground plane's sea and sand colours.*

This fantastical beast was named after a patient, a four-year-old boy who has had 20 operations at the hospital. Sam Burt's mother, Deborah, was a leading force in the creation of the garden, knowing at first-hand the importance of it: 'When your kid is hooked up to an IV drip day after day, the sound of the birds and the wind in the trees is like heaven.'

Other creatures featured in the garden include a giant sea-horse fountain rising from a sea-blue concrete floor gently shooting jets into shallow pools, and 300 ceramic sea animals set into the walls. There is also a rainbow-coloured windmill with mechanically driven birds inside its open structure. Within the garden, the Celestial Wall is inset with the signs of the zodiac and the Constellation Wall is decorated with 158 glass stars glowing in the afternoon sun. Other walls have glass discs in the shape of ducks, horses, bats and mice casting scampering shadows on the ground and providing a focus during the day for partially sighted children. At night, the glass beasts are back-lit by coloured concrete spheres representing the planets on the edge of the street so that they can also be seen from the hospital windows overlooking the garden area.

The garden's ground planes of crushed granite are swirls of soft, sandy ochres, yellows, blues and teal greens. These were inspired by the shore and the waves of the Pacific Ocean.

There are plenty of places to sit and relax in the garden: mosaic seats, serpentine, concrete benches, movable wheelbarrows with fixed umbrellas and 'rainbow' rocks. From all of these seats, families can enjoy the medicinal plants and shrubs attractive to bees and butterflies.

Three small lawn areas are used for picnics. Shade and height are provided by mature palms and eucalyptus; large bird-of-paradise plants continue the bold colours and fantasy themes.

Within the garden is a story-telling room for the hospital's resident story-teller. On its walls the shadows of animals are cast by large metal cut-outs. Anecdote as antidote! Story-telling is another purposeful activity, an antidote to the clinical confines of the hospital, providing both a welcome distraction to the children, and short-term mental solace for visiting parents. This and other areas of the garden bring to mind images from twentieth-century art based on colourful, abstract fantasy – the works of Joan Miró, Antonio Gaudí and Niki De Saint-Phalle.

The Healing Garden in San Diego is unique in that it was built entirely from donated funds, labour and materials. Paul Hagin, who is the director of facilities at the hospital, was responsible for much of the fund raising. He also enlisted the help of an agency which specializes in the employment of high school students in crisis, who built the walls dividing the different areas of the garden.

The client and the contractor were the hospital which, together with the Bereavement Committee, collaborated with designers at each stage of the design and installation. The garden is now complete and it is a great success. The use has been extended to severely handicapped children and they are now able to share it with the other children and their families.

Right *Scented plants attract bees and butterflies to the garden. The star benches in the foreground are made of limestone and mosaic. 'Sam the Dinosaur' can be seen in background.*

Below *The Constellation Wall is set with 158 glass stars. The planets, coloured concrete spheres with lights inset, bring glass star configurations inside the garden wall to life at night.*

George Hargreaves

The Dayton Garden, Minneapolis, Minnesota

You don't walk in and say, 'This is my way', because if that's all it is, it's not a very good project. Landscape design expresses how our culture meets nature. It's not about architectural ideas. It's about people.

George Hargreaves

In a brilliant and mind-opening lecture on the contemporary landscape given at the Royal Institute of British Architects, London, in November 1993, George Hargreaves described his average brief: 'Garbage 60ft [18m] deep on landfill or post-industrial sites for eventual public use is where we are most often asked to design, not on idyllic, green-valley sites for corporate villas.'

The search for meaning in the landscape is the key to the designs created by Hargreaves Associates. Nature and culture, culture and nature, the interplay and variations between these macro-concepts, has led George Hargreaves towards his interpretation of landscape architecture. He sculpts the earth and envisions forms in the land of a site. Initially, in the early part of the design process, he seeks for shapes either on, in or around the site. This approach makes his team sensitive to the existing, natural landscape. They can find their inspiration for the design in the configurations and contours within view of the site. A deep and thorough enquiry into the given circumstances and natural processes of a site, such as the land, the light, the shadow, the water, the wind and the rainfall, a thorough understanding of its larger, natural context, combined with research into its history, all yield shapes and design elements for a Hargreaves project. The layout which evolves from this data is not based on an earlier pattern. It is a site-generated design. In Hargreaves' view, 'The truths we uncover in the analysis of environmental phenomena should be the fodder – the subject – of design.'

Hargreaves Associates was established in San Francisco, California, in 1983. When Hargreaves became Head of Landscape Architecture at Harvard University Graduate School of Design, a second

Far right *Richard Serra's* Garden Arc, *made in 1986, is set against a background of trees. The lake, the climax of the vista, can just be seen within the filigree line of trees.*

GARDEN STATISTICS

Client: Kenneth and Judy Dayton

Budget: Withheld at clients' request

Designer: Hargreaves Associates

Area: 0.3ha (0.75 acre)

Climate: Midwest USA

Soil type: Glacial Till

Aspect: North/south

Date of completion: 1997

Right Snakearm *by Peter Shelton stands at the far end of an allée of honey locusts.* Untitled (Triptych), *by Ellsworth Kelly, 1982, is seen in profile in the foreground of the picture.*

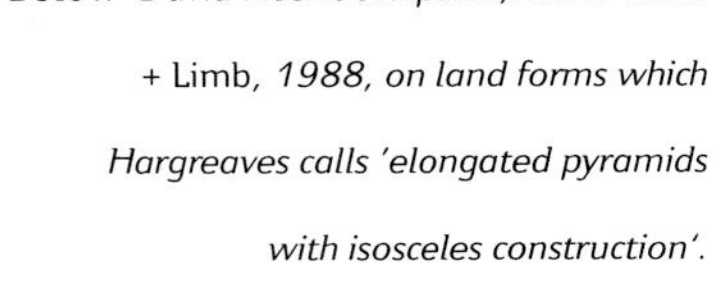

Below *David Nash's sculpture,* Stand Trunk + Limb, *1988, on land forms which Hargreaves calls 'elongated pyramids with isosceles construction'.*

studio was opened in Cambridge, Massachusetts. Many of the company's Californian projects display an ability to emphasize the elemental in the landscape. At Byxbee Park, Palo Alto, the profile of land forms was taken from distant hills. The existing site was covered in rubbish to a depth of 18m (60ft). They solved this problem by spreading 60cm (2ft) of good soil sown with native grasses and wild flowers over 30cm (12in) of impenetrable clay sealer. At Candlestick Cultural Park, south San Francisco, strong winds and their sounds were harnessed to the concrete Wind Gate. At Prospect Green, Sacramento, a flat valley was sculpted into land forms from earth ravaged by gold dredging.

George Hargreaves has designed gardens for just two private houses. The first was a stunning series of spirals and serpentines of contrasting grasses and wild flowers, set in a forest clearing of holm oaks and mesquite. The design contrasted with a large, white stucco, angular, asymmetric, Modernist house – Villa Zapu – on a hillside at the end of the Napa Valley in California.

The second is the subject of this Case Study. It is the Dayton residence, a rectilinear, Modernist villa in Minneapolis, Minnesota. Its setting, overlooking some of Greater Minneapolis' many lakes, recalls two other International style villas: the Farnsworth House by Mies van der Rohe outside Chicago and its Connecticut offspring, the Glass House by Philip Johnson. In our view, this building by local architects Vincent James Associates also has echoes of the Villa Savoye, designed by Le Corbusier outside Paris.

The history of this project is rooted in the Daytons' decision to leave their house at Wayzata and move into the city. The grounds of their old home had been the setting for a modern sculpture collection. The sculptures were arranged at intervals along a path that bounded their 5-hectare (13-acre) property. Many of their favourite pieces made the move into the new garden nearer the city. This slightly smaller collection included works by Siah Armajani, Scott Burton, Ellsworth Kelly, Richard Long, David Nash, Martin Puryear, Richard Serra, Joel Shapiro and Peter Shelton. The new sculpture circuit designed by Hargreaves is on a smaller, urban scale.

Hargreaves' landscape concept is based on a series of areas which extend the indoor–outdoor, house–landscape connection already achieved by the glass walls of the main rooms of the house. From inside the house, the different areas of the garden appear as gallery spaces for the sculptures.

Arriving at the house, the visitor is led up the immaculately paved driveway of granite sets which leads to the car court. On the left of the driveway Hargreaves has placed three low, sculpted and grassed land forms (a signature of his singular design philosophy) which he calls 'elongated pyramids with an isosceles construction'. The shapes, which are his opening statements in this garden, are enclosed by a right angle of small-leafed lime trees. The sculpted ground plane subtly signals the clients' interest in contemporary sculpture. Two pieces of sculpture, *Ferndale Ladder* and *Standing Trunk + Limb,* both by David Nash, are set asymmetrically within the grassed mounds. Hargreaves' land forms are particularly beautiful in the summer when they cast low, dark shadows from the setting sun. In the winter, the depressions between the shapes make longer-lasting, Minimalist, horizontal bas-reliefs in the snow.

Below *Master plan of the Dayton Garden.*

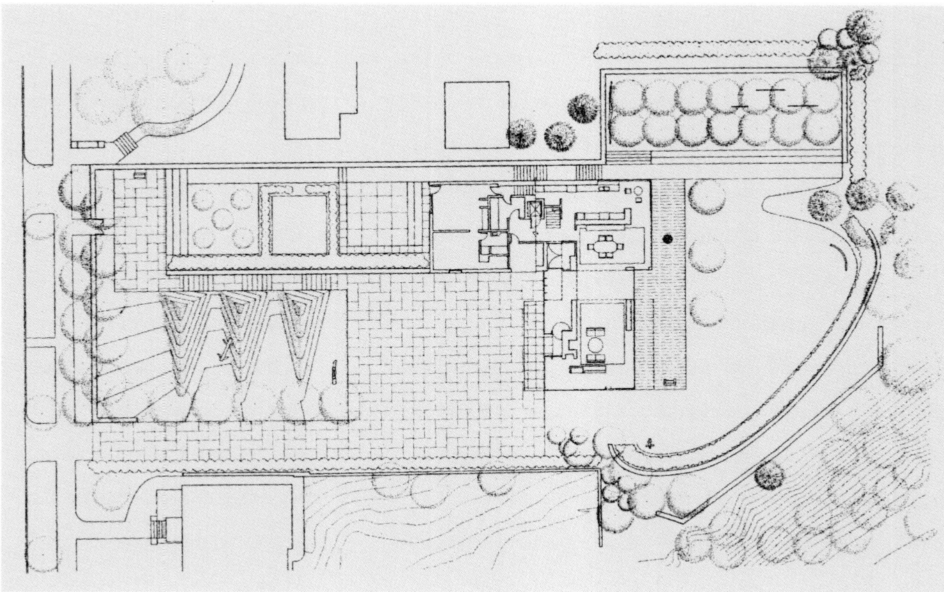

When asked about the genesis of the sculptured ground plane, Hargreaves admitted that the clients were unsure about it when it was first mentioned. He suggested it again six months later, nine months later, and finally after about a year. At this point they said that the ground work could begin. When it was half built the Daytons became uncertain again. Once more, Hargreaves 'donned his spurs', as he puts it. He finally persuaded them to accept the grassed land forms, which they could now perceive as Modernist, planar, sculptural surfaces – clean and green, and right for the garden.

Hargreaves revelled in the residential scale of this project in contrast to the large-scale, cultural and ecological projects on reclaimed sites:

> This was a scale you can touch and feel. It wasn't 50, 100 or 200 acres. It wasn't a ten-year project. It was a project that was all going to be done at one time, and I knew it was going to be done well. It was of such a scale that you could stake things out. We staked those mounds [land forms] out and tested the size of them. We staked out the lens shape [lawn plateau] and the curves. We were out there actually doing it.

Hargreaves' other major stroke with the garden footprint is the large area which the main rooms overlook. The view through the glass walls of the living room, dining room and kitchen is out across the narrow granite terrace and grassed plateau – or lens as Hargreaves calls it. At its furthest extreme is the elegant curve forming the edge of the plateau, the climax of the lawn. Beyond it are the lakes and their forested shores. The plateau and curved edge were worked out by the architect and Hargreaves. As he says, 'It's not an arc, it is its own shape. It is a clean shape that comes from a view of the lakes.'

A robust retaining wall supports it, and below the plateau is a road leading up to the house. The arc of a steel sculpture by Richard Serra is a splendid counterpoint to Hargreaves' plateau curve. Growing up from below the curve are some existing riparian hardwood trees. The gaps between the trunks give miniature framed views of the lakes, the centrepiece of the main vista. They also act as an exquisite line of filigree between the house, lawn and the lakes, echoing the landscape pictures of Camille Corot.

Above *This* Small Green Stone Circle, *was made in 1985, by Richard Shelton.*

The change of level between the plateau and the footprint of this garden could be read as a Post-Modernist, late twentieth-century, American version of the British eighteenth-century ha-ha. Then, it was a ditch and retaining wall separating the garden of a country house from adjacent grazing land, while giving an uninterrupted view over the open countryside beyond. Hargreaves has adapted this historical garden incident in order to create a wonderful, uninterrupted lake view.

The design and construction of the garden took two-and-a-half years from start to finish. Hargreaves worked closely with the Daytons, the contractor and the gardener who now maintains the garden:

> All of the key players were involved with the project from the beginning, so no one can say, 'I didn't know that'. The client would ask good basic questions: 'How much does it cost? Is it maintainable? Does it make sense with the house?' Pretty much questions that a major mid-Western retailer would ask, very sharp. The collaboration was an interesting discipline, for the client asked those questions throughout the process, and having the gardener in on the meetings meant we had the opinion of the man who's going to maintain it.

When asked about any constraints on those 'wonderful, necessary and constant givens of any landscape project – good ol' Time and Money', Hargreaves comments:

> Yes, there was a constraint on time. The clients had sold their property and they had to move into the new house by a certain date, so we had to be out by that date. We fast-tracked a couple of things, like we were building things before we had a full set of drawings and stuff like that. Money, I was never

Below *Ellsworth Kelly's sculpture,* Untitled (Triptych) *1982, in the foreground and Richard Serra's* Garden Arc.

> really given a budget, but everything was sort of vetted...A lot of things that were concrete were slowly turned to stone. It pushes up the cost, but they were interested in the longevity... So in a meeting we'd sit and say that concrete was $7.00 per foot and limestone was $25.00 a foot. I'd give a recommendation and as we got closer and closer to building, the process would tip, and the *right* decision would be made.

As for the general guidelines he followed in designing the garden, Hargreaves says that the client wanted both a serene environment and a place to live gracefully. Then they hammered away at him for a year to make sure that they got exactly what they wanted. He would propose and the Daytons would dispose!

Above *A view from the drawing room out to the terrace, with Scott Burton's witty marble bench,* Six Part Settee, *1984. Beyond it lies the lawn and the top of the curved retaining wall. The climax of the view is the lake, seen through a Corotesque filigree of bare trees.*

Daniel Urban Kiley

A Connecticut Estate

I find direct and simple expressions of function and site to be the most potent. In many cases, though not all, this has led me to design using classic geometries to order spaces that are related in a continuous spatial system, that indicates connections beyond itself, ultimately with the universe.

Daniel Urban Kiley

Once, when Kiley was on the point of giving a presentation, a fellow architect urged him to 'go easy on the geometry because you're thought of as a neo-classicist'. Kiley snapped back, 'Forget the "neo".' This Case Study deals with a country site set in low, rolling hills with spectacular views to the forested Taconic Range of mountains – a brilliant east-coast autumn panorama of colour when the leaves of the maples turn their brilliant shades of red and yellow.

This is a case of Le Nôtre comes to New England. Alternatively, one could apply Mark Twain's *A Connecticut Yankee in King Arthur's Court.* Daniel Urban Kiley could feel very much at home as 'A Vermont Yankee in King Louis XIV's Court'.

In this formal design, Daniel Urban Kiley has brought the shade of André Le Nôtre to Connecticut. Louis XIV's garden designer for Versailles would appreciate Kiley's use of the formal landscape language of geometry. Kiley acknowledges the Frenchman as a major design 'ancestor'.

Kiley has made a splendid classical design for the large garden of this grand American country house. Remembering back to the very beginning of the project he said:

> Upon viewing the site, my first thought was of a nice Beefeater martini with lemon twist . . . Seriously, my first visit with the client was a bit strange; time the architect was let go. I saw that the house was quite large, 14,000sq ft [1,300sq m] and stained a dull brown. It rankled with the peaceful countryside of south-western Connecticut. I said, "You know you have to paint this white"?' After initial shock, the clients agreed and the entire structure is now a pure, harmonious traditional white and sits well in the New England countryside.

Far right *A panorama of meadow, lake and the glorious Taconic Mountain range seen from the formal terrace in Kiley's garden for a Connecticut estate.*

GARDEN STATISTICS

Client: Withheld at clients' request
Budget: N/A
Designer: Office of Dan Kiley
Area: 242 ha (600 acres)
Climate: Zones 4–5
Soil type: Clay/loam
Aspect: South/west
Date of completion: 1996
Number of gardeners: 2

Right *The pergola on the lawn terrace which is used for croquet. A jet rises from a sleek, contemporary plane of water which mirrors the sky and clouds. The rectilinear, black slate block carries 7.6cm (3in) of recycled water falling down copper-sheathed sides.*

Below *The serpentine retaining wall creates a crucial plinth of formal terraces. Kiley sees this as a means of defining the house complex in relation to the surrounding sylvan landscape of the estate.*

Kiley was commissioned to deal with the 20 hectares (50 acres) nearest to the house, creating a balanced transition between this area and the untouched countryside beyond. He explained his approach to the creation of this transition in the following way:

> What inspires me is to develop the undiscovered relationships between the house and the land and let these be the diagram for the landscape design. One never needs to make up a design – just go to the site with clear eyes, listen to the client's needs with an open mind and seek the highest solution. . . it evolves!

When asked about the constraints set by the client on time or money, Kiley replied:

> None. When we began the project in 1993, the client was almost as old as I was [83]. He told me, 'I don't want any green bananas.' In other words, the project was to appear fully mature on installation, therefore, we selected large-girthed trees: 15in-calliper [the US tree nursery reference to the circumference of the trunk] sweet chestnuts, 14in-calliper gingko, 8ft-high hornbeam hedges and other wonderful plants to ensure that structural elements of the landscape – *allées,* bosques, lines of trees and other shapes – imparted the full effect of the design immediately.

When we asked Kiley about his ideas regarding the concept of space in the project he gave the following explanation:

> The concept and treatment of space is the same for all projects. . . in terms of shaping and creating dynamic spatial volume with screens and lines of hedges and trees, ground cover, grass, water and

crushed stone panels, etc. The use of light and shadow, and seasonal effects are essential to developing clarity of relationships. I celebrate space in the same way: integrate the existing with the new; interpret the client's programme and the site's characteristics within a spatial order of unity and clarity; develop details and nuance which bring the essence of spiritual connection to the universe and beyond. I try to access the delight and mystery in daily life and in seasonal change, to be revealed in the design.

The major classical details near to the house are a simple but hefty pergola, some formally set trees, lawns and a couple of raised water features. Each water feature is 30m (100ft) long. Together, they form part of massive, poured-concrete retaining walls which bound the house on two sides at a height of 2m (6ft) and create the perimeter of the north terrace.

The pergola has poured-concrete columns and wooden lintel crosspieces. Wisteria is planted at each of the columns. The paving under the pergola is square, carnelian granite pavers set with wide grass 'mortar' courses. This stone–grass design is a Kiley signature in

Above *Kiley's early elevation sketch shows the juxtaposition of the serpentine retaining wall and rectilinear water feature.*

Left *Immaculately designed and installed retaining walls with Barbara Hepworth sculpture* Two Figures, *1968, bronze with colour.*

Above *Formal serenity created with a few, well-considered garden elements.*

many of his gardens. The grass between the pavers makes a softer effect than closely set, mortared stones, and appears to be an extension of the lawn ground plane. Maintenance is simplified also, for the grass 'mortar courses' can be mowed when the lawn is cut.

Trees are set formally in pairs, *allées, bosques* and lines. A pair of *Gingko biloba* in circles of periwinkle are in the arrival court, only becoming visible after going up the main drive through an *allée* of red maples. This is the east side of the house, and the entry court opposite the front door is defined by a square *bosque* of crab-apples underplanted with periwinkle and cotoneaster. A two-lane *porte-cochère* shelters the main door; the round columns are painted black and the roof has two triangular skylights. On the east side there are two lines of limes shielding the conservatory from the setting sun.

The long retaining wall, which bounds the site on two sides, serves to focus and define the house and garden within the larger landscape. Abutting the wall are other large areas of grass and adjacent to it is agricultural land which merges into the rolling hills and the mountains of the horizon.

The historic precedent for massive walls used to level and retain the soil near a house can be found in both Italy and France. Huge retaining walls were designed by Michelozzo for Cosimo de Medici at the sixteenth-century Villa Medici in Fiesole. They are considered to be the first such constructions during the Italian Renaissance. In seventeenth-century France, Le Nôtre's redesign of the gardens of Chantilly for Louis II de Bourbon, 'Le Grand Condé', included the construction of retaining walls for new terraces and for the gigantic grand canal.

Long rectangular canals and basins were another common feature in many French gardens of the seventeenth century. Kiley has installed his own version of the formal canal in this garden. It consists of two rectangular, granite water features, set at a right angle and retained by the rampart. A very shallow depth of water falls down over three narrow steps on the face of the granite, making three long, gentle waterfalls. The smooth water on the surface of dark granite rectangles mirrors the changing sky. At the angle where two 'canal' shapes meet, Kiley has designed a square pool from which shoots a tall and vigorous jet that he calls a 'roiling fountain'. The jet creates a dramatic end stop. The fountain by the house also feeds a woodland runnel which cascades down the west slope through a grove of birch and ferns. This runnel spills into a constructed bog, ringed with black spruce and swamp azalea, sited at one end of the pond. Discussing the versatility of the water used in the garden, Kiley explained:

> . . . water is used in several forms to express varied character. Each interpretation of water expresses a specific purpose – cool and elegant on the terrace, rich, fragrant and cloistered in the bog; bubbling

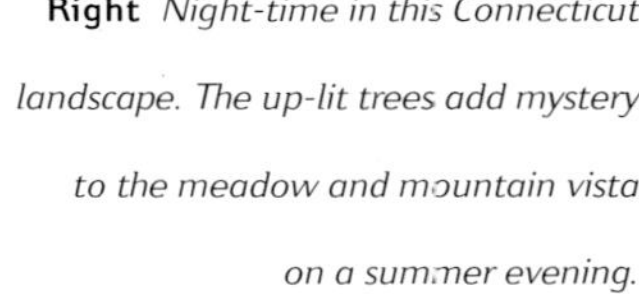

Right *Night-time in this Connecticut landscape. The up-lit trees add mystery to the meadow and mountain vista on a summer evening.*

and playful as the fountain which is viewed from within the library and bar of the house.

In his use of water, Kiley shows the mature mastery of his art. If the rectangular water features had been conventional pools, they would need high maintenance, with algae, leaves and other detritus for the gardeners to remove. Here they must deal only with the narrow pool at the base of the raised rectangle of granite.

Daniel Urban Kiley is the most respected landscape architect in the United States. His career has spanned 60 years. In 1997 he was awarded the National Medal of Art, for distinguished service to landscape architecture. Over the decades he has designed some 1,500 private and public gardens, often in collaboration with some of this century's leading firms of American architects: Skidmore Owings and Merrill, Roche-Dinkeloo, Louis Kahn, Philip Johnson, I.M. Pei and Eero Saarinen. Many of his designs have become twentieth-century landmarks. As Pei says:

> Kiley is the best. He belongs to that tradition of, let's say, the big thinkers in the field. He is not just limited to doing a small house and garden. He also has tremendous scope and breadth in his thinking about landscape. He treats landscape with grand gestures.

Kiley/Pei projects have included Fountain Place, Dallas, Texas, the John F. Kennedy Library, Dorchester, Massachusetts and the East Wing of the National Gallery, Washington DC. At the time of writing Kiley is 86 years old and he is working again with Pei and Mario Bellini on a 3.2-hectare (8-acre) site in Kyoto, Japan. Over the whole site he has designed a grid of 8.5m (28ft) squares of gravel, moss and water across which diagonals of raised, mounded shapes intervene. Seeing the plan at his studio in woods near Charlotte, Vermont, we said that we thought he must have been inspired by an intricate Japanese silk kimono or the *obi* of a court lady from medieval Japan. He laughed and replied that it was a garden and nothing more. But, we think he was interested by the comparison.

Studying the designs of Dan Kiley and other leading classicists, we have been struck by the wonderful congruence or 'fit' between architecture of the International style and the geometry of the ancient formal style and its variations through the history of garden design. As Dan Kiley, America's master landscape architect, says: 'Landscape is not mere adornment but an integral part of the disposition of space, plane, line and structure with which it is associated.'

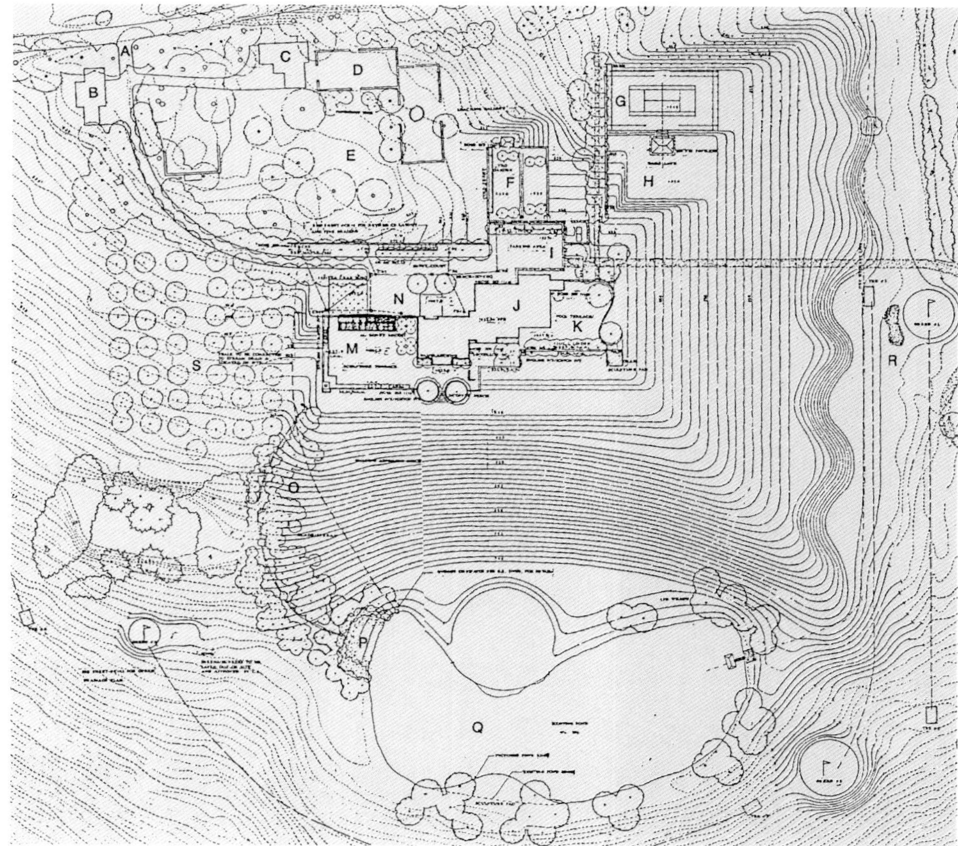

Above *Kiley's master plan, which clearly shows the relationship of the square and rectilinear elements of the house and adjacent gardens to the gentle land contours, lake and wilder elements of the landscape. As Kiley says, 'The challenge was to develop an effective exterior sequence which would respond appropriately to its physical and historical setting.'*

The conical volume is a familiar form in the language of the desert. It becomes a point of reference in the endless procession of horizons. By creating conical volumes that are precise geometrical forms, their origin moves into the realm of the mysterious . . . the moment they are completed, they become an instrument to measure the passage of time.

D.A.ST.

D.A.ST. Art Team: Danae, Alexandra, Stella

Desert Breath, El Ghouna, Egypt

D.A.ST. consists of three artists, Danae Stratou, sculptor, Alexandra Stratou, industrial designer, and Stella Constantinides, architect. The group was formed in the spring of 1995 in order to collaborate on an installation in the desert. They envisioned a site-specific work on such a scale that it could only be fully experienced on foot. It takes 40 minutes to walk around the finished structure.

In June 1995, they went to Egypt in search of a suitable site. They settled upon a large expanse of desert six hours south of Cairo. It lies between the coast of the Red Sea and a ridge called the Eastern Mountains. Here, in an atmosphere of great excitement and enthusiasm, they reached an agreement about the concept for the project, Desert Breath.

When they returned to their homes on the Greek island of Paros, one of the windiest places in the Mediterranean, they spent the rest of the summer testing their concept using sand models and computer-generated sketches. In September their proposal was approved by Mr Samih Sawiris, the president of Orascom, a construction and development company based in Cairo. Sawiris and his enthusiasm proved to be fundamental to the eventual success of the project.

Far right *An aerial view of the site-generated landscape project, Desert Breath, which is located near to the Red Sea in Egypt.*

Until the September of 1996, D.A.ST. worked with architects, engineers, mathematicians and geologists on final detailing. The team returned to the site several times to discuss exact site selection and construction methods.

The construction of Desert Breath began in June 1996 and was complete nine months later. The finished project covers an area of 100,000sq m (320,000sq ft) and has a total diameter of 450m (1,460ft), resulting in the displacement of 8,000 cu m (280,000cu ft) of sand. The two

GARDEN STATISTICS

Client: Mr Samih Sawiris, Orascom Construction PTD, Cairo

Designer: D.A.ST.

Area: 100,000sq m (1,076,426sq ft)

Climate: Desert

Soil type: Sand

Aspect: West

Date of completion: 1997

interlocking, logarithmic spirals consist of 178 cones. They have a single centre with a phase difference of 180 degrees in the same direction of rotation. One spiral is made from 'positive' cones, rising above the desert grade. The other is made from 'negative' cones, which were excavated below the desert grade. The positive cones are formed from the sand which is displaced to make the negative ones. They range in height from 50cm to 4m (20in to 12ft).

The concept of the cone shapes was first inspired by piles of sand spoil which had resulted from road building in the area. D.A.ST. noticed that when the wind-blown sand collected at the feet of desert plants,it created a cone shape around the base. This natural combination of sand and wind inspired the team to create cone shapes themselves. Our interest in site-generated design makes this aspect of the project particularly exciting for us.

The correct compaction of the sand used to construct both the positive and negative cones was crucial. It was achieved through a combination of manual labour and earth-moving equipment. Initially, D.A.ST. thought that the cones could be dug and compacted at random. However, it soon became clear that they had to be worked on as a series. The team give full credit to the skills of their digger driver, Ahmed. His control of the machine was such that he was able to judge the correct depth of each negative cone by eye. In order to make the positive cones it was crucial to calculate the exact angle of deposition. This is the critical point of mass at which the sand falls away, and getting it wrong would ruin the cone shape.

Water is another major element of the design. The lack of water in the desert and a view of the Red Sea inspired the notion of a circular pool. It is a beaten-earth concavity with a diameter of 30m (100ft). The centre of the pool was filled with a giant cone calculated to have only its tip above the finished water level. When the pool is filled to the brim, the protruding cone becomes the central incident of the design and can be read as a small island on the horizon. It is the mathematical starting point of the double spiral cones.

It was crucial to D.A.ST. that all of the elements should be finished at exactly the same time. They wanted the moment of completion to be time zero, before the forces of nature began their inevitable transformation.

Desert Breath represents an important moment for Land Art in the 1990s. As with the projects of the 1960s and 70s, documentation will be crucial. The

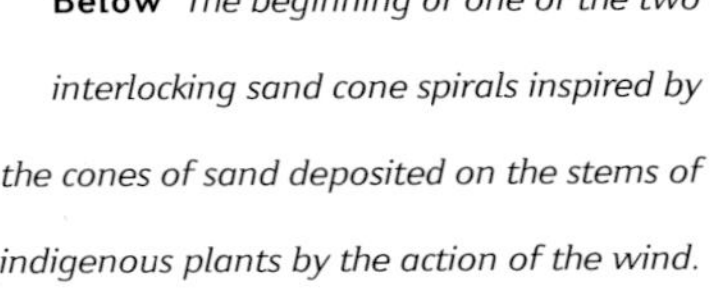

Below *The beginning of one of the two interlocking sand cone spirals inspired by the cones of sand deposited on the stems of indigenous plants by the action of the wind.*

Left *While constructing the double spiral cones, the D.A.ST. team found that the positive and negative cones had to be dug in height and depth sequence: from the largest to the smallest.*

team has returned frequently to the site over the past two years, using videos and photographs to record the gradual changes wrought on Desert Breath, the 'harmonic cohabitation of the precision of human geometry with that of nature.'

The choice of location was vital to the concept of this project. The desolate site meant that D.A.ST.'s 'marks' should remain undisturbed by humankind. They will be 'disturbed', however, by that most pervasive of natural elements of the desert, the wind. The mobility of the sand controlled by the wind will eventually change, if not obliterate, the cones. This is yet another perfect example of the universe's principle of construction and destruction.

Finally, the D.A.ST. Art Team should have the last words on their fantastic land creation:

> The project is rooted in our common desire to work in the desert. The lack of objects in the surrounding area renders one unable to rely on customary means in order to determine scale, space, distance and orientation, so that these acquired senses have to be re-learned based on experience with earth (gravity), sky (motion), light (change), water (level). Simultaneously, one experiences a feeling of isolation and completeness. One can feel time go by yet provide no resistance. The vastness of the horizon becomes the only visual reference to equilibrium.

Below *Walking the spiral pathway. The D.A.ST. Team has documented the inevitable changes to Desert Breath since its construction using photos and videos.*

ONE

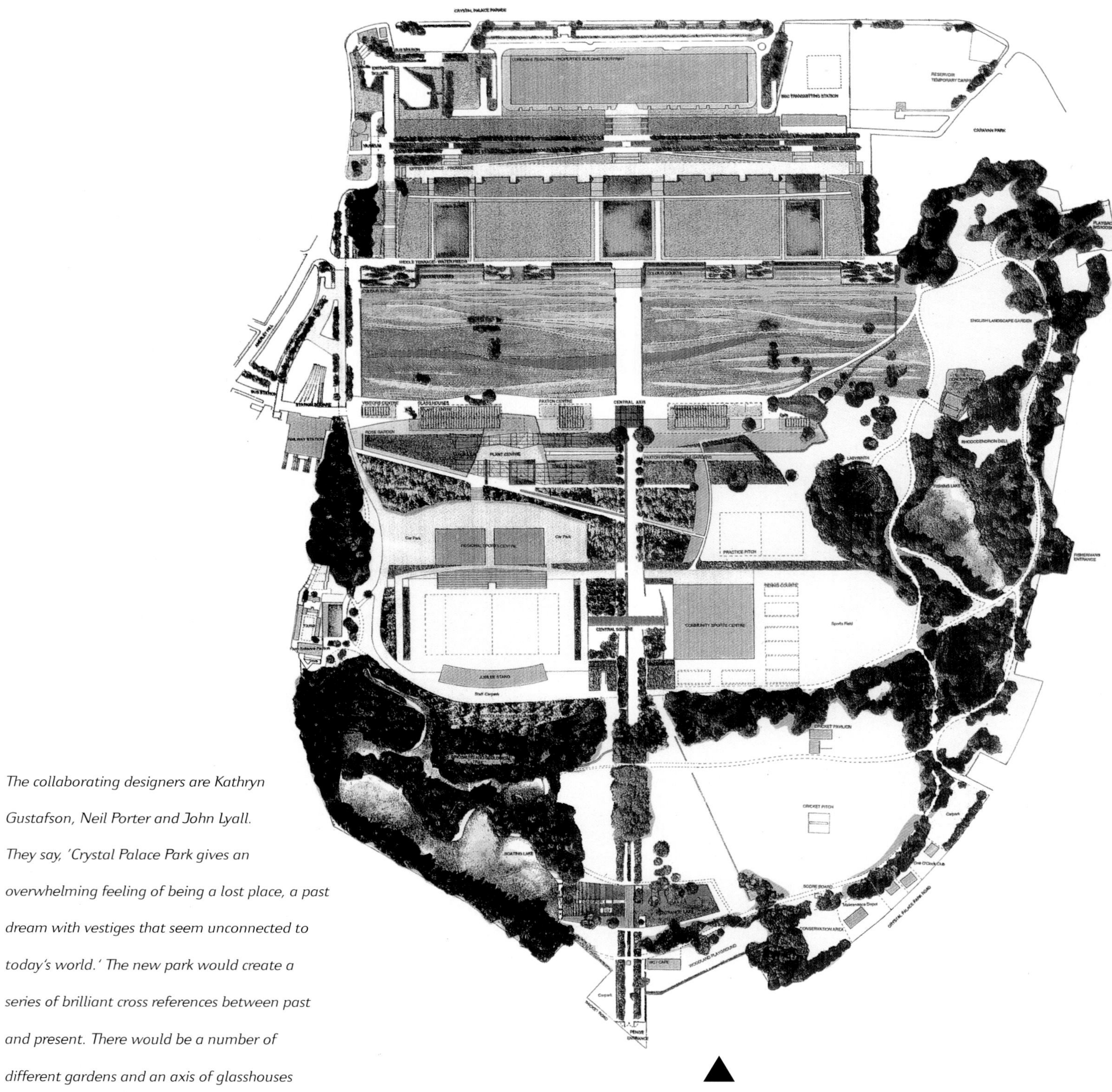

The collaborating designers are Kathryn Gustafson, Neil Porter and John Lyall. They say, 'Crystal Palace Park gives an overwhelming feeling of being a lost place, a past dream with vestiges that seem unconnected to today's world.' The new park would create a series of brilliant cross references between past and present. There would be a number of different gardens and an axis of glasshouses

The New Crystal Palace Park Project London

relating to Joseph Paxton's original terraces. The first phase has received partial funding to cover the restoration element of the project.

Park Detski Moscow, Meshcherjakov & Tolkachev

This was the winning entry for the children's park competition in 1990–1991. It was created by the design team of the late Alexei Mescherjakov and Oleg Tolkachev, trained in the landscape course of Professor Kraskov at the Moscow Architecture Institute. It is one of many theme park projects designed in Russia after Khrushchev's visit to Disneyland, Los Angeles, in 1959. Russian mysticism, historicism and a strong eighteenth-century formal grid are all elements of the design. Most Russian landscape architects present their work as paintings like this, rather than in drawing form.

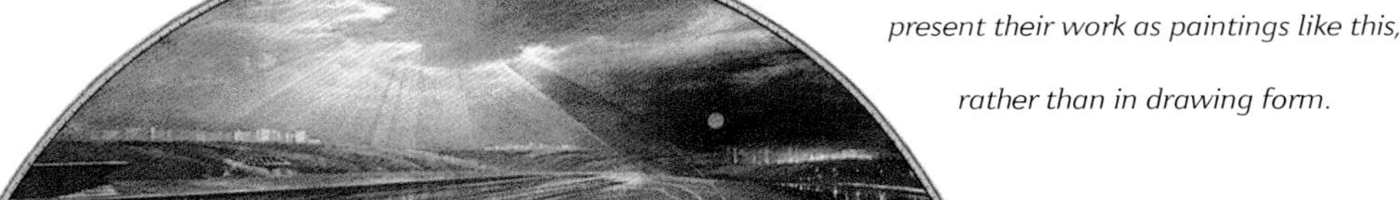

On the former site of the medieval walls of the city and its Friesentor (an important city gate), Foster & Partners, London, has designed

Gerling-Ring Cologne, Desvigne & Dalnoky

a mixed-use project of offices, flats and shops. The landscape improvements, or 'greening', of the five internal open spaces and the tops of the flat roofs have been designed by Desvigne & Dalnoky, Paris. There are large-scale water features in various conformations: pools – including plinths for sculpture – and a large terrace, canals and water walls. There are also areas of dense plantings of azaleas and rhododendrons which will all contrast with the rectilinear architecture.

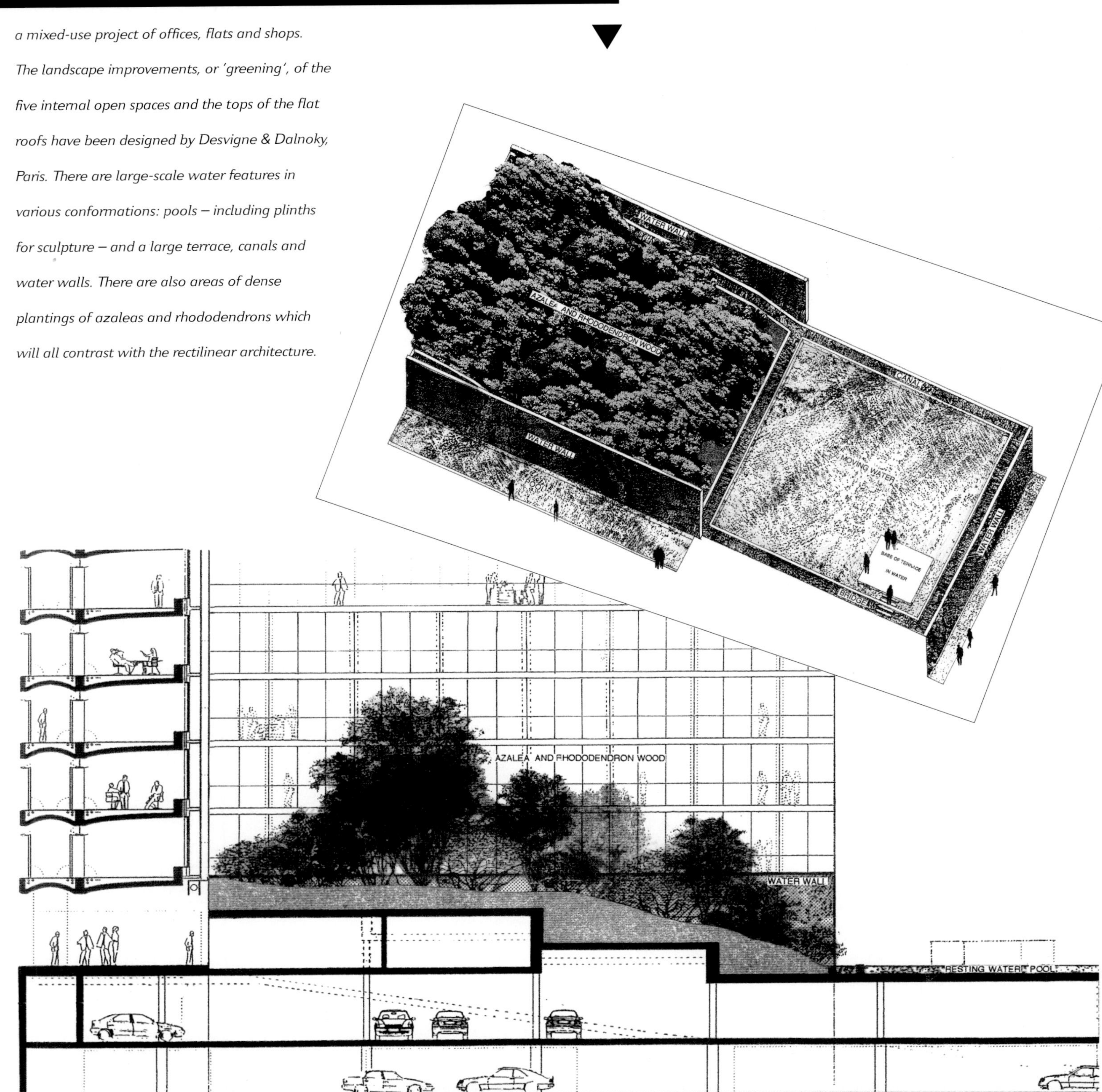

Mid-Kyoto Master Plan, Daniel Urban Kiley

A 3.2-hectare (8-acre) redevelopment in Kyoto, including office, hotel, commercial and cultural complex. The architects involved are I.M. Pei and Mario Bellini. Kiley's master plan, in three layers, is a reinterpretation of Japanese gardens and culture. The primary layer is a 8.1 x 8.1m (25 x 25ft) grid across the site. Two walkway systems follow the grid lines reinforced by lines of moss and ground cover. Between the grid lines are alternating grid panels of grass and clipped azalea, with a ground cover of bulbs and water. The second layer is created by quartets of trees planted in grid panels. The third layer, placed across the grid, is serpentine mounds of moss, azalea and other plantings.

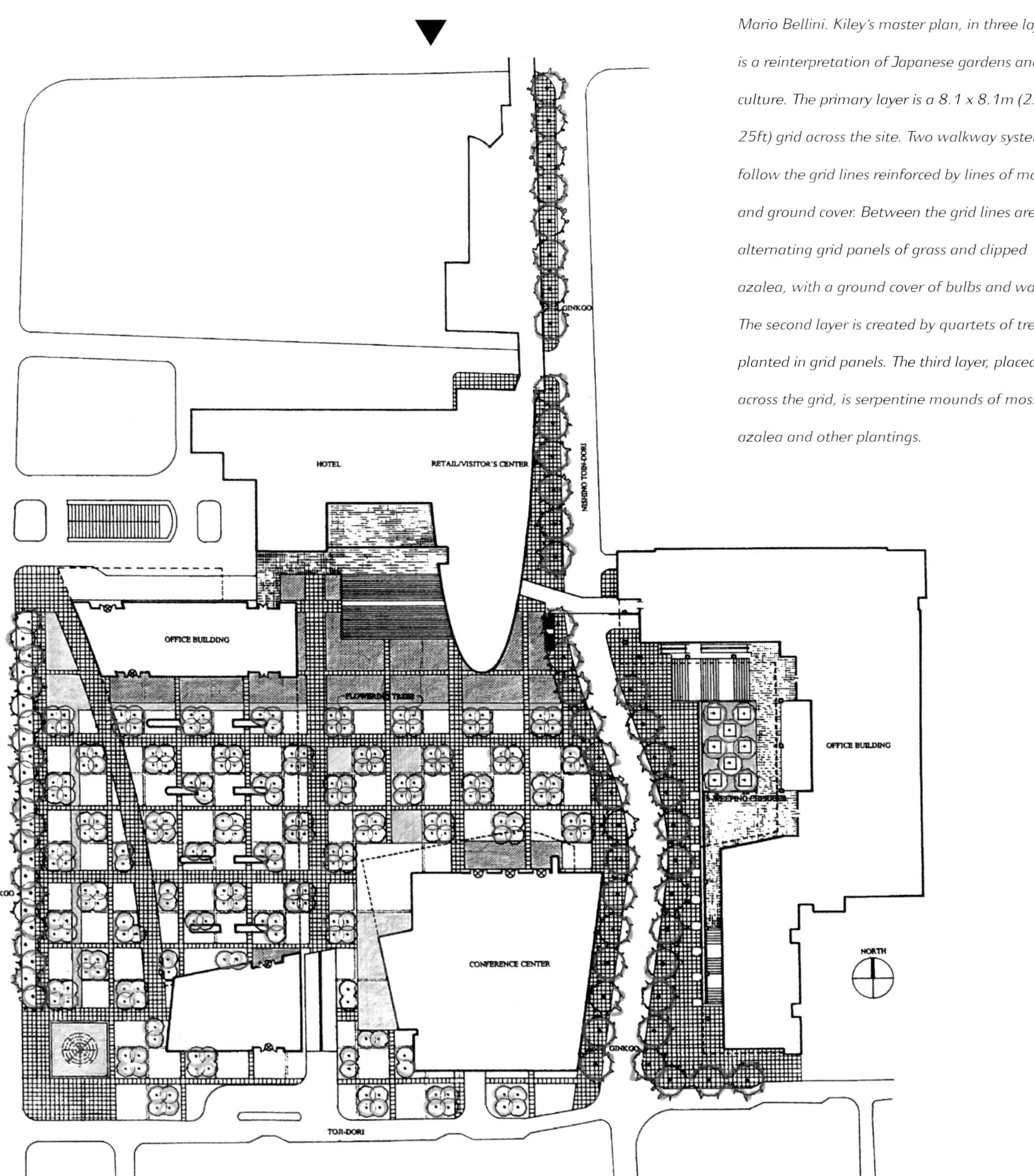

The Trekroner School Copenhagen, Stig L. Andersson

A Danish schools-of-the-future competition was won by Stig L. Andersson, a leading Danish landscape architect. The school is part of a new town project. Andersson's view of the landscape is contextual and flexible. The school yard will be replaced by a school garden. An asphalt basin lake can be emptied for roller blading and skateboarding, artificial rock is provided for climbing and there are areas for flower and vegetable gardens.

Le Meuble Qui Pousse *(The Growing Building) Montpelier, by Edouard François and Associates, winner of Millennium 2000, France, Projects for*

Le Meuble Qui Pousse Montpelier, Edouard Francois & Associates

Architecture. Sited on the River Lez outside Montpelier, Edouard François' building is green and growing. It is in a grove of mature plane trees. The roofless rooms on stilts are among the branches. Gabion stone walls and a second skin of Turkish volcanic stone create soil pockets for growing drought-resistant succulent plants. The entire façade was sprayed with water, pig manure and seeds. This visionary, verdant seven-storey apartment block cost Ff 22million; purchasers queued up to buy.

A public park on the river Nervion, adjacent to the Guggenheim Musem. John Beardsley describes Diana Balmori's work in the following way: '[She]

Abandoibarra Park Bilbao, Balmori Associates

has worked to reveal as many of the natural and cultural layers as possible that are evident in a site, encompassing ecology, history, the demographics of adjacent communities, and the social uses of the landscape. She has made herself attentive to the various possibilities for environmental remediation, from the restoration of derelict urban landscapes to the repair of damaged ecosystems.'

1:00pm Square New York, West 8 and Adriaan Geuze

Adriaan Geuze established his Rotterdam-based office in 1987. The practice is named from the strong wind which sweeps across the Netherlands' polder. The designs are site-generated and contextual. Geuze says 'We love popular culture, we love the dock culture, the technical effects, we love the aesthetics of non-design.' 1:00PM Square is a design for Madison Square in the heart of Manhattan. Giant topiary constructions would humanize this area of the city's grid; instead of lunchtime among a few trees, it would become a 'green village'.

Afterword

A received prevailing attitude in the landscape architecture profession, over the past 20 years or so turns on the view that it is without a sufficient body of critical writings, that it is without models, that it has no focused direction and, finally, that twentieth-century landscape design lacks art.

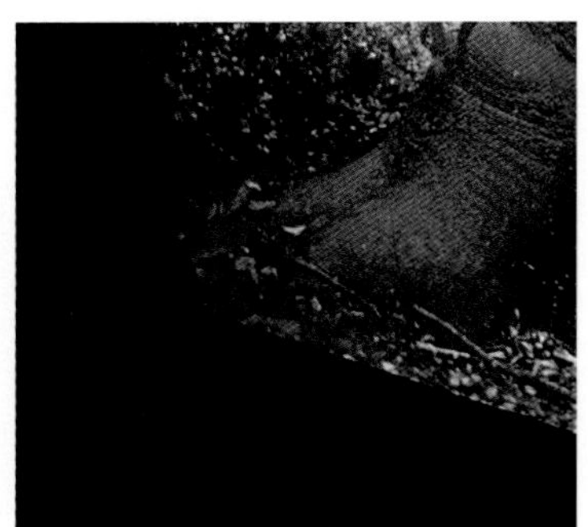

Art in the garden and landscape does *emerge, but not because some landscape designers and architects proclaim self-consciously about art, and question endlessly whether or not theirs or a very few practitioners' work is art. George Hargreaves explains another view:*

> *I dislike the drive towards everything to do with metaphors and art meanings. Well, you know, a row of trees being simply a row of trees, they don't have to represent the essence of life or some grounding in nineteenth-century or twentieth-century thought, they can simply be a row of trees. You can then bring whatever interpretation you want to bring to it, from nothing, to 'I like it', and the row of trees can stand simply as elements. They don't have to be skewed into metaphors, they don't have to have a purpose as, or be in something else, they can simply be themselves, a row of trees; it has taken me 20 years to get to that.*

Some gardens and landscapes can be called art or have fulfilled an aspiration towards art, for they are uniquely expressive, or the projects have solved problems of human activity both usefully and aesthetically within the reality of a site, or perhaps, they just 'are', in some way to enough people, exquisite or beautiful. Maybe, they emerge only from landscape designers who have what Philip Johnson called in a lecture, 'the fire in the belly', that mysterious source of creative energy and vision.

Some garden and landscape designs of the twentieth century do have that vision, we feel, and 'sing' to us. The landscapes we would define as art are: Dan Kiley's Miller Garden, Isamu Noguchi's California Scenario, George Hargreave's Villa Zapu, Charles Jencks' Garden of Cosmic Speculation and Robert Irwin's Lower Central Garden at the Getty Center.

A.A.Gill, one of Britain's most perceptive and controversial critics offered this opinion of contemporary art, when reviewing a recent television series.

> *The trajectory of modern art is plainly all downhill. It is a medium in steady, precipitous decline, running on empty. The conclusion is inescapable; art has painted itself into a box of its own devising, from where it has no vision or talent or the will to find a response to the real world.*

Gill's view could be called extreme, and even blinkered, but we do think the work of the landscape architects and designers shown in this book is evidence of 'a response to the real world', as opposed to some of the accepted leading-edge art of the past 10 years in Britain: a pharmacy cabinet filled with boxes of medicines, a fried egg and sausage on a pine wood table, or a small canvas tent inside of which there are embroidered the many names of the conceptual craftperson's lovers. These were exhibited in the Sensation *exhibition at the Royal Academy, London, 1998.*

Is contemporary art really without models and focus, other than those approved by the mutually self-interested group of curators, collectors, dealers and critics, all of whom need, in some way, to find and promote ever newer products for their consumers. As opposed to another accepted view which many landscape

architects and designers hold about their work, namely, that it is always following other major design, art and cultural activities, we think there are signs that quite the opposite is happening.

In fact, it seems that over the past 20 years, landscape and garden design has been, in certain aspects of thinking and practice, leading, not following the other arts, in this difficult and complicated cultural assessment. Landscape and garden design appear now to have more direction and focus than current contemporary art. Designs for the landscape embody a connectedness, being concerned with an actuality, the land we walk on, where we live, work and play, all materialized through a responsiveness to the real world.

Several of the Case Studies, along with some of the Future Designs in the final section, are inspired by the philosophy of the site-generated or contextual. This approach is the advance in the late twentieth century on all of the past, for these designs can reflect directly the context of our lives within contemporary culture.

Tree Lung of the Earth *by the D.A.S.T. Art Team. The viewer walks into a large dark room. There is the scent of earth-covered floor and moist air. Unifying elements are the sounds: forest mixed with a breathing accentuated by a single drop on an amplified drum. In the centre is a large cubical volume: 6 x 6 x 3 m-high walls on which are projected video images shot in real time over one day and projected in real time. Sun filtering through tree and plant movement creates a suspension of time.Landscape into art? Art into landscape?.*

Index

Page numbers in italics refer to illustrations.

Bibliography

Abington Art Center Sculpture Garden, *Winifred Lutz, A Reclamation Garden 1992-1993. Winifred Lutz, A Reclamation Garden 1993-1995.* USA: Abington Art Center Publication, 1996.

Abington Art Center, *'The Garden Matrix'.* USA: Abington Art Center Publication, 1996. (Program to support the creation and installation for outdoor sculpture.)

Adams, William Howard, *Denatured Visions: Landscape and Culture in the Twentieth Century.* Museum of Modern Art, 1991

Adams, William Howard, *Roberto Burle Marx, The Unnatural Art of the Garden.* USA: Museum of Modern Art, 1991.

Anderton, Frances, 'Avant-Gardens'. U.S.A: *Architectural Review,* September, 1989. (Peter Walker and Martha Schwartz)

Arriola, Andreu, Adriaan Geuze, Steen Hoyer, Bernard Huet, Peter Latz, David Louwerse, Norfried Pohl, and Clemens Steenbergen, *Modern Park Design, Recent Trends.* Holland: Thoth Publishers, 1995 (Second Edition).

Atkins, Robert, *Art Speak.* USA: Abbeville Press, 1990.

Atkins, Robert, *Art Spoke.* USA: Abbeville Press, 1993.

Baljon, Lodewijk, *Designing Parks.* UK: Garden Art Press, 1992.

Barnett, Rod, 'Rod Barnett Examines a Contemporary Landscape and the Politics of Place'. (Quay Park, Ted Smyth design). New Zealand: *Landscape New Zealand,* Nov/Dec 1997.

Beardsley, John, *Earthworks and Beyond. Contemporary Art in the Landscape.* USA: Abbeville Press, 1998 (Third Edition).

Beardsley, John, 'Making Waves'. USA: *Landscape Architecture,* March 1998. (Charles Jencks's Garden)

Begley, Adam, 'Secret Garden'. USA: *Connoisseur,* April 1991. (Millbrook Garden)

Bennett, Paul, 'Big Ideas Down Under'. USA: *Landscape Architecture,* February, 1999. (George Hargreaves' Olympic Park in Sydney).

Brand, Jan, Catelijne de Muynck and Jouke Kleerebezem. *Allocations: Art for a Natural and Artificial Environment.* The Hague-Zoetermeer, Holland: Floriade Foundation, 1992.

Caploe, David, 'The Pros and Cons of Miami Style'. USA: *New Miami,* July 1990. (Raymond Jungles and Debra Lynn Yates).

Celan, Paul, *Selected Poems.* USA: Penguin Books,1996.

Cerver, Francisco Asensio, *World of Environmental Design: Landscape Art.* Barcelona: Arco,1995.

Cerver, Francisco Asensio, *World of Environmental Design: Landscape of Recreation II (Amusement Parks)* Barcelona: Arco, 1994.

Compton, Tania, 'Gardening a la Mode'. UK: *House & Garden,* April 1998. (Chanel Garden at Chelsea Flower Show).

Corbett, Sue, 'Large but Perfectly Formed'. UK: *Country Life,* January 28, 1999. (Modern sculptors working in gardens).

D.A.ST. Art Team, *Desert Breath.* Athens, Greece: D.A.ST. Art Team, 1997.

Deitz, Paula, 'Fearless Gardening'. USA: *House Beautiful,* May, 1995. (LongHouse, Jack Lenor Larsen).

Deitz, Paula, 'Recultivating the Tuileries'. USA: *Design Quarterly,* Spring, 1992. (Jacques Wirtz and Peter Wirtz).

Domaine de Kerguehennec, Catalogue of Site Specific Sculpture Collection. Brittany, France.

Don, Montagu, 'Chanel's Natural Look'. UK: *Observer Life,* (Chanel's Chelsea Flower Show Garden). May 31, 1998.

Ducas, Jane, 'Come into the Garden, Karl'. (Chanel Chelsea Flower Show Garden). UK: *Saturday Telegraph Magazine, May 23, 1998.*

Eckbo, Garrett, 'Is Landscape Architecture?'. USA: *Landscape Architecture,* May 1983.

Eckbo, Garrett, 'Garrett Eckbo: Philosophy of Landscape'. Tokyo, Japan: *Process: Architecture, No. 90,*1990.

Edwards, J.G., 'The Constancy of Change'. Japan: *Mainichi Daily News,* December 10, 1987. (Arata Isosaki).

Edwards, Lawrence, *The Vortex of Life.* UK: Floris Books, 1993.

Elle Decoration, 'Le Monde Etrange de Monsieur Jencks'. France: *Elle Decoration,* No.58, October 1995. (The lifestyle of Charles Jencks).

Emmet, Alan, 'How Green is His Valley'. USA: *House & Garden,* March, 1999. (Robert Irwin Design of Lower Central Garden at Getty Centre, Los Angeles).

Evans, Barrie, 'The Well-Tempered Environment'. UK: *The Architects' Journal,* July 27, 1994. (Ian Ritchie Architects' design for a park building in the Dordogne).

Everdell, William R, *The First Moderns.* USA: The University of Chicago Press, 1997.

Filler, Martin, 'The Recent Work of Arata Isozaki: Part I'. USA: *Architectural Record,* October 1983. (Business Design Engineering, a McGraw-Hill Publication).

Finch, Paul, 'Combining Artifice and Nature in the Dordogne'. UK: *The Architects' Journal,* November 9, 1995. (Ian Ritchie's design for a park building in the Dordogne).

Flanagan, Barbara, 'A Healing Place in the Sun'. USA: *The New York Times,* January 15, 1998. (Topher Delaney).

Futagawa, Yoshio, *Bernard Tschumi. GA Document Extra 10.* Japan: A.D.A. EDITA, Tokyo, 1997.

Gerlach-Spriggs, Nancy, Richard Enoch Kaufman and Sam Bass Warner, Jr., *Restorative Gardens: The Healing Landscape.* New Haven & London: Yale University Press, 1998.

Gill, A.A., 'Corset Makes Sense'. UK: *The Sunday Times, (Culture),* June 13, 1999. (TV Programme Review: 'What is Modern Art?').

Gillette, Jane Brown, 'Kiley Revisited'. USA: *Landscape Architecture,* August, 1998.

Gillette, Jane Brown, 'Pure Design, Pure Image'. USA: *Landscape Architecture,* October, 1998. (The Dayton Garden designed by George Hargreaves).

Glancey, Jonathan, 'The Hole in the Heart'. UK: *The Guardian,* January 27, 1999. (Daniel Libeskind's Jewish Museum, Berlin).

Goldsworthy, Andy, *Touching North.* UK: Fabian Carlsson, Graeme Murray, 1989.

Goldsworthy, Andy, *Stone.* UK: Viking, 1994.

Goodwin, Stephen, 'Garden Grows in Fertile Soil of Science and the Senses'. UK: *The Independent,* November 17, 1997. (Charles Jencks's garden).

Grant, Bill and Paul Harris (editors), *Natural Order. Visual Arts & Crafts in Grizedale Forest Park.* UK: The Grizedale Society, 1996.

Greenberg, Stephen, 'Libeskindbau Leads Where Other Museums Should Follow'. UK: *The Architect's Journal,* February 28, 1999. (New Jewish Museum in Berlin).

Griswold, Mac, 'A History of the Sanctuary Garden'. USA: *Design Quarterly 169,* Summer 1996.

Griswold, Mac, 'Brooding Forest As Artist's Medium'. USA: *The New York Times,* November 20, 1997. (Reclamation Garden at Abington Art Center).

Griswold, Mac, 'The Therapeutic Garden'. USA: *Landscape Architecture,* 1996. (Healing Garden at Wellesley, MA.).

Hammerslough, Jane, 'The Children's Garden' USA: *Garden Design,* June/July, 1997. (Healing Garden at Wellesley, MA.)

Heizer, Michael, *Germano Celant.* Italy: Fondazione Prada, 1997.

Hirsch, Jeffrey, *Seeing the Getty Gardens.* 1998. (Getty Centre, Los Angeles).

Hoffman, E. T. A., *The Life and Opinions of the Tomcat Murr.* UK: Penguin Books, 1999. (Hoffman Anthology)

Holden, Robert, *International Landscape Design.* UK: Laurence King Publishing, 1996.

Hortus Third: A Concise Dictionary of Plants Cultivated in the United States and Canada. USA: Macmillan Publishing, 1976

Hughes, Robert, *The Shock of the New.* UK: Thames and Hudson, 1991.

The Hutchinson Encyclopedia (New 8th Edition). UK: Century Hutchinson Ltd, 1988.

Imbert, Dorothee, *The Modernist Garden in France.* USA: Yale University Press, 1993.

International Kunstcentrum deSingel, *The Landscape, Four International Landscape Designers (Hargreaves Associates, Desvigne & Dalnoky, West 8 Landscape Architects, Torres & Lapeña).* (Museum Catalogue). Holland: deSingel, 1995.

Iovine, Julie V, 'Sermon on the Mound' USA: *The New York Times Magazine,* February 4, 1996. (Charles Jencks's Garden).

Iovine, Julie V, 'Fountain Fantasies, From Cascades to Curbs'. USA: *The New York Times,* June 11, 1998. (Dan Kiley and Water Features).

Irwin, Robert, *Retrospective Exhibition: 1993.* Catalogue. Museum of Contemporary Art, Los Angeles & Rizzoli International Publications, New York, 1993.

Jaffe, Matthew, 'Acropolis Now'. US: *Sunset,* January 1998. (The $1-billion Getty Center).

Jellicoe, Geoffrey and Susan, Patrick Goode and Michael Lancaster, *The Oxford Companion to Gardens.* UK: Oxford University Press, 1986.

Jencks, Charles, 'New Science – New Architecture'. Japan: *A+U,* June 1995. (Charles Jencks's Philosophy).

Johnson, Jory, 'Martha Schwartz's 'Splice Garden': A Warning to a Brave New World'. USA: *Landscape Architecture,* August 7, 1988.

Karson, Robin, 'Conversation with Kiley' USA: *Landscape Architecture,* December, 1988.

Karson, Robin, *Fletcher Steele, Landscape Architect, an account of a garden maker's life.* USA: Abrams, 1989.

Kaster, Jeffrey, and Brian Wallis, *Land and Environmental Art.* UK: Phaidon, 1998.

Kaufman, Ann, 'A New Expression of Japan Emerges Through a Collection of Western Themes'. (Isosaki's Civic Centre in Tsukuba). Japan: *Far Eastern Economic Review,* May 31, 1984.

Kearton, Diane, (Editor), *Art & the Garden.* UK: Academy Group Ltd., 1997.

Dan Kiley: Landscape Design II – in Step with Nature. Process: Architecture, No. 108. Japan: 1993.

Kiley, Dan and Jane Amidon, *Dan Kiley in His Own Words.* UK: Thames & Hudson, 1999.

Kindt, Sven and Eric Messerschmidt, *The Danish Wave.* Exhibition Catalogue. Copenhagen: The Danish Center for Architecture, 1998.

Klein, Marjorie, 'Fahkahatchee Kid'. USA: *Home & Garden,* February 1988. (Visualist Raymond Jungles designs a sub-tropical dream).

Lacey, Stephen, Article on the Ton ter Linden garden- Holland. UK: *Daily Telegraph,* July 13, 1996.

Lacey, Stephen, 'How Wirtz Proved to Be the Best'. UK: *Weekend Telegraph,* June 6, 1992.

Landecker, Heidi, (Editor), *Martha Schwartz: Transfiguration of the Commonplace.* USA: Spacemaker Press, 1997.

Lane Fox, Robin, 'Weather Puts the Heat on Chelsea'. UK: *Financial Times, Weekend May 23/24, 1998* (Chelsea Flower Show).

Larsen, Jack Lenor, *A Weaver's Memoir.* USA: Harry N Abrams, Inc., 1998.

Leccese, Michael, 'Nature meets Nurture'. USA: *Landscape Architecture.* January 1995.

Leviseur, Elsa, 'Hargreaves Weaves'. USA: *The Architectural Review.*

Levy, Leah, *Kathryn Gustafson, Sculpting the Land.* USA: Spacemaker Press, 1998.

Libeskind, Daniel and Helene Binet, *Jewish Museum, Berlin.* Germany: G + B Arts International, 1999.

Lloyd, Christopher, 'In My Garden'. UK: *Country Life*, December 18/25, 1997. (Charles Jencks's garden).

Logan, William Bryant. 'Making the Stones Dance'.USA: *Garden Design*, December 1994/January 1995. (Innisfree Garden).

Lowry, Suzanne, 'The Unknown Garden Guru'. (Gardens Created by Jacques Wirtz). UK: *Telegraph Magazine*, February 4, 1995.

Lund, Annemarie, *Abstract & Book for 36th World Congress of the International Federation of Landscape Architects*. Copenhagen: Danish Architectural Press, June 1999.

Lund, Annemarie, *A Guide to Danish Landscape Architecture: 1000 –1996*. Copenhagen: Arkitektens Forlag, 1997.

Mariage, Thierry, *The World of André Le Nôtre*. USA: University of Pennsylvania Press, 1990.

Marton, Deborah, 'History Moved Forward'. USA: *Landscape Architecture*, January, 1999. (Gantry Plaza, designed by Thomas Balsley).

McCormick, Kathleen, 'Realm of the Senses'. USA: *Landscape Architecture*, January 1995.

Melloan, Joan, 'A Belgian Shows the French How It's Done'. UK: *The Bulletin*, August 8, 1991. (Jacques Wirtz's Work at The Tuilieries).

Merser, Cheryl, 'Lake Water Lapping'. USA: *Preservation*, November/December 1997. (Innisfree Garden).

McGeorge, Pamela, 'An Artist as Landscaper'. New Zealand: *NZ Gardener*, May 1998. (Ted Smyth).

Miyake, Riichie, 'The Afterimage of Ruins'. Tokyo: *The Japan Architect, No.* 8703. (Arata Isosaki).

Muschamp, Herbert, 'Where Iron Gives Way to Beauty and Games'. USA: *The New York Times*, December 13, 1998. (Gantry Plaza State Park, designed by Thomas Balsley).

New Eden: The Contemporary Gardens Magazine. UK: May/June 1999.

Needleman, Deborah, 'Shadow and Act'. USA: *House and Garden*, March 1999. (Dan Kiley Garden in Connecticut).

Needleman, Deborah, 'Recycled Memories'. USA: *House & Garden*, March 1999. (Andrew Cao's Garden).

Owen, Jane, 'Unearthing the Seeds of Chaos Theory'. (Charles Jencks's Garden) UK: *The Times Weekend*, Saturday December 6, 1997.

Owen, Jane, 'Twists and Turns'. (Charles Jencks's Garden). UK: *The Garden*, May 1998.

P/A Profile, 'Peter Walker and Martha Schwartz'. USA: *Progressive Architecture*, July, 1989.

P/A Profile, 'Hargreaves Associates'. USA: *Progressive Architecture*, July, 1989.

Papier, Deborah, 'Avant Gardeners'. USA: *Avenue*, June/July, 1990. (Revolution in landscape design and the Avant-gardeners).

Pearson, Dan, 'The Healing Garden'. UK: *Gardens Illustrated*, August/September, 1998. (San Diego Children's Hospital Healing Garden, designed by Topher Delaney).

Pelle, Marie-Paule, 'Zen a Madrid'. Paris: *Vogue Decoration*, Edition Internationale No.10, May 1987. (Fernando Caruncho Garden).

Pegg, John, 'Martha Schwartz: Learning to Build Big Art'. UK: *Landscape Design Extra*, March, 1998.

Perlman, Heidi B, 'When Helping Children, Therapist Says Nature is the Key', *Townsman*, USA: Wellesley, MA., 1996

Pigeat, Jean-Paul, 'Les Jardins du Philosophie'. France: *Vogue Decoration*, Paris: Edition Internationale No.38, June/July 1992. (Fernando Caruncho Gardens).

Pigeat, Jean-Paul, *Festival de Jardins*. France: Editions du Chene – Hachette Livre, 1995.

Pollak, Sally, 'The Natural'. USA: *The Burlington Free Press*, Sunday, November 30, 1997. (Daniel Urban Kiley).

Popham, Peter, 'Teaching the Japanese to Relax'. UK: *Blueprint*, May, 1988. (Interview with Arata Isosaki).

Popham, Peter, 'Dreams of Rome'. Japan: *Mainichi Daily News*, July 18, 1983. (Tsukuba 'New Town').

Powers, Alan, 'Figures in the Garden'. UK: *Country Life*, January 14, 1999. (Modern Art in Public Parks).

Randall-Page, Peter. *Boulders and Banners*. UK: Exhibition Catalogue, Reed's Wharf Gallery, London SE 1, London: 1995.

Raver, Anne, 'In Mystical Innisfree'. USA: *The New York Times*, September 1, 1994.

Raver, Anne, 'When Hope Falters, Balm for the Soul'. USA: *The New York Times*, December 29, 1994. (Healing Gardens).

Read, Emily, 'Green Peace'. USA: *American Vogue*, August, 1997. (Fernando Caruncho Gardens).

Reed, Douglas P, 'The Therapeutic Garden: An Environment of Sensory and Symbolic Experiences'. USA: *Art New England*, August/September, 1995.

Richardson, Martin, 'A Sense of Hard Reality in an Empty Landscape'. UK: *The Architects' Journal*, November 9, 1995. (Rotterdam Practice, West 8).

Richardson, Tim, 'Editor's Manifesto'. *New Eden, The Contemporary Garden Magazine*, UK: May/June 1999.

Richardson, Tim, 'How to Garden in a Jumping Universe'. UK: *Country Life*, October 23, 1997. (Charles Jencks's Garden).

Rodriguez, Alicia, 'Celestial Connections'. USA: *Landscape Architecture*, April 1998. (Rios Associates' Design at Satellite Garden, Long Beach).

Rodriguez, Sol, 'Paisajes y Piscinas'. Spain: *Casa & Estilo*, Ano II, No.8.

Schama, Simon, *Landscape and Memory*. USA: Knopf & Co., 1995. (Raymond Jungles and Debra Yates).

Schneider, Bernard, *Daniel Libeskind Jewish Museum Berlin, Between the Lines*. Germany: Prestel Verlag, 1999.

Scully, Vincent, *Architecture the Natural and the Manmade*. USA: St Martin's Press, 1991.

Shields, Hatsy, 'Artfully Tropical'. USA: *House Beautiful*, February, 1997. (Raymond Jungles and Debra Yates).

Shopland, Alice, 'Downtown Space Place'. New Zealand: *NZ Herald*, December 3, 1997. (Ted Smyth's Quay Park Design).

Shrady, Nicholas, 'Landscapes in Spain'. USA: *Architectural Digest*, March 1998. (Fernando Caruncho Design at Mas de les Voltes).

Sitwell, Sacheverell, Osbert Sitwell, Sir George Sitwell, and Reresby Sitwell, *Hortus Sitwellianus*. USA: Michael Russell (Publishing), 1984.

Smithson, Robert, *The Collected Writings*. (Editor: Jack Flan). Berkeley & Los Angeles: University of California Press,1996.

Spens, Michael, 'Berlin Phoenix'. UK: *Architectural Review*. February, 1999. (Daniel Libeskind Jewish Museum in Berlin).

Spens, Michael, *Landscape Transformed*. UK: Academy Editions, 1996.

Spirn, Anne Whiston, *The Language of Landscape*. USA: Yale University Press, 1998.

Steadman, Todd A, 'Touch of Burle Marx'. USA: *Landscape Architecture*, October, 1992. (Raymond Jungles' garden in Coconut Grove).

Stevens, Margaret, 'Life in Fast-Forward Reverse'. USA: *Landscape Architecture*, January 1995.

Stewart, Ian, *Life's Other Secret*. UK: Allen Lane, The Penguin Press, 1998.

Stichting Rotterdam-Maaskant Foundation, *Adriaan Geuze/West 8*. Holland: 1995.

Stocker, Carol, 'Journey into the Spirit'. USA: *The Boston Globe*, October 10, 1996. (Innisfree).

Strong, Sir Roy and Julia Trevelyan Oman, *A Celebration of Gardens*. UK: HarperCollins, 1991.

Stuart-Smith, Tom, 'Le Bosquet de Chanel: Camellias at the Chelsea Flower Show'. UK: *International Camellia Journal*. No. 30, 1998.

Stungo, Naomi, 'Germany Recalling'. UK: *The Observer Review*, January 24, 1999. (Daniel Libeskind's New Jewish Museum).

Swaffield, Simon, 'A Thoroughly Modern Man'. USA: *Harvard Design Magazine*, Summer, 1998. (Ted Smyth).

Taylor, Patrick, 'Visions of a Flemish Master'. UK: *The Sunday Telegraph Magazine*, November 15, 1998. (Jacques Wirtz).

Taylor, Patrick, 'Good in Beds'. UK: *The World of Interiors*, April 1993. (Ton ter Linden).

Thacker, Christopher, *The History of Gardens*. UK: Croom Helm Ltd. Publishers, 1979.

Thomas, R.S., *Selected Poems: 1946-68*. UK: Bloodaxe Publishing, 1992.

Thompson, D'Arcy, *On Growth and Form*. UK: Cambridge University Press, 1961.

Thompson, Elspeth, 'High Society'. UK: *The Times Magazine*, August 22, 1998. (Tom Stuart-Smith, Garden Designer).

Tilberghien, Gilles A., *Land Art*. USA: Princeton Architectural Press, 1993.

Treib, Marc, 'Fragments on a Void, Tsukuba Center'. USA: *Landscape Architecture*, July/August, 1985. (Plaza designed by Arata Isosaki).

Treib, Marc, *Modern Landscape Architecture: A Critical Review*. USA: The MIT Press, 1998 (third printing).

Treib, Marc and Dorothee Imbert, *Garrett Eckbo: Modern Landscapes for Living*, Berkeley, Los Angeles & London: University of California Press, 1997.

Uide, A., 'Greenhouse Effect'.UK: *The Architectural Review*, May, 1998. (Greenhouse and park, Terrasson - Lavilledieu, Dordogne).

van de Kaa, Romke, 'Floating on Air'. UK: *The Garden Illustrated*, Oct/Nov, 1995. (Ton ter Linden's Impressionistic Dutch Garden).

Walker, Peter, *Minimalist Gardens*. USA: Spacemaker Press, 1997.

Watson, James, 'Color Celebration'. USA: *Florida Home and Garden*, April, 1989. (Raymond Jungles, Tropical Garden Rooms).

Way, David, and Hanne Cannegieter, 'The Art of Gardening'. UK: *The Garden*, August 1995. (Ton ter Linden).

Webb, Michael and Francisco Ascenso Cerver, *Redesigning City Squares and Plazas*. USA: Hearst Books International for Arco (Spain), 1997.

Weilacher, Udo, *Between Landscape Architecture and Land Art*. Germany: Birkhauser, 1996.

Weschler, Lawrence, 'When Fountainheads Collide'. USA: *The New Yorker*, December 3, 1997. (Robert Irwin and Richard Meier tangle over the Getty Center's Garden).

Whitney Library of Design, *Desvigne & Dalnoky*. USA: Watson-Guptill Publications, 1997.

Wilson, Karen C., 'Plenty of Merit' USA: *San Diego Union-Tribune*, November 16, 1997. (Douglas Reed Therapeutic Garden, Wellesley, MA.).

Wortz, Melinda, 'Robert Irwin: Aesthetic of Context'. USA: *Artforum*, November 1981.

Yoos, Jennifer, 'Conversation with Vincent James, George Hargreaves and James Carpenter'. (Dayton Residence). Japan: *Architecture and Urbanism, (A&U)*, December, 1998.

Picture acknowledgments

The publisher would like to thank the following photographers, landscape architects and organisations for their kind permission to reproduce the photographs in this book.

1 Supplied by Robert Irwin (Designer: Robert Irwin)
2–3 Designer: Thomas Balsley
4 *above* Leigh Clapp (Designer: Steve Martino); *below* Marianne Majerus (Designer: Jacques Wirtz)
5 *above* Nicola Browne (Designer: Martha Schwartz); *below* Richard Felber (Designer: Steve Martino)
8–9 *above* Marianne Majerus (Designer: Jacques Wirtz); *below* Designer: Robert Irwin
10–11 Curtice Taylor (Designer: Fletcher Steele)
12–13 Pepijn Langedijk (Designer: Huub Kortekaas) © DACS 2000
14 Mise au Point/Noun (MetB Zuburchen, Henz, S Nedir, V. Schmoker, Willi)
14–15 J C Mayer - G Le Scanff (Designers: Claire Gardet & Philippe Nigro)
16 Nicola Browne (Designer: Steve Martino)
16–17 Nicola Browne (Designer: Andrew Cao)
18 Nicola Browne (Designer: Isamu Noguchi)
19 Tim Street-Porter (Designer: Luis Barragan)
20–21 E.T Archive/Nicolas Sapieha (Designer: Gianfranco Brignone)
22 *below left* T. Delaney, Inc
22–23 Nicola Browne (Designer: Steve Martino)
23 *below* Harpur Garden Library (Designer: Topher Delaney)
24–25 Nicola Browne (Designer: Martha Schwartz)
25 Nicola Browne (Designer: Steve Martino)
26 *above* Deidi von Schaewen (Designer: Vendeuvre)
26–27 photograph courtesy of the estate of Robert Smithson © VAGA, New York/DACS, London 2000
27 *right* Makoto Sei Watanabe/ Architects Office
28–29 Marianne Majerus (Designer: Paul Cooper)
30 left Undine Prohl (Designer: Philippe Stark);
30–31 Nicola Browne (Designer: Martha Schwartz)
32 Deidi von Schaewen (Designer: Tschumi)
32–33 Hargreaves Associates
34 Jeroen Musch (Designers: West 8 Landscape Architects and Urban Planners)
34–35 Courtesy of Martha Schwartz, Inc
36 *left* Michael Latz
36–37 Sven Ingvar Andersson
38–39 Richard Felber (Designer: Steve Martino)
39 T. Delaney, Inc
40 *left* Richard Felber
40–41 Marijke Heuff (Designer: Mien Ruys, Holland)
41 *right* L. Toussaint (Designer: Fernando Caruncho)
42–43 *above* Marianne Majerus (Designer: Paul Cooper)
42–43 *below* Helen Fickling/The Interior Archive (Designer: Patrick Watson)
43 *right* Erica Lennard (Designer: Hiroshi Teshigahara)
44–45 T. Delaney, Inc
46–47 Nicola Browne (Designer: Dan Pearson)
48 Nicola Browne (Designer: Topher Delaney)
49 supplied by T. Delaney, Inc
50–51 Andreas Sterzing
52 Ron Sutherland/The Garden Picture Library(Designer: Anthony Paul)
53 Peter Bodhynek (Designers: Latz + Partners)
54 Andrew Lawson (Designer: Arabella Lennox-Boyd)
55 *above* Robert Irwin
55 *below* Nicola Browne (Designer: Steve Martino)
56 Marianne Majerus (Designer: Stephen Woodham)
56–57 Claire de Virieu (Designer: Kathryn Gustafson)
58 Derek Fell (Designer: Roberto Burle Marx)
58–59 Piet Oudolf
60 Deidi von Schaewen (Designer: Patrick Genty)
60–61 Marianne Majerus(Designer: Jacques Wirtz)
62–63 Deidi von Schaewen (Designer: Pasal Cribier)
63 Tim Harvey (Designer: Martha Schwartz)
64–65 Courtesy of Beverly Pepper
66 *above* Pierre Vivant
66 *below* Jaques Dirand/INSIDE (Designer: Tori Winkler)
66–67 Pierre Vivant
68 Alan Ward (Designer: Martha Schwartz)
68–69 J C Mayer - G Le Scanff (Designers: Liliana Motta & Jean-Christophe Denise)
69 J C Mayer - G Le Scanff (Designer: Eric Ossart)
70 *left* Deidi von Schaewen (Designer: Rosenberg)
70–71 Nicola Browne (Designer: Andrew Cao)
72 *left* Hargreaves Associates
72–73 Gil Hanly (Designer: Ted Smyth)
74 Jose Antonio Martinez Lapeña : Eliaz Torres Tur
75 Harpur Garden Library (Designer: Topher Delaney)
76 Bill Wood/UM Photo Services (Designer: Maya Lin)
76–77 Claire de Virieu (Designer: Kathryn Gustafson)
78–79 James Pierce (Pratt Farm, Clinton, Maine)
80–81 Curtice Taylor (Designer: Tom Stuart–Smith)
82–83 Mise au Point (Designers: Judy & David Drew)
84–85 Hargreaves Associates
86 *above* J C Mayer - G Le Scanff (Designer: Eric Ossart); *below* James Pierce
86–87 David Walker (Designers: Peter Walker and Partners (1995)
88 Bart van Leuven (Designer: Jan Joris)
88–89 Supplied by Martha Schwartz, Inc
89 Christine O'Loughlin
90 *left* T. Sato/Balmori Associates,Inc
90–91 Shigeo Anzai (Architect: Arata Isosaki; Sculptor: Aiko Miyawaki)
92 *left* Clive Nichols (Sculptor: Thomas Nordstrom & Annika Oskarsson/Designer: Julie Toll
92–93 J C Mayer - G Le Scanff (Designer: Kathryn Gustafson)
93 J C Mayer - G Le Scanff (Designers: Michele Elsair/Jean-Pierre Delettre)
94 Nicola Browne (Designer: Faith Oquma)
94–95 Gary Rogers (Artist: Tage Andersen)
96 Artist: Anne Jones
96–97 Tiziano Canu (Sculptor: Mauro Staccioli)
98 *above* W. Volz/Bilderberg Archiv der Fotografen/Network (Christo and Jean Claude Wrapped trees for the Beyler Foundation, Reihen, Switzerland); *below* Peter Randall-Page (Photographer Jerry Hardman-Jones)
99 Franz Schachinger/The Lisson Gallery (Artist: Dan Graham)
100 Andrea Jones (Sculptor: David Begbie; Hannah Peschar Garden)
101 J C Mayer - G Le Scanff (Designer: Latz + Partners)
104–106 Charles Mann (Designer: Robert Irwin)/Conran Octopus
106–107 Robert Irwin
108–111 Charles Mann (Robert Irwin)/Conran Octopus
112–113 Jerry Harpur (Designer: Douglas Reed)/Conran Octopus
115 Douglas Reed
116–117 Jerry Harpur (Schematic Design and Landform: Child Associates Inc., project designer Douglas Reed/Conran Octopus)
118–121 Bitter Bredt Fotografie (Designer: Daniel Libeskind)
122–125 Gert Tabak (Designer: Ton Ter Linden)
126–127 Betsy Pinover Schiff (Designer: Thomas Balsley)
128 Thomas Balsley
129 *above & below* Betsy Pinover Schiff (Designer: Thomas Balsley)
129 *centre* Thomas Balsley
130 Betsy Pinover Schiff (Designer:Thomas Balsley)
131 Betsy Pinover Schiff (Designer: Thomas Balsley)
132 Andrew Lawson (Designer: Ted Smyth)
33–136 Gil Hanly (Designer: Ted Smyth)
136–137 Andrew Lawson (Designer: Ted Smyth)
138–141 Gerard Dufresne (Designers: Desvigne & Dalnoky)/ Conran Octopus
142–144 Derek Rath (Designers: Rios Associates)
144–145 Rios Associates
145 Derek Rath (Designers: Rios Associates)
146–147 Marianne Majerus (Designer: Charles Jencks)/ Conran Octopus)
148–149 *above* Liane Wilcher
148–149 *below* Marianne Majerus (Designer: Charles Jencks)/ Conran Octopus
149 *above* – **151** Marianne Majerus (Charles Jencks)/ Conran Octopus
152–153 Christian Moutarde (Designer: Jacques Wirtz)
154 Jacques Wirtz
155 *above* Christian Moutarde (Designer: Jacques Wirtz)
155 *below* Jacques Wirtz
156–157 Curtice Taylor (Designer: Jack Lenor Larson)/ Conran Octopus
158 Jack Lenor Larson
159–161 Curtice Taylor (Jack Lenor Larson)/Conran Octopus
162–165 Yasuhiro Ishimoto (Designer: Arata Isosaki)
166–167 Lanny Provo (Designer: Raymond Jungles)
168 *above* Raymond Jungles
168–169 Lanny Provo (Designer: Raymond Jungles)
170 Kathryn Gustafson
171 J C Mayer - G Le Scanff (Designer: Kathryn Gustafson)
172–173 *above* Kathryn Gustafson
173 *below* Gustafson Porter
174–175 Kathryn Gustafson
176–178 *above* L. Toussant (Fernando Caruncho)
178 *below* – **179** *above* Fernando Caruncho; *below* L. Toussant (Designer: Fernando Caruncho)
180–182 Curtice Taylor (Designer: Lester Collins)
183 *above* Lester Collins; *below* Curtice Taylor (Designer: Lester Collins)
184–185 Andrew Lawson (Designer: Topher Delaney)
186 *above* Harpur Garden Library (Designer: Topher Delaney) *below* T. Delaney, Inc
187 Harpur Garden Library (Designer: Topher Delaney)
188 Andrew Lawson (Designer: Topher Delaney)
189 Harpur Garden Library (Designer: Topher Delaney)
190–193 *above* Don F. Wong (Designer: George Hargreaves)
193 *below* – **194** Hargreaves Associates
194–195 Don F. Wong (Designer: George Hargreaves)
196–200 Jerry Harpur (Designer: Daniel Urban Kiley)/Conran Octopus
201 Daniel Urban Kiley
202–205 D.A.S.T. ART TEAM
206–207 Jeroen Musch (Designers:West **8**)
208 Gustafson Porter (John Lyall Architects)
209 Alexei Mescherjakon and Oleg Tolkachev
210 Desvigne & Dalnoky (Architects: Foster & Partners)
211 Daniel Urban Kiley
212 Stig L. Andersson (Photographer: Jakob Skou-Hansen)
213 Edouard François
214 Balmori Associates (photographer: Enrique Pelli, CP&A)
215 Jeroen Musch (Designers: West **8**)
216–217 D.A.S.T. ART TEAM

Every effort has been made to trace the copyright holders and we apologise in advance for any unintentional omission and would be pleased to insert the appropriate acknowledgment in any subsequent edition.

Authors' acknowledgments

The authors would like to thank the following:

Stig L. Andersson,
Helena Attlee for superb editing;
Elizabeth Benbrooks: Rios Associates;
Evelyn Bergaila: Martha Schwartz Inc.;
Paul Bonomini
Susan Cahill-Aylward, librarian of *Landscape Architecture;*
Kate Campbell,
Fernando & Maru Caruncho Torga,
Archie Carr,
Carlos Caster,
Rob Cassy & Valerie Scriven: Garden Bookshop, London;
Stuart Cooper,
Topher Delaney,
Prof. Peter Docherty,
Charlotte Frieze: *House & Garden*, USA;
A. A. Gill & The Blonde;
Theresa Go: Daniel Libeskind office, Berlin;
Frazier Horton,
Robert Irwin,
Charles Jencks,
Dodie Kazanjian: *VOGUE*, New York;
Gavin Keeney: Landscape Agency, New York;
Pauline Levy: Desvigne & Dalnoky office, Paris;
Nicholas Logsdail & Elly Ketsea of Lisson Gallery, London:for Robert Smithson sketch & Dan Graham photo;
Annemarie Lund,
Marianne Majerus,
Anne M. W. Manson: fine administrative assistance;
Kaki Martin: Hargreaves Associates, Cambridge, MA.;
Sarah Gray Miller & Stephen Whitlock: *Garden Design*, USA;
Michael Mushak,
Ines Auge Navas,
Simon Nicol, our techno-dude;
Sal Patel,
Richard Pierce,
Jean-Paul Pigeat, Chateau-de-Chaumont International Garden Festival, Tours, France;
Rebecca Price,
Anne Raver,
Tim Richardson: editor of *new eden*, UK;
Eve Ritscher,
Staff, John Sandoe Books, London;
Martha Schwartz
Sir Roy Strong,
Curtice Taylor,
Tom Todd,
Rob Tokar,
Deborah & Bruce Walther,
Jess Walton,
Patricia Holden White: our always helpful literary agent;
Liane Wilcher,
David Williams: title collaborator;
Peter Wirtz of Wirtz International,
& for Conran Octopus: Helen Woodhall, Mary Staples, Tony Seddon, Liz Boyd, Rachel Davies, Alex Kent.

The subtitle 'Gestures against the Wild' was inspired by the poem 'The Garden' by Rev. R.S. Thomas.

Guy Cooper and Gordon Taylor can be contacted at:
Landscape Design Limited
31 Harley Street
London W1N 1DA

First published in 2000 by
Conran Octopus Limited
a part of Octopus Publishing Group
2-4 Heron Quays
London E14 4JP

www.conran-octopus.co.uk

Reprinted in 2002

Commissioning Editor: Stuart Cooper

Senior Editor: Helen Woodhall

Copy-Editor: Helena Attlee

Editorial Assistant: Alexandra Kent

Art Editors: Mary Staples, Tony Seddon

Picture Research: Liz Boyd, Jessica Walton

Production: Suzanne Sharpless

British Library Cataloguing-in-Publication Data
A catalogue record for this book is available from the British Library

1 84091 087 9

Colour origination by Sang Choy International, Singapore

Printed in China.